THE RIGHT TO AN AGE-FRIENDLY CITY

MCGILL-QUEEN'S STUDIES IN URBAN GOVERNANCE
Series editors: Kristin Good and Martin Horak

In recent years there has been an explosion of interest in local politics and the governance of cities – both in Canada and around the world. Globally, the city has become a consequential site where instances of social conflict and of cooperation play out. Urban centres are increasingly understood as vital engines of innovation and prosperity and a growing body of interdisciplinary research on urban issues suggests that high-performing cities have become crucial to the success of nations, even in the global era. Yet at the same time, local and regional governments continue to struggle for political recognition and for the policy resources needed to manage cities, to effectively govern, and to achieve sustainable growth.

The purpose of the McGill-Queen's Studies in Urban Governance series is to highlight the growing importance of municipal issues, local governance, and the need for policy reform in urban spaces. The series aims to answer the question "why do cities matter?" while exploring relationships between levels of government and examining the changing dynamics of metropolitan and community development. By taking a four-pronged approach to the study of urban governance, the series encourages debate and discussion of: (1) actors, institutions, and how cities are governed; (2) policy issues and policy reform; (3) the city as case study; and (4) urban politics and policy through a comparative framework.

With a strong focus on governance, policy, and the role of the city, this series welcomes manuscripts from a broad range of disciplines and viewpoints.

1 Local Self-Government and the Right to the City
Warren Magnusson

2 City-Regions in Prospect? Exploring Points between Place and Practice
Edited by Kevin Edson Jones, Alex Lord, and Rob Shields

3 On Their Own
Women, Urbanization, and the Right to the City in South Africa
Allison Goebel

4 The Boundary Bargain
Growth, Development, and the Future of City–County Separation
Zachary Spicer

5 Welcome to Greater Edendale
Histories of Environment, Health, and Gender in an African City
Marc Epprecht

6 Still Renovating
A History of Canadian Social Housing Policy
Greg Suttor

7 Order and Disorder
Urban Governance and the Making of Middle Eastern Cities
Edited by Luna Khirfan

8 Toward Equity and Inclusion in Canadian Cities
Lessons from Critical Praxis-Oriented Research
Edited by Fran Klodawsky, Janet Siltanen, and Caroline Andrew

9 Accountability and Responsiveness at the Municipal Level
Views from Canada
Edited by Sandra Breux and Jérôme Couture

10 A Neighborhood Politics of Last Resort
Post-Katrina New Orleans and the Right to the City
Stephen Danley

11 Shaping the Metropolis
Institutions and Urbanization in the United States and Canada
Zack Taylor

12 China's Urban Future and the Quest for Stability
Edited by Rebecca Clothey and Richardson Dilworth

13 Big Moves
Global Agendas, Local Aspirations, and Urban Mobility in Canada
Anthony Perl, Matt Hern, and Jeffrey Kenworthy

14 The Right to an Age-Friendly City
Redistribution, Recognition, and Senior Citizen Rights in Urban Spaces
Meghan Joy

THE RIGHT TO AN AGE-FRIENDLY CITY

Redistribution, Recognition, and Senior Citizen Rights in Urban Spaces

MEGHAN JOY

McGill-Queen's University Press
Montreal & Kingston • London • Chicago

ISBN 978-0-2280-0394-6 (cloth)
ISBN 978-0-2280-0395-3 (paper)
ISBN 978-0-2280-0467-7 (ePDF)
ISBN 978-0-2280-0468-4 (ePUB)

Legal deposit fourth quarter 2020
Bibliothèque nationale du Québec

Printed in Canada on acid-free paper that is 100% ancient forest free (100% post-consumer recycled), processed chlorine free

This book has been published with the help of an Aid to Research Related Events grant from Concordia University.

Funded by the Government of Canada | Financé par le gouvernement du Canada | Canada

Canada Council for the Arts | Conseil des arts du Canada

We acknowledge the support of the Canada Council for the Arts.
Nous remercions le Conseil des arts du Canada de son soutien.

Library and Archives Canada Cataloguing in Publication

Title: The right to an age-friendly city : redistribution, recognition, and senior citizen rights in urban spaces / Meghan Joy.
Names: Joy, Meghan, 1983- author.
Series: McGill-Queen's studies in urban governance ; 14.
Description: Series statement: McGill-Queen's studies in urban governance ; 14 | Includes bibliographical references and index.
Identifiers: Canadiana (print) 20200306456 | Canadiana (ebook) 20200306537 | ISBN 9780228003946 (cloth) | ISBN 9780228003953 (paper) | ISBN 9780228004677 (ePDF) | ISBN 9780228004684 (ePUB)
Subjects: LCSH: City planning—Social aspects—Ontario—Toronto. | LCSH: Population aging—Social aspects—Ontario—Toronto. | LCSH: Urban elderly—Services for—Ontario—Toronto. | LCSH: Urban elderly—Civil rights—Ontario—Toronto. | LCSH: Urban elderly—Ontario—Toronto—Social conditions. | LCSH: Urban policy—Ontario—Toronto.
Classification: LCC HT169.C32 T67 2020 | DDC 307.1/216—dc23

For Brad. My partner in this and everything else.

CONTENTS

THE RIGHT TO AN AGE-FRIENDLY CITY

INTRODUCTION

What Are Age-Friendly Cities?

My interest in the topic of population aging was ignited personally as I experienced the aging of my loved ones and noticed the behaviours of senior citizens around me. In the space of a few years, my Grandma passed away from ALS and my Nana from dementia. I witnessed the toll that informal caregiving takes on a family, even when some formal supports are present. At the same time, my elderly neighbour was taking care of her ailing husband, whose wish was to die at home. She also cherished the familiarity of aging at home, which we witnessed in the way she continued to prepare her husband's favourite meal of roasted rabbit and carefully plucked the ripened pears from their backyard tree in late summer. Yet, this caregiving role also left our neighbour with feelings of intense sadness and anxiety, which she would often express to me and my partner across the backyard fence. She suffered from arthritis, which affected her mobility, and once we saw her severely bruised from a fall. My partner was called on several occasions to help our neighbour carry her husband to bed and to fetch her arthritis medicine from the pharmacy down the street when her pain was unbearable. She did not drive and though living close to downtown Toronto and a short walk from a grocery store, she struggled to carry bags of food home. This couple had children who lived outside the city and visited only on occasion. On those visits, we heard them begging their parents to consider moving to a long-term care home, but the couple wanted to age in place in their beloved neighbourhood and private residence. One cold and icy winter, after weeks had gone by without seeing our neighbour, we learned from her son that she had passed away after a bad fall. This caused me to reflect on the number of people living in her situation. I began to ask whether there was more that we could have done, collectively as a society, to support this couple.

As I walked around my Toronto neighbourhood, I became more conscious of barriers in the urban environment and the behaviours seniors took to adapt to them. How the old Portuguese men would sit chatting on the often-broken benches at the top of Christie Pits Park but never venture down the steep embankment into the ravine. I found myself increasingly angry having to move large bins from the middle of the sidewalk on garbage day so that neighbours with walkers and wheelchairs would not have to cross the street to get by. One early morning while walking our dog, my partner and I encountered an old lady who had fallen on her step bringing bags of rubbish out to the curb for collection. We helped her up and led her back into the house, wondering who would be there to assist her the next time, as she appeared to live alone in an old Victorian building.

On my way to an appointment via the subway one day, I was approached by an old woman at the St Patrick stop who inquired with exasperation whether there was an elevator to take her above ground as the escalator was under repair. All I could do was instruct her to go back one stop and walk to her destination. I found this incident particularly egregious because there are several hospitals and medical facilities in this part of Toronto, making it essential that nearby stations be fully accessible. I wondered if this lady would ever use the subway again and was reminded that if she did not have a car or a family member to take her or could not afford a taxi, she had little choice. Would she forgo her next medical appointment or perhaps wait until her ailments got so bad that she would qualify for the subsidized accessible transportation provided by Toronto's Wheel Trans service? I wondered whether this was the invisible reality of aging in urban environments and therefore how more people would face these daily difficulties, given the aging of the baby boom population. It seemed to me that these personal experiences were political. I began to search for a public response.

A Public Response to Aging in Urban Environments

A public response that meets the needs of senior citizens is particularly important and timely, given census figures that illustrate the largest increase in those aged sixty-five and older since confederation (Statistics Canada 2017). With urbanization, much of this aging is taking place in big cities. This is true of Toronto. There were 700,000 residents over the age of fifty-five in 2013 and this number is estimated to jump to 1.2 million by 2041 (ibid.). By 2031, those over the age of sixty-five will represent 20 percent of the city's population (City of Toronto 2015). As my observations could attest, population aging is a multifaceted issue that transforms everyday needs in a variety of intersecting social and physical infrastructure domains such as health care, social services, housing, and transportation. How were governments responding to this?

I learned that in 2013, Toronto City Council had passed a strategic plan for population aging, the *Toronto Seniors Strategy*, which sets out a series of policy actions for local government. Shortly after its release, the *Toronto Star* published an opinion piece by reporter Carol Goar, who harshly criticized the city for a strategy that simply re-states what they are already doing in areas that "affect seniors only peripherally," that offers a limited number of small-scale and vague actions, and that fails to connect to broader trends around urbanization and housing access linked to inner-city gentrification (Goar 2013). Goar warned that "without vision and leadership, Toronto will become the kind of city whose residents leave – or get left behind" (ibid.). The latter point reflects an important observation that seniors in Toronto are a diverse population group, some of whom may be able to leave while others may not. According to Goar, the seriousness of the issue of population aging in Toronto did not seem to match the policy response, and I became increasingly interested in exploring this further.

The *Toronto Seniors Strategy* is informed by the Age-Friendly Cities (AFC) policy movement. The AFC program was developed by the World Health Organization (WHO) in 2006–07 based on research in several pilot cities across the world, including some in Canada. Focus groups were undertaken with senior citizens, their caregivers, and service providers from the public, non-profit, and private sectors to identify the defining characteristics of an age-friendly city (Plouffe and Kalache 2010;

Rémillard-Boilard 2019). AFCs are part of a longstanding movement at the WHO to shift from a medical model of treating seniors as a health problem to "a more socio-ecological approach to health" (Rémillard-Boilard 2019, 14) that focuses on the social and environmental determinants of healthy aging (Kalache 2016). This led to the conceptualization of "active aging," which places emphasis on the continued social, economic, and political participation of citizens throughout the life-course (Kalache 2016). Active aging thus became an important policy goal for the WHO, with the AFC program presented as a policy solution to the challenges associated with population aging. In particular, the AFC program serves to enhance the fit between seniors and the environments in which they live, supporting them to age in place (i.e. in their own homes and/or neighbourhood) rather than in medical institutions like hospitals and long-term care homes.

The WHO's research on age-friendly cities culminated in the design of the document *Global Age-Friendly Cities: A Guide* (2007) which consists of an "Active Aging Framework" of recommended policy improvements to support seniors to remain "active participants in society" (Senate of Canada 2009, 84). The "Active Aging Framework" includes the following eight priorities:

1. respect and inclusion, including combating and preventing ageism
2. civic participation, mainly conceptualized as volunteering and paid employment
3. efforts to encourage social participation with family, friends, neighbours, and communities
4. community supports and services that encourage public health prevention and meet the needs of diverse seniors, including nutrition, recreation programming, and access to health services and home care
5. the availability of housing that is affordable, accessible, and adaptable in design
6. accessible, affordable, and flexible transportation options, including investments in walkability
7. outdoor spaces and public buildings planned through the participation of older adults

8. accessible communication and information sharing that outreaches to older adults.
(WHO 2007; Golant 2014)

The WHO also convenes the Global Network for Age-Friendly Cities and Communities in order to share knowledge between members who have committed to becoming more age-friendly.

Canada's Federal Public Health Agency was an active participant in the development of AFCs at the WHO, helping to design and endorse the "Active Aging Framework" (see Plouffe et al. 2016). In 2007, the agency also supported the federal, provincial, and territorial ministers responsible for seniors by publishing *Age-Friendly Rural and Remote Communities: A Guide*, and in 2012 designed the *Age-Friendly Communities in Canada: Community Implementation Guide* and associated *Toolbox* of best-practice resources. The concept of age-friendly "communities," as opposed to cities, is more commonly used in Canada to remain inclusive of rural places. The agency does not provide funding to support AFC development, though community-based non-profits and local governments can apply to the Federal Ministry of Employment and Social Development's New Horizons for Seniors grant program, where they compete for up to $25,000 in funding for a one-time twelve-month grant, and smaller grants of up to $5,000.

All ten provinces claim to officially support AFC development (Public Health Agency of Canada 2016). The Ontario Seniors Secretariat (now Ministry), a body that convenes provincial policy initiatives related to seniors, made "Senior-Friendly Communities" a key pillar of its 2013 *Action Plan for Seniors*. In 2013, the province released an information guide on AFC development called *Finding the Right Fit: Age-Friendly Community Planning*, which encourages local policy actors from the municipal and non-profit sectors to invest in age-friendly environments and voluntarily adopt the AFC program (Ontario Government 2013). This commitment also includes a Seniors Community Grant Program that provides between $1,000 to $25,000 to non-profit organizations who compete for funding to deliver supports and services to senior citizens (Ontario Government 2015; Ontario Government 2019). The *Finding the Right Fit* guide also directs non-profits and local governments interested in developing AFC initiatives to "consider reaching out to potential funders such as the Ontario Trillium Foundation or other non-profit and private foundations" (Ontario Seniors Secretariat 2013, 8).

AFC development is supposed to begin with a "custom needs assessment" of local environments that locates gaps, identifies opportunities, and outlines areas where additional research is needed. This process is intended to support the development of an action plan that includes concrete strategies to address gaps and incorporates implementation and evaluation procedures (Ontario Government 2013). To be officially recognized as age-friendly in Canada, the Federal Public Health Agency has developed a "milestone approach" that includes: establishing an advisory committee that incorporates senior citizens; passing a municipal council resolution to commit to age-friendly work; developing an action plan that corresponds to local needs; posting the action plan publicly; and measuring and publicly reporting on outcomes (Public Health Agency of Canada 2016). Once this process is complete, municipalities can apply to the WHO to become members of the Global Network for Age-Friendly Cities and Communities.

AFC Claims

As I began my review of reports and literature on AFCs, I found the topic studied mainly by public health and gerontology scholars and professionals, and it was exploratory, descriptive, and highly optimistic. Illustrating this optimism, the WHO claims that "active ageing in supportive, enabling cities will serve as one of the most effective approaches to maintaining quality of life and prosperity in an increasingly older and more urban world" (WHO 2007, 75). I found this optimism expressed through three interrelated claims:

1. AFCs will *improve local environments* for everyone
2. AFCs will *promote a positive aging identity* that challenges societal ageism
3. AFCs will *empower local policy actors* who deliver supports to senior citizens in cities and communities

AFCs are part of a movement in gerontology to consider the geography in which people are aging and whether it supports their everyday needs.

Plouffe and Kalach (2010) suggest that seniors are a resource, and that "to tap the potential that older people represent for continued human development, cities must ensure their inclusion and full access to urban spaces, structures, and services" (734). Thus, to enhance inclusion, the AFC framework incorporates big-ticket policy domains such as health care, housing, and transportation available in local places as well as the active participation of seniors in identifying changes needed. The AFC discourse also emphasizes the need to create environments that promote population health throughout the life-course; hence focusing on population aging as a policy issue encourages governments to improve local environments for all population groups (Golant 2014; Ontario Government 2013). Here, Barusch (2013) characterizes AFCs as representative of a "paradigm shift" in public policy that reorients aging from a negative to a positive social reality by promoting a model of healthy and active "lifelong citizenship" (469).

Secondly, there is an explicit emphasis on changing societal understandings of seniors as passive, invisible, and unhealthy to active citizens who continue to contribute politically, economically, and socially (WHO 2007; Kalache 2016). Gonzoles and Morrow-Howell (2009) applaud the AFC movement for its effort to meet the demands of seniors who want to continue contributing to the labour market, their families, and their communities. Rather than understanding seniors as inherently dependent, Halvorsen and Emerman (2013) argue for an "age abundancy ratio," in which baby boomers and older adults, armed with a lifetime of experience, are engaged to solve some of society's most pressing social problems – and while they're at it, continue to contribute to the tax base" (33). Thus, ensuring that the local environment meets the needs of senior citizens through the AFC framework enables continued contribution in this later phase of the life-course, and this is considered fundamentally positive for seniors, communities, governments, and economies.

Finally, AFCs illustrate a policy approach that conceptualizes policy solutions, and their associated investments, at the geographic and governmental scale of the local. Here, Ontario's *Finding the Right Fit* guide notes that "a community's history, size or preferred approach to decision-making may mean choosing a process led by local government, while others may find an approach driven by the collaboration of volunteers and community organizations more desirable" (Ontario Government 2013, 15). The terminology is thus not limited to local government but is also used to refer to more informal groups of volunteers and non-profit organizations situated in geographic communities who are, in theory, enabled and empowered through the program to support seniors. The phrase age-friendly "community" rather than city may also be used so that the program remains inclusive to these non-governmental participants.

Gaps in AFC Practice

While generally applauding the aims of the AFC movement, a growing body of research has begun to identify gaps in program realization. In 2012, Scharlach conducted a preliminary scoping of the number and types of AFC initiatives underway in the United States through a comprehensive internet search. Of the 292 initiatives located through this methodology, the majority were led by municipal governments and focused on identifying local problems and designing solutions, though actual implementation and impact were unclear. Of those initiatives that did seem to promote actual action and change, the majority were small pilot projects led by non-governmental organizations in receipt of ad hoc funding from philanthropic foundations (Scharlach 2012). Scharlach's investigation indicated that the highly localized and voluntary nature of the AFC program was dividing those places that had the capacity and resources to sustain age-friendly initiatives and those that did not, as success appeared dependent on having non-profit and foundation leadership and funding which did not necessarily correspond to need. Literature on AFCs has continued to highlight similar challenges in cities worldwide, including initiatives that are small-scale, short-term, heavily reliant on voluntary labour, lacking in clear leadership and responsibility, poorly funded, inequitably distributed both within cities and between cities as well as rural areas, and that target only particular sub-groups of seniors (Golant 2014; Ball and Lawler 2014; Winterton 2016; Lehning 2014; Kendig et al. 2014; Neal et al. 2014; Buffel et al. 2012; Buffel et al 2014.; see cases in Moulaert and Garon 2016; see cases in Buffel et al. 2019). In a recent review article, Buffel and Phillipson (2016) note that "although age-friendly cities (AFCs) have many achievements to their name, their material impact on older people has been more limited" (98).

Although AFC practice appears to reflect more of a piecemeal response to addressing the fit between seniors and their local environment and not the revolutionary policy project extolled by the WHO, there is a dearth of analysis on the program directed to explaining these gaps. Buffel et al. (2012) argue that a major problem is that the mainstream academic and professional approaches to AFCs tend to rely on a mechanistic framework or checklist of features that can be disconnected from the everyday experiences of diverse seniors navigating local environments. Particularly absent, according to these researchers, is a fulsome understanding of "the context of the complexities and contradictions that beset modern cities, especially those that arise from accelerated global social and economic change" (598). In more recent work, Buffel and Phillipson (2016) continue to find that "the study of urban society and population ageing has tended … to be kept separate in research and policy" (96). Specifically, they argue that there is a lack of integration between the literature lauding AFCs and the everyday effects on seniors of urbanization, the shift from a manufacturing to a service-oriented economy where many urban services and amenities have become privately owned commodities, and public-sector austerity (ibid.). Buffel et al. (2012) and Buffel and Phillipson (2016) call for a research agenda that advances the AFC literature through analyses that explore how the urban political economy challenges the AFC program from having a greater material impact on the everyday lives of senior citizens in specific places. For these scholars, this critical analysis is fundamentally normative at its root; a better understanding of actual problems and opportunities is sought to inform the development of a more substantive AFC program. Here, Buffel and Phillipson (2016) make "a strong case for incorporating issues about ageing in urban environments with debates concerning spatial justice" (98–9). Buffel et al. (2012) emphasize the need for a counter AFC movement based on a new form of urban citizenship for seniors grounded in "right to the city" theories from urban geography that seek to "de-commodify urban life" (612).

AFCs as a Right to the City

Urban geographers coming from a political economy perspective understand cities as spaces of private profit-making, facilitated by state policy, and thus mired by inequitable class relations. Biggs and Carr (2015) argue that this intersects with age relations, as cities are designed for a predominantly working-age population and, as such, the needs of both young and old citizens are often left out of urban decisions. Harvey (1989) notes that the dominant mode of capitalist economic development has shifted from state-led managerial projects of industrial development to a service-oriented model of neoliberal urban entrepreneurialism where the city itself, including its services, amenities, and infrastructures, becomes private commodities. Cities are constructed as economic engines and are expected to compete domestically and globally for businesses, investment, human capital, and tourism (Boudreau et al. 2009). State policy focuses on facilitating the market through lowered taxation, reduced social spending, and the use of market values and metrics (including outright privatization) in physical and social infrastructure such as public transportation and affordable housing (Harvey 1989; Andrew 2003; Keil and Kipfer 2003). This neoliberal economic policy package results in inequities between those who can pay out of pocket for services and amenities and those who cannot, leading to differential access to the city and thus spatial injustice (Soja 2010). Buffel et al. (2012) are concerned that the competitive demands placed on cities will create even greater risks that those population groups considered "unproductive," such as seniors, will not be considered in urban decisions. Yet, paradoxically, it is in this context that the AFC program has become increasingly popular worldwide, with 500 cities and communities now part of the WHO's Global Network for Age-Friendly Cities and Communities (Rémillard-Boilard 2019, 17). How can we make sense of this?

Answering this question requires understanding the urban governance dimensions of AFCs. AFCs can be understood as an example of another modern trend that has not been acknowledged in the dominant AFC literature: the trend to "place-based" policymaking. Due to a complex mix of economic globalization, urbanization, and ideological communitarianism and localism, the central state (which in Canada can be understood as both the nation-state and the provinces) and its institutional role in enhancing access to key services and amenities through a centralized collective response is "unbundling" (Clarke 2004; Mahon and Keil 2009; Brenner 2009). As the state is decentred, the domain of responsibility over collective provisioning is at once reduced and expanded, from more centralized to fragmented funding and coordination by local governments, non-profit organizations, private businesses, and active citizens (Newman and Clarke 2009). There is a greater emphasis on distinct policy "problems" that occur in place, such as homelessness, neighbourhood poverty, or the social isolation of seniors, and a "task specific" rescaling of public responsibility to local actors to target and solve these problems (Horak 2013; Bradford 2007). An increasingly popular "new localism" governance paradigm beckons a revolution in which cities are understood as drivers of change because they are spaces that convene a variety of local partners to solve today's most complex policy challenges (Barber 2013; Katz and Bradley 2013). This paradigm attributes a pragmatic and democratic nature to local government actors as ideal agents who partner to design and deliver innovative programs. This localism thus draws on theories of governance (Isett et al. 2011; Osborne 2010) that claim a new normal in the realm of governing, policy design, and implementation where networks of partnered public, private, and non-profit actors work together to problem-solve in ways that include local communities and citizens.

In theory, place-based policy is meant to target need in specific places, while still involving collaboration between actors within and between local and central governments in both policy design and service provision (Bradford 2005). However, in his study on Toronto, Horak (2013) finds that while place-based policymaking to address complex problems is indeed a growing trend, policy innovations are weakly institutionalized both locally and, especially, intergovernmentally. This weak institutionalism can lead to a dismissal of place-based policy as a symbolic response on the part of local governments to efforts by central governments to cut costs via policy devolution in areas such as social housing and public transit. Here, Peck (2012) warns that the devolution of responsibility to local governments and non-profit organizations with more limited financial and human resources can represent a neoliberal cost-cutting strategy on the part of other levels of government that facilitates municipal budget cuts, the privatization of formerly public services, as well as "materially hollow" symbolic policy initiatives. Harvey (1989) argues that at best, these policies consist of meagre social programs that target the local symptoms of structural problems. Similarly, Jessop (2009) warns that policy rescaling may contain and localize problems, disconnecting them from wider structures of power. Despite these critiques, the everyday practices of place-based policy have not been the subject of detailed and systematic empirical analysis by urban geographers and political scientists (Sancton 2015). I posit that much can be learned about how projects of neoliberal austerity "actually exist" (Brenner and Theodore 2002), including the tensions and inconsistencies that might create openings for alternative understandings, through an inductive analysis of the urban governance of place-based policy programs such as AFCs.

I work from the assumption that local governments operate in a "landscape of antagonism" (Newman 2014) where they are not unitary actors following a single political script, such as neoliberalism, but a complex web of different institutions and actors. This means that they retain their own political ideas, translate and challenge the political ideas of others through their role in policy design and implementation, and engage in this work while facing administrative constraints. A multiplicity of political projects, of which neoliberalism is just one, take shape in local spaces and we can learn about these projects through an inductive study of place-based policy. For instance, place-based policy may operate to extend neoliberalism through cost cutting, as is highlighted by critical geographers above, but also via discourses of responsibilization. Here, Clarke and Newman (2012) note that political projects of austerity require consent, which may work through place-based policymaking to responsibilize "active" citizens, "dutiful" families, and "innovative" non-profit organizations and local governments to take on more public responsibility with limited political tools and resource support. We can thus learn about how neoliberalism actually works through a detailed study of the values, techniques, and practices of place-based projects. This includes an examination of the ways in which any potentially expansive elements of localism, such as active community participation and local problem-solving that meets diverse needs, may be co-opted by the neoliberal project.

At the same time, Clarke (2004) notes that state unbundling is also linked to projects that seek to expand social welfare services to better accommodate diverse voices and experiences. Applied to cities, this might include expansion to social and physical infrastructure that fails to accommodate diverse needs, particularly those of a non-working population (Biggs and Carr 2015). Policy that seeks to locate the root causes of a lack of access to urban space may present openings for citizens to work with local policy actors to make demands based on their rights as inhabitants. Urban geographers remain hopeful that lack of access to city services and amenities might force new forms of participation in defining the terms of urban policymaking based on a citizen's "right to the city" (Lefebvre 2003; Purcell 2003).

Given these insights, I understand AFCs as a contradictory place-based policy, not a fundamentally progressive approach challenged in implementation by cost-cutting trends associated with neoliberal austerity. The different political ideas behind AFCs are expected to result in tensions and contradictions in practice that create significant conflict for local policy actors operating in real "landscapes of antagonism." AFC policy may legitimate and extend neoliberalism more deeply into urban governance through strategies that responsibilize local actors with limited support. At the same time, the AFC program offers a framework that helps to highlight problems of inadequate access to local services and amenities, and a space to link those problems to public policy and broader political, social, and economic conditions. It is only by teasing out these contradictions, challenges, and potentials that a right to the city for senior citizens can be achieved through the AFC program.

A "right to the city" framing offers the opportunity to link the AFC program, both conceptually and practically, to the current movement to design and adopt a United Nations Convention on the Rights of Older People. The proposed treaty is the subject of considerable advocacy among international non-profit organizations on aging as well as some nation-states, and is driven by systemic gaps in domestic rights protection for senior citizens as well as the fragmented international human rights landscape as it applies to older adults (see HelpAge International 2019). Canada is among a list of nation-states that does not support such a convention due to skepticism about the capacity of the United Nations to implement an additional treaty and an apparent lack of evidence that additional legislation is needed (DiGiacomo et al. 2017). While the rights of older Canadians are protected under the *Canadian Charter of Rights and Freedoms*, the *Canadian Human Rights Act* and provincial human rights codes, the proposed treaty would mean regular assessment by an independent expert and would place the onus on the federal government to explain any gaps in treaty obligations (ibid.). As we will see in this book, it is at the local scale that gaps in human rights protection become most acute for seniors as well as for local service providers. Aligning local and international pressure on central governments to protect the rights of older adults is crucial to the development of substantive public policy that fills these gaps.

I use Isin's (2008) work on the right to the city as a framework to guide my analysis. According to Isin, a right to the city means that the wants and needs of urban residents are met through forms of collective redistribution. This *redistribution* meets both universal needs and includes "positive discrimination" for certain groups so that they can achieve the same outcomes as others; what Antonnen et al. (2012a) term "universal inclusion." Inequities in access to everyday needs based on intersections of class, age, race, gender, and sexuality (among others) can differentiate citizens and spark mobilizations and new claims to social and material rights to the city (Isin 2008; Clarke et al. 2014; Soja 2010; Lefebvre 2003; Purcell 2003).

Secondly, for a right to the city based on universal inclusion to exist, the life experiences, wants, and needs of urban residents must be recognized (Isin 2008). This *recognition* requires that urban residents have a right to define the problems to be addressed through collective redistribution (Bacchi 2009). This necessitates forms of participatory policymaking with citizens and their non-profit agency representatives.

Finally, Isin (2008) argues that a right to the city can only be achieved when local policy actors have the legal authority and financial capacity to undertake the tasks demanded of them by citizens. He terms this the rights *of* the city. It is this aspect of urban governance analysis that has been particularly under-assessed in the AFC literature to date. Because achieving a right to the city based on universal inclusion requires resource devotion and policymaking by different political authorities, it is a multiscalar endeavour that requires some form of "translocal" or intergovernmental authority (Isin 2008). I argue that it is also crucial to understand the rights of non-profit organizations given the important role of the sector in local service delivery and policy advocacy. Clavel's (2010) work on the progressive city reiterates the importance of an institutionalized base of non-profits who develop an urban agenda based on the recognition and redistributive needs of their membership and work in collaboration with local government administration.

Isin's (2008) framework of redistribution, recognition, and rights of the city can be used to examine the ways in which AFCs promote a right to the city for senior citizens by dissecting the three claims that AFCs improve local environments, promote a positive aging identity, and empower local policy actors. An outline of this analysis, including key themes and questions, is highlighted in Table 1.

TABLE 1

AFC claims	*Right to the city*	*Guiding question*	*Sub-questions*
AFCs improve local environments	Redistribution	How do AFCs promote the redistribution of services and amenities to senior citizens in local environments?	» How do AFC programs serve to identify inequities in access to services and amenities based on old age? » How do AFC actions include both universal and more targeted improvements to local environments for senior citizens?
AFCs promote a positive aging identity	Recognition	How do AFCs promote the recognition of senior citizens and their needs in local environments?	» How are similar and different life experiences, wants, and needs of senior citizens recognized in AFC programs? » How do AFCs promote the participation of senior citizens and their non-profit organizations to define policy problems and solutions?
AFCs empower local policy actors	Rights of the city	How do AFCs promote the rights of local policy actors?	» How do AFCs enable local governments and non-profit organizations to undertake the tasks demanded of them by senior citizens? » How do local governments and non-profit organizations work together to meet the needs of senior citizens? » How are central governments supporting AFC policy work?

The purpose of this analysis is to better understand and explain lingering challenges with the AFC program rooted in a more holistic understanding of urban policy and governance. There is also a normative dimension to my research: I want to offer insight into how the AFC program can work better for senior citizens through an expansive form of redistribution, recognition, and the rights of the city.

AFCs in Toronto

Research for this book consists of an in-depth qualitative case study (Merriam 1988; Flyvbjerg 2006) of AFCs in the City of Toronto. My research is guided by Magnussen's (2011) recommendation that political analysis shift from describing public institutions, or "seeing like a state," to "seeing like a city." The latter analysis encourages an academic focus on underexplored political sites such as cities and neighbourhoods, and actors such as municipal and non-profit staff, as well as the citizens who experience policy on an everyday basis. This approach is inherently multi-actor and multi-scalar as it hones the focus on how policy is experienced in place, including how and by whom it is enacted, and how it produces social equity or inequity for different groups. I expect that the challenges that we are witnessing with AFCs more generally and the *Toronto Seniors Strategy* specifically reflects a broader landscape of antagonism (Newman 2014) in a complex big-city context of advanced capitalism and state unbundling that must be better understood to support the development of meaningful policy.

The case study method allows me to retain the complexity and contradictions of the actual context (Yin 2009) of place-based policymaking, which has been identified as a notable gap in pre-existing AFC research by several scholars (Buffel et al. 2012; Buffel and Phillipson 2016; Novek and Menec 2014). Specifically, while the endeavour of developing and implementing an AFC in big cities with large bureaucracies is highly complex – a mixed social service landscape with a dizzying array of non-profit organizations, a diverse population, multiple neighbourhoods with a mix of land uses, and intense pressure to be economically competitive – little focus has been placed on the challenges of large cities in the AFC literature (Buffel and Phillipson 2016). In the Canadian case, central governments have shown particular concern with aging in smaller cities and rural areas, perhaps reflecting an underlying assumption that big cities can take care of themselves given that they have a larger tax base and more non-profit and private sector partners. This book explores whether this is, in fact, the case in Toronto.

As will be outlined in more detail in the following chapter, Toronto is similar to other large cities facing the pressure of economic restructuring, the rescaling of policy responsibility, and the growing needs of diverse seniors. My empirical findings about the challenges and opportunities for achieving a right to the city for seniors through the AFC program in Toronto thus has generalizable insights for other large cities. Toronto is also an ideal case because it has recently taken the political initiative to develop the *Toronto Seniors Strategy*, which has the stated purpose of enhancing equity for senior citizens (City of Toronto 2013). The strategy is informed by the WHO AFC framework and the province of Ontario's Seniors Strategy, offering an opportunity to understand the multi-scalar dynamics of place-based policy on aging.

My fieldwork was undertaken between May and November 2014, one year after the *Toronto Seniors Strategy* was passed by city council and the bureaucracy was in the process of implementation. The *Toronto Seniors Strategy* acts as an embedded case within a broader case of age-friendly work in Toronto. This approach was chosen strategically to ensure as wide a scope as possible on all the actors involved in the practice of AFCs to capture this complex policy domain through a "seeing like a city" lens. I wanted to gain a deep understanding of how policy actors themselves, involved in different capacities and institutional locations understand, experience, and mediate the AFC policy program in Toronto. I was particularly interested in both the similarities and differences of meanings and experiences with the AFC program and the struggles and inconsistencies of practice (Stake 1995) and how this related to the institutional location of the different actors involved.

My research method consisted of a textual analysis of key reports on aging in the City of Toronto, including the *Toronto Seniors Strategy* (2013) and the city's two previous reports on aging: *City of Toronto Roundtable on Seniors: Housing Toronto Seniors* (2006) and *Toronto – Building a City for all Ages* (1999). I also analyzed notes taken during my attendance at a mayoral forum on the *Toronto Seniors Strategy* in advance of the 2014 local elections. Textual analysis was also undertaken on seventy-seven interview transcripts from a total of eighty-two participants, whose names, save for politicians, remain confidential. Participants included four current or former city councillors (population A), twenty-four city staff members (population B), four senior citizen members of the Toronto Seniors Forum advisory group (population C), thirty-five employees from non-profit organizations (population D), eight academic and other research-oriented policy experts (population E), and seven representatives from other levels of government (population F). These include actors involved in various capacities in the development and implementation of the *Toronto Seniors Strategy*, those involved more broadly in the practice of implementing AFCs in Toronto, as well as representatives from other levels of government and policy experts who could offer a broader perspective on AFCs as a place-based policy concept.

My interview guide (see Appendix) was qualitative, in-depth, and semi-structured, and my line of questioning made room for participant stories, allowing them to speak at length about how they made meaning of the AFC program both conceptually and practically through their day to day work (Stake 1995; Thompson et al. 2010; Flyvbjerg 2006). I selected semi-structured questions because I was interested in description of how AFCs actually work as well as comparing responses within and across population groups to see how they understood different aspects of AFCs. At the same time, the questions were broad, allowing room for unique stories, interpretations, and differences of opinion (Stake 1995). I began the interviews with "what" questions about how their everyday work relates to population aging. I then asked "how" questions that sought to establish an in-depth understanding of the meanings actors made of the policy issue of population aging, the uniqueness of aging as a policy issue in a big-city context in Toronto, their understanding of the importance of place-based responses to population aging, the changing role of policy agents and their relations with other agents engaged age-friendly work. I ended the interviews with more delicate questions about policy capacity after we had built a rapport throughout the conversation. The interview guides differed slightly depending on the population group in question to reflect their level of involvement in AFCs in Toronto specifically and as experts more broadly and to reflect their level of involvement in the embedded case of the *Toronto Seniors Strategy* (Stake 1995; Berg 2009; Vromen 2010). To ensure an accurate representation of participant voice, my consent form provided the opportunity for participants to review and revise our interview transcript.

My fieldwork and data analysis was a co-constitutive process, as is the case with inductive qualitative research. The interviews were electronically recorded[1] and transcribed immediately. During the transcription process, I began to pull out preliminary themes. The same process was applied to the city report texts and my notes from the mayoral forum. I created separate word documents, or memos (Maxwell 2005; Maxwell 2012; Charmaz 2006), for each of these themes where I plugged in keywords and quotations as well as my own interpretations, which included highlighting differences between the population groups and the relationships between themes. I ended up with twenty-six thematic memos, which served as a coding template that I used to analyze subsequent interviews, and which were also refined through the interviews as new insights became available. Once the analysis was complete, I organized my thematic memos into broader organizational categories (Maxwell 2005), or chapters, which include the case description and the AFC claims to improve local environments, promote a positive aging identity, and empower local policy actors. The thematic findings associated with each chapter were analyzed through Isin's (2008) "right to the city" framework of redistribution, recognition, and the rights of the city. This data provides a rich analysis of the opportunities and challenges to enact AFCs as a place-based policy based on a right to the city in the Toronto case.

Chapter Breakdown

In chapter 1, I introduce the Toronto case by scoping the landscape of age-friendly work conducted by local government and non-profit organizations in the city and providing an overview of policy work on aging, including the *Toronto Seniors Strategy*. I offer an initial understanding of the content of AFCs in a big city context and begin to explore the critique that the *Toronto Seniors Strategy* is more symbolic than substantive. In chapter 2, I examine the first claim that AFCs

1 Recording was optional and one interview was not electronically recorded, on the request of the participant. In this case, I took extensive handwritten notes. One interview was done electronically, with written answers sent by email.

improve local environments. I contrast how participants understand the importance of local environments to support the universal and diverse needs of senior citizens with gaps in the *Toronto Seniors Strategy* policy and practice to address this. Chapter 3 examines how the AFC approach in Toronto is supporting a positive aging identity by exploring the meanings interview participants make of the place of seniors in society, how they understand their diverse needs, and how they understand the policy issue of population aging and consider it a challenge and/or an opportunity. I present inconsistences in the ways that older adults are recognized that correspond to different ways of understanding the purpose of the AFC approach, and particularly its redistributive potential. I outline how this relates to the various ways in which seniors themselves have defined the problems they face in local environments through participatory AFC processes. Chapter 4 explores the claim that AFCs empower local policy actors to support seniors by outlining how participants understand the institutional mechanisms at their disposal to design and action effective AFCs, how they work with other "partners" in different sectors, and the power relations within and between these sectors. I offer important insight into the needs for the rights of local government and the non-profit sector to support them to design and implement place-based age-friendly policy. Finally, the concluding chapter brings the findings together to offer insight for what changes need to be made both conceptually and practically to achieve a right to the city for senior citizens through the AFC program.

CHAPTER ONE

A Case Study of Toronto's Age-Friendly Landscape

Introduction

The purpose of this chapter is to map the urban governance landscape of age-friendly work within the geographic boundaries of the city of Toronto from a multi-scalar and multi-actor "seeing like a city" perspective. This contextualization is essential to the study of AFCs because the WHO's Active Aging Framework incorporates multiple policy domains, many of which are the overlapping responsibility of local government departments, central government agencies and ministries, and non-profit organizations. Mapping this "landscape of antagonism" requires an identification of who is doing what and according to which rules; where there is overlapping jurisdiction; where there are partnerships; and the ways in which roles and partnership relations might be changing and being challenged.

As such, this chapter includes an initial examination of the roles of both local government and the non-profit sector in the governance of age-friendly environments, including how these roles intersect with the work of central governments. I begin by mapping these roles and then analyze how this work is coordinated across Toronto through age-friendly policy. The latter includes a historical analysis of age-friendly policy in Toronto and additional detail on the development of the *Toronto Seniors Strategy*.

Through description, I identify challenges as well as opportunities in the actualization of AFCs as a right to the city that is the subject of in-depth analysis in the chapters to come.

The Role of Local Government in Producing Age-Friendly Environments in Toronto

There is scarcely a realm of local government responsibility that is not relevant to the production of an age-friendly environment. Rather than listing the role of each city division and agency, I have grouped this work into the following policy fields: health, transportation, housing, recreation, and social planning. The work undertaken in these fields is either governed directly by municipal council and operates through a City of Toronto division or is governed via a municipally-funded special-purpose body that retains its own governance structure, such as the Toronto Transit Commission or the Toronto Community Housing Corporation.[12]My definition of local government includes both the work of the municipal government and these special-purpose bodies.

Much of the work of local government in these fields is mandated by the Ontario provincial government through legislation. Here it is important to highlight that provincial governments in Canada have constitutional authority over local affairs and local governments are "creatures of provincial statute and therefore possess no autonomous or inalienable status" (Eidelman and Taylor 2010, 314). While Toronto remains a creature of the province, with its powers limited to those which are granted to it, provincial legislation often comes with room for local discretion and policy autonomy (Sancton 2015). Furthermore, local governments engage in policy work and service provision that is driven by citizen needs and demands, which may reflect a new need for programming or may be the

1 Toronto's administrative structure is led by a council-appointed city manager; three deputy managers from the human services, hard services, and internal finance clusters who oversee the work of forty-one divisions; and 122 special-purpose bodies (also known as agencies, boards, commissions, and corporations) such as the Toronto Board of Health, Toronto Police Services Board, Toronto Transit Commission, and the Toronto Community Housing Corporation who direct service provision and are governed by a board of councillors and citizens (Joy and Vogel 2015).

result of inadequacies in urban policymaking by central governments. In fact, much pre-existing provincial and federal legislation on issues in the fields of housing and infrastructure, for instance, emanated from needs, service gaps, and policy fragmentation in urban environments as well as from advocacy by local actors (Marutto 2004; Mahon et al. 2007).

The responsibility of Toronto's local government in many of the social and physical infrastructure policy domains that are crucial to the production of age-friendly environments increased in 1998 because of a provincially imposed amalgamation. Ontario's Conservative premier, Mike Harris, merged the six municipalities of Metro Toronto (Toronto, York, East York, North York, Scarborough, and Etobicoke) into a new megacity. Institutional amalgamation was combined with policy devolution that transferred full costs and operating responsibility for social housing, libraries, water, sewers, roads, public transit, mental health group homes, shelter and hostel beds, as well as the operating costs of social assistance and half the costs of social services, public health, and ambulances to the megacity (Joy and Vogel 2015, 41). Toronto relies on the property taxes, user fees, and transfers from the province (and to a lesser extent, the federal government) to fund these new public responsibilities. The province has been criticized for providing neither commensurate financial assistance nor new substantive revenue-generating powers to local government to ensure the redistribution of adequate service and infrastructure provision to their citizens (Frisken 2007; Joy and Vogel 2015; Fanelli 2016).

HEALTH

While health care is officially under provincial jurisdiction, Toronto engages in a considerable component of this work through the provision of paramedic services, long-term care homes, and public health programming. Toronto Paramedic Services is the municipal provider of ambulance and paramedic services. Staff explain that the division pays special attention to seniors, as almost half of their calls are for people over the age of sixty-five. Paramedic Services offers specific support through a community para-medicine program that targets vulnerable seniors, many living in local government social housing buildings, and refers them to non-profit home care service providers. There is also a pilot program where paramedics notify non-profit agencies when the seniors they serve interact with paramedics and may be taken to hospital. Both projects are funded by the province to facilitate aging in place and a more active role on the part of local government and the non-profit sector to meet the needs of seniors in local environments.

Since 1949, the province has required its municipalities, no matter their size, to operate one long-term care home (Association of Municipalities of Ontario 2011). Given its size and the extent of its population need, the city has decided to operate ten long-term care homes. The province regulates these homes through the *Long Term Care Homes Act 2007* and the Ontario Ministry of Health and Long Term Care provides funding per resident for nursing and personal care. As part of its regulatory role, the province has mandated redevelopment in six of Toronto's long-term care homes to bring them up to new standards and is providing some funding for this endeavour (City of Toronto 2015a). At the time of my interviews, the city's Long Term Care Homes and Services division was undertaking a capital renewal plan, and one home had been extensively redeveloped. The division also provides programs for the broader community, including adult day programs for seniors in three of its homes; homemakers and nurses services (housekeeping, laundry, shopping, meal preparation) to low-income individuals coordinated through community contracts with non-profit agencies; and supportive housing services (personal care, housekeeping and laundry, medication reminders, security checks, meal preparations) to eligible tenants in designated social housing buildings (City of Toronto 2016a).

Toronto Public Health also provides community health support for vulnerable seniors, as well as work on falls prevention. This work is governed by the Toronto Board of Health under the provincial *Health Promotion and Protection Act 1990*. While the act directs municipal public health provision broadly, it does not mandate services to vulnerable seniors (City of Toronto 2002). Local government has illustrated policy autonomy to meet needs here as Toronto Public Health established a Vulnerable Adults and Seniors Team in 2011 as part of its mental health promotion work. This team consists of a group of nurses who respond to calls about citizens over fifty-five who, according to the website, are "living in a challenging situation," which may include mental and physical ailments, experiences of bed bugs and hoarding, a risk of eviction and homelessness, low income, and little informal support (City of Toronto 2016b). The team does some short-term home visiting and follow-up during extreme weather events, links people to other support services based on client assessments of needs, and provides some basic health care through two non-profit community health centres for seniors who have no provincial health coverage (ibid.). Toronto Public Health also covers dental services to low-income seniors in community health centres and through a mobile dental clinic (ibid.). According to the Toronto Public Health website, a bulk of the Vulnerable Adults and Seniors Team work is "prevention-oriented" and consists of presentations to community groups on topics such as safety during extreme weather, safe medication use, nutrition and food security, social isolation, home and personal safety (ibid.).

Although Toronto Public Health does work on intimate partner violence against women, it does not focus specifically on elder abuse. Instead, elder abuse is under the domain of the enforcement services of the Toronto Police Service, and Ontario's *Police Services Act* requires local police to have procedures and processes in place for criminal investigations of elder abuse. Toronto Police Services has a Vulnerable Persons Coordinator who raises awareness through a social media presence, is involved in broader advocacy work through Ontario-wide committees, and does trainings and updates procedures for police officers on elder abuse.

Toronto Public Health also has a Chronic Disease and Injury Prevention Directorate and a small piece of this work is falls prevention for seniors. The Toronto Public Health website includes tips and links on how individuals can keep their homes safe and can stay active and well-equipped for home and winter safety (City of Toronto 2016c). On this topic, it is important to note that the city of Toronto provides uneven coverage of sidewalk snow-clearing within its borders, a legacy of amalgamation before which this service was provided in some former municipalities but not others and was not redistributed as a mandatory public service. Those aged sixty-five and above can apply for free snow-clearing and the city provides some funding for non-profits to do this work, though the Chronic Disease and Injury Prevention Directorate website says nothing about this assistance and simply urges city-dwellers to keep their paths clear. At the time of my interviews, the directorate was also working on providing training on falls prevention to the personal support workers and family member carers of seniors.

HOUSING

Local government supports the provision of housing services for vulnerable seniors through Toronto Community Housing; the Shelter, Support and Housing Administration division; the Affordable Housing Office; and City Planning. Toronto's social housing service provider, Toronto Community Housing, provides housing for low-income seniors and 25 per cent of its residents are over the age of fifty-nine (Toronto Community Housing 2016; Ombudsman 2013). At the time of my interviews, Toronto Community Housing was developing a Vulnerable Seniors Action Plan which includes measures to address the potential eviction of vulnerable seniors facing challenges paying their bills, as well as those who experience issues with hoarding and bed bugs. This action plan stems in part from an Ombudsman investigation on seniors evicted from public housing for non-payment of rent (Ombudsman 2013). To provide supportive housing services for vulnerable seniors, Toronto Community Housing works with the city's Long Term Care and Paramedic Services divisions as well as community non-profit providers. The extent of vulnerability in the city and the growing senior population aging in place has led to the development of a new protocol, SPIDER (Specialized Interdivisional Enhanced Response), which targets individuals who might struggle, for instance, with hoarding, pest infestations, and unsafe living situations (City of Toronto 2016d). A city representative explains that SPIDER is "meant to bring together all the divisions of the city around problematic issues in the community" (B20) where in the past they have lacked a coordinated response.

The Hostel Services section of the city's Shelter, Support and Housing Administration division provides support to people experiencing homelessness on the streets and in the shelter system, including seniors. A considerable and growing number of their clients are aging, and through partnership with the city's Long Term Care division they are adapting to provide for the specific needs of seniors in the revitalization of Seaton House, a large downtown shelter. Hostel Services also has several contracts with non-profit agencies that provide housing and shelter services to seniors. They can support seniors in the private rental market by targeting "some housing allowances for seniors … to try to get them out of shelters and into the community with supports or to target housing allowances to people who may be at risk of losing their housing" (B20).

Hostel Services has also produced a *Services for Seniors in Toronto* guide directed to vulnerable seniors and their caregivers that outlines government and non-profit services available in Toronto.

The city's Affordable Housing Office, which is charged with creating and maintaining affordable housing through partnerships with the non-profit and private sector, operates a homeowner's renovation grant for low-income seniors that receives minor funding from the province. Also in the domain of housing, the Strategic Initiatives, Policy and Analysis section of the City Planning division are working towards the creation of affordable housing in new condominiums by allowing developers more density (a.k.a. density bonusing) and a city-wide zoning bylaw that allows for the creation of secondary basement suites. City Planning also does demographic projection work through *Toronto Plan Flashforward* that can facilitate planning, design, and policy needs for senior citizens. The division's review of planning applications may require applicants to conduct a Community Services and Facilities study that identifies a demographic profile of the geography and existing maps and projected social infrastructure needs based on this profile, which may include seniors.

TRANSPORTATION

Transportation in Toronto is managed mainly through the city's Transportation Services division and the Toronto Transit Commission. The Public Realm section of the Transportation Services division has a Pedestrian Projects unit that works to enhance walkability and accessibility enhancements such as street furniture, signage, fixing sidewalks and crosswalks, and snow-clearing standards are part of this. The Public Realm section has also created new accessibility protocols for city infrastructure in response to provincial accessibility requirements. The Ontario government released the *Accessibility for Ontarians with Disabilities Act* (AODA) in 2005 and all businesses, local government bodies, and non-profit organizations must comply with the legislation fully by 2025, though no funding support is provided by the province to ensure implementation.

Also in response to AODA requirements, the Toronto Transit Commission has been working to enhance the accessibility of the transit system by making all of its buses accessible; has started to operate accessible streetcars; intends to retrofit all subway stations to be accessible;

is working to make more seats designated for priority groups, which includes seniors; and is improving its public communication system in the stations. There is a small seniors' discount for regular subway service and people with a support assistance card can receive free travel for their accompanying attendant. The Toronto Transit Commission also operates Wheel Trans, which provides rides to those with accessibility challenges based on eligibility requirements. This also includes the operation of five Community Bus Routes, which according to a city representative are "a fixed route service that circulates locally within a community typically hooking up say seniors homes and community facilities whether it is a shopping mall or a local medical clinic or some retail area where there is a lot of services or libraries" (B22).

RECREATION

Both the Toronto Public Library and the city's Parks, Forestry and Recreation division have relatively new staff and divisional teams to look at servicing for older adults. A particular focus of this work is to align and ensure a redistribution of programs for seniors in the former municipalities of the City of Toronto post-amalgamation. The Toronto Public Library has hired a seniors' services coordinator who works with a cross-city team to coordinate all library programming for seniors, including a mobile library and a great variety of programs on health and wellness, technology, and financial needs. The library has also reached out to a local non-profit to assist them to train staff on seniors' issues, and they have an older adult committee that helps design services and programs to meet the needs of seniors.

The Community Recreation Older Adults Service Team has representation from frontline community-recreation programmers from across the city as well as their supervisors to support existing and new programming for seniors. The recreation division is also one of the city's "largest landlords" (B15A) and permits space for non-profit programming for seniors through partnership work. The city also has several community centres within the boundaries of the former municipalities that are known as agencies of the City of Toronto and that provide seniors with social and recreational programming. The city covers the administrative costs of these organizations, but the programming and program-specific staff are funded through separate grants from all three levels of government.

SOCIAL PLANNING

The city's non-service operating divisions, Equity, Diversity and Human Rights and Social Development, Finance and Administration, also undertake work relevant to seniors. The Equity Division works to "ensure that city policies are responsive to the City of Toronto's diverse communities" (B13) and all city policy and program reports are required to include an equity impact statement based on an equity analysis of the policy. This analysis identifies potential barriers and impacts for specific groups, attempts to remove these barriers, and measures whether efforts to remove barriers are working (City of Toronto 2014). A city representative explains that aging is "another lens that we would place on our work just as we might use the other lenses which would be ability, access, race, sexual identity, just to name a few. Also, intersections of age … with other diversity considerations in terms of policy, program development, and also in terms of how the city communicates with seniors and vice versa" (B13). There is a Human Rights section within the Equity division that hears and deals with human rights complaints, and one of the prohibited grounds of the *Ontario Human Rights Code* is age and disability. The division put in place training and advice on how to prevent code violations via public and internal protocols such as the *Equity Lens and Equity Impact Statements*, and *Accessibility Design Guidelines* that apply to renovations and retrofits to city-owned buildings. At the time of my interviews, staff were in the process of reviewing the *Equity Impact Statement* due to problems such as equity being considered secondarily rather than a crucial component of early program development and evaluation, the uneven application of the *Equity Impact Statement* in different city divisions, and a failure on the part of the city to keep track of and enforce this equity work (City of Toronto 2014).

The city has an internal resource, *The Guide to Good Practice: Providing Equitable Services to Individuals of All Abilities,* which includes a guide, content for staff training, meetings to coordinate joint protocols among staff, and division-specific responses to support the work of frontline staff who engage with population groups with diminished cognitive abilities. The protocol stemmed from a City of Toronto Ombudsman investigation called *A Duty to Care* (2010) on a case where a bylaw enforcement officer ordered the cutting down of a tree on a property of a homeowner who was a senior with advanced Alzheimer's.

Finally, in its social planning and social policy development role, the city's Social Development division is charged with coordinating the design and implementation of city-wide social policy strategies, including the *Toronto Seniors Strategy*. The division's Community Funding unit coordinates the Community Service Partnerships grants, the main pool of funding for the non-profit sector. The Community Funding unit employs agency review officers to monitor the agencies, obtain feedback on service needs, and connect agencies to share information about programming. It is through these grants that the city fulfills is municipal legislative requirement to fund 20 percent of elderly persons' centres, which is cost-shared with the province. Through the *Elderly Persons Centre Act*, the Province of Ontario provides money to municipalities to distribute to community organizations to provide recreational and educational programming. I will now briefly outline the role of these non-profit organizations in producing age-friendly environments in Toronto.

The Role of the Non-profit Sector in Producing Age-Friendly Environments in Toronto

The non-profit sector in Ontario is a major provider of community-based services for senior citizens of varying levels of need and a great many of these organizations operate in the City of Toronto. Many non-profit participants talked about their longstanding history of service provision for seniors, with one employee describing this historical evolution thus: "Many non-profits, cultural groups, and church groups started providing services to vulnerable seniors long ago that needed care and were socially isolated. Many started developing seniors' apartments and then started to include different services based on needs, like meals on wheels and congregate dining" (D3). Non-profits serving seniors vary greatly in size, as some agencies provide a full basket of these services and others specialize in one or two areas. In defining the work of the non-profit sector in the realm of elder care, we can distinguish between non-profits providing community support services and those doing more civic engagement work.

COMMUNITY SUPPORT SERVICES

The community support services sector helps seniors remain in their own homes and provides long-term care in an institutional setting for those who are no longer able to age in their own homes. Services that help seniors remain at home vary according to need and may be provided directly in the home or in a neighbourhood community centre. This work includes:

» prevention-oriented group-based social and recreational programming such as computer courses, meal sharing, excursions, and health promotion lectures

» personal home-based supports such as case management and referral to other services, homemaking, nutrition counselling, chronic illness management, personal care, meals on wheels, transportation for those who do not qualify for public accessible transit, escort to medical appointments, friendly visits, and security checks

» intensive supports such as day programs in non-profit community facilities for those with dementia and Alzheimer's, which also act as respite for informal caregivers who support seniors in the home.
(United Way 2001)

Non-profits also provide services for seniors with specific needs, including prevention and crisis response for those facing situations of abuse. However, there is only one agency in Toronto that specializes in this work, and it operates one "safe haven" apartment and "an elder abuse consultation team which is a forum for service providers to come to if they are dealing with cases of abuse in the community" (D31B). Non-profits also operate affordable housing and shelters for vulnerable seniors experiencing addiction and mental health challenges. Many smaller agencies specialize in providing supports to seniors of different linguistic and ethno-cultural backgrounds, offering translation services between seniors and medical support services and organizing groups of seniors for social activities in their preferred language. There is one agency of the

City of Toronto that specializes in active living groups and classes as well as more informal personal interventions such as check-ins and referrals for LGBTQ+ seniors.

Funding for community support work is provided to non-profits by all three levels of government as well as by non-government sources such as the United Way. Some agencies also organize fundraising events and charge user fees for their services. Many of the community support services for seniors are provided on a volunteer basis, though with increased demand, these organizations have hired social workers to run activities, coordinate volunteers, and manage funding.

Over the last few decades, many of these non-profits have shifted to provide more professionalized and health-related services such as nursing, physiotherapy, occupational therapy, and psychological services (United Way 2001); mobile medical teams that bring nurses and doctors to seniors; 24–7 supportive housing, such as specialized facilities for seniors with dementia; and long-term care homes and palliative care hospices. Several medium to large agencies provide a basket of social support and medical home care services in distinct areas of the city.

The blurring of provision between community support services and more medicalized services is an outcome of health care restructuring. To meet community needs and reduce health care costs, the Government of Ontario shifted health care services from hospitals and long-term care homes "into the community" beginning in the early 1990s (United Way 2001). The closure of hospitals and limitation of beds – 18,500 have been lost since 1990 (Ontario Health Coalition 2011) – as well as the increase in short-stay procedures and quick discharge of patients augmented the demand for home care in the community (United Way 2001). By 2011, there was a waitlist for home care of more than 10,000 people across the province (Ontario Health Coalition 2011). To gain greater control over the changing home care landscape, as well as to bring in a competitive bidding system of "managed competition" in the new home care and long-term care "markets," the provincial government created forty-three localized Community Care Access Centres (CCACs) to contract with non-profit and private care providers and designed eligibility criteria for those receiving care (United Way 2001). Personal care and homemaking services, as well as more professionalized medical services, long-term care, and palliative care are also being provided by private sector organizations (ibid.). While those that are eligible for public CCAC services do not pay out of pocket, home care is not covered under the *Canada Health Act* and funding limitations have meant that publicly provided care is rationed to those with the most acute needs (ibid.), while those who do not qualify must pay out of pocket for non-profit and private services. Those who cannot afford to pay may go without or rely on city Homemakers and Nurses services, which during this period of restructuring began to introduce waitlists (City of Toronto 1999). According to the report *Living Longer, Living Well* (2012), commissioned by the province and prepared by a leading gerontologist, while funding for CCACs has increased by 69 percent over the past decade, the number of patients demanding service has increased by 83 percent and these patients have more acute and complex needs.

In 2006, the provincial government sought to align the funding and planning of all local health care provision (hospitals, community care, and long-term care) through fourteen new special-purpose bodies known as Local Health Integration Networks (LHINs), five of which are within the boundaries of Toronto. LHINs funnel money from the Ontario Ministry of Health and Long Term Care to fourteen associated CCACs to support people to age at home through the province's 2007 *Aging at Home* strategy (Sinha 2012). LHINs also directly fund community support services, with a new focus on innovative wellness programs that encourage aging in place. The emphasis on patient-centred prevention, specifically focused on the most acute patients, and addressing the local fragmentation in health provision in the context of the priority to age in place, has continued with the 2012 *Ontario Action Plan for Health Care.* However, remaining challenges include a lack of clear standards and access to care (as well as publicly available information on these issues); staff shortages, in part because of low wages and working conditions; and a reduction of public home care funding in the community as a percentage of health care, even as the number of hospital beds are reduced and as the population is aging and its needs are increasing (Ontario Health Coalition 2011).

Ontario has the most privatized home-care market in the country, and there has been a consolidation of large private companies providing this care, with small non-profits struggling to compete and losing key contracts (Ontario Health Coalition 2011; United Way of Greater Toronto 2001; O'Connor 2004). While the ratio of non-profit to private home care was 82–18 in 1995, this ratio became 42–58 by 2011, illustrating a dramatic shift towards private provision (Ontario Health Coalition 2011). Before the shift to managed competition and before amalgamation, home care delivery was coordinated locally by the Home Care Program of Metropolitan Toronto based on a service partnership between local public health divisions, hospitals, and community agencies (United Way 2001; Brown 1968). As other services were devolved to the new megacity of Toronto post-amalgamation, home care was uploaded from the former metropolitan government to the province and then marketized.

CIVIC ENGAGEMENT

In addition to service provision, non-profits do civic engagement work. Engagement includes the creation of senior citizen committees to inform programming and having seniors deliver programming through volunteerism, as well as policy advocacy work. This advocacy is undertaken by service agencies to inform public policy based on their expertise and by a small number of organizations that exist specifically to inform policy on the rights of senior citizens. Some non-profits also offer workshops with seniors on how to strengthen their autonomy and policy voice. There are also large policy advocacy organizations that represent home care and long-term care providing agencies before government. One Toronto-based volunteer-oriented organization offers educational workshops and training for both the private and public sectors on how to work with seniors and conducts facility and site assessments through an aging lens.

The first section of this chapter has illustrated the rich array of service work undertaken by local government and non-profit organizations to produce age-friendly environments in Toronto. I will now explore how this work is coordinated through local age-friendly policy initiatives. I begin with a brief history of this policy work in Toronto before moving on to examine the development of the *Toronto Seniors Strategy* in more detail.

Past Age-Friendly Policy Initiatives in Toronto

Toronto has a history of developing coordinated policy strategy on population aging. Post-amalgamation, a Toronto Seniors' Taskforce, which included seven city councillors and eighteen seniors, was struck and the group produced the 1999 report *Toronto – Building a City for All Ages*. The report is grounded in the voices of Toronto seniors and identifies the everyday challenges they face in accessing key services and amenities in the new geographic boundaries of the City of Toronto (City of Toronto 1999). The historical context of amalgamation and policy devolution is important, because seniors identified concerns around the loss of crucial city- and non-profit-provided services and sense of familiarity and community in the new megacity (ibid.). The recommendations, based on the needs identified by seniors and developed in consultation with city councillors and staff, are directed to multiple levels of government based on everyday experiences of limited access to health services, affordable housing, and affordable and accessible transportation (City of Toronto 1999; City of Toronto 2002). The taskforce report also recommended the establishment of a Toronto Seniors Assembly which would act as a formal advisory body to a political Toronto Seniors Advocate who could coordinate with city staff (City of Toronto 2002). Councillor Anne Johnston was appointed to be the first advocate and chaired the Toronto Seniors Assembly. While the initial taskforce report and its follow-up progress report in 2002 placed emphasis on the city continuing to advocate to other levels of government, there was no clear advocacy strategy on the part of the city and in partnership with non-profits outlined in the report. The focus on local government bureaucracy and its specific role is also underdeveloped in the reports, as there is no clear action plan.

The megacity's second mayor, David Miller, established a Roundtable on Seniors in his first term that convened from 2003 to 2006, which replaced the Toronto Seniors Assembly and political seniors advocate model. A senior citizen participant with institutional memory explains that the roundtable had the "big heads of different departments and also heads of seniors organizations and big agencies providing services. So basically, it was sort of a service provider network" (C2). The more professional nature of the roundtable model sparked "an interest and a concern that there were many other voices of seniors that were not heard. The newcomers, the people who are low-income, those living in the periphery of the city" (C2). As a result, a new Seniors Advisory Group to Toronto City Council was convened with an effort to achieve representation of Toronto seniors in all their diversity. A former member of the group explains that it was always a "second-class seniors' group" (C2) that had less access to decision-making power than the professional roundtable. The roundtable produced a report in 2006 titled *The City of Toronto Roundtable on Seniors: Housing Toronto Seniors*. This report barely mentions the previous taskforce reports and, rather than emanating from the voices of seniors highlighting their everyday needs, there is an undertone of aging as an expensive issue for local government (City of Toronto 2006). While the report offers a detailed focus on housing policy, mapping out the complexity of the area and the roles of different players, it does not include the voices of seniors experiencing housing instability. While it outlines recommendations, including a critique of provincial devolution in the realm of housing and recommendations for policy changes to support tenants and more resources for the city in social housing, a concrete action plan was not fully established (ibid.).

Mayor Miller's direction of convening people-based roundtables (he had one on children as well) quickly dissolved and failed to make the priority list for his second term in office. Although Miller is considered by many to have had a legacy of progressive policy, it was under his leadership that "a number of advisory groups disappeared" and were "declawed" (D49). When the roundtable on seniors disappeared in Miller's second term of office, the Seniors Advisory Group was suddenly "left with the responsibility to respond, be up to date, question, inquire, advocate, inform, and all of the above. With more or less the same makeup of the group" (C2). At the end of Miller's second term, the Seniors Advisory Group morphed into its current iteration: the Toronto Seniors Forum. The forum receives some city staff support in its efforts to facilitate civic engagement, to represent a voice for seniors not often heard, and to ensure that Toronto provides public services equitably.

The Toronto Seniors Strategy

AGENDA SETTING

My interviews highlight a wide array of factors that brought designing a new seniors' strategy to the policy agenda in Toronto, illustrating the complex multi-scalar and multi-actor nature of municipal policymaking and the diverse motives underlying age-friendly policy work. Several participants spoke to "top-down" or external drivers such as the WHO's work on AFCs, and particularly the rapid spread of the movement in surrounding cities such as Hamilton, Waterloo, London, and Ottawa.

Here participants speak to how local politicians seeking the recognition of WHO age-friendly status felt pressure to compete with other cities. The work of central governments encouraging AFCs through grants and information guides is also cited as a factor influencing *Toronto Seniors Strategy* initiation. Finally, several participants believed that local senior strategies are motivated to support provincial priorities in the health care sector as they aim to prevent admission to hospital and long-term care homes as well as to reintegrate citizens back into the community after hospital procedures.

Many participants note what they see as more "grassroots" motivations for the *Toronto Seniors Strategy*, though there is debate as to whether this was initiated by citizens themselves, external advocacy organizations, the city bureaucracy, or by a politician. Several participants point to the changing demographics and population needs sparking budget pressures around community facilities and programs. City representatives spoke about the need to support Toronto's most vulnerable populations, who are increasingly senior citizens. Two municipal bureaucrats spoke about the AFC concept first being raised by bureaucrats in the city's Long Term Care division in the context of the provincially mandated redevelopment of six of their facilities. However, other staff members recall that it was Councillor Josh Matlow who pushed the *Toronto Seniors Strategy* forward, which suggests the motivation was also political. Creating a strategy for seniors was a key election platform for Councillor Matlow, as he explains: "When I was running for office, it was obviously not the number one thing that people talk about at the door because it's not the wedge issue, it's not an issue that the media obsesses about, but it's something that I talked about. How one of the things that I wanted to do if I was elected was to create a strategy for seniors in Toronto. Actually, a lot of people, even though they hadn't talked about this initially, once we had that conversation, they said, 'Wow, that makes a lot of sense.' Because everybody has somebody in their life who [is] arriving there" (A1).

Councillor Kristyn Wong-Tam agrees that, while it was Councillor Matlow who passed the motion to develop the *Toronto Seniors Strategy*, it could have been many others as councillors are beginning to think about aging, especially if they have many seniors in their wards. Several participants also spoke to the political expediency of the AFC concept motivating the *Toronto Seniors Strategy*, many noting that seniors tend to vote. I also learned that there were a few non-profit organizations who advocated for the AFC concept in Toronto after it was announced by the WHO. In particular, Charlotte Maher, now deceased, is cited by several interview participants as having lobbied Councillor Matlow to pass the motion to develop the *Toronto Seniors Strategy*, though this was not mentioned in my interview with the councillor himself.

POLICY DEVELOPMENT

In April 2011, Josh Matlow got council to pass a motion directing staff to prepare the *Toronto Seniors Strategy*. Matlow had to engage councillors individually to pass the motion because the City of Toronto is prevented by the province from operating political parties in local politics.[23] Councillor Matlow speaks to the unique political context in Toronto at the time, under the leadership of controversial mayor Rob Ford: "One of the first major initiatives that I moved when I became a councillor was to create a Toronto Seniors Strategy. So, I brought a motion to council. At that time, it was quite an interesting time, to understate it. It was an incredibly divisive council; we had a new mayor with a mandate that had nothing to do with any of this. This isn't about gravy; this is about people. We had a distinct right-wing and left-wing and centre. I was able to get unanimous support to go ahead with this" (A1).

Councillor oversight for the development of the *Toronto Seniors Strategy* was provided through the Seniors Strategy subcommittee of the Community Development and Recreation Committee of Council which, according to a former member, is charged with directing the planning of city services that are people-oriented in nature.[34]Councillor Matlow was the chair of the subcommittee and worked with city staff to develop its strategy. The Social Research unit of the city's Social Development, Finance and Administration division led the strategy; the staff team

2 At the time, city council consisted of forty-five members elected to represent wards of about 54,000 people and a mayor elected at large (Joy and Vogel 2015).

3 Toronto has a council-committee structure of government and six standing committees that lead the functional work of council and hear citizen deputations on their agenda items (Joy and Vogel 2015).

consisted of one planning analyst and two policy officers. The planning analyst was tasked with bringing together demographic data on Toronto seniors to illustrate trends and project service impacts. This included data collected from non-profit agencies with whom the city has a funding relationship, such as the number of clients they serve in their programs and how often they frequent the programs. Reflecting on this data-gathering process, a city representative explains that "in terms of population aging, we ran some demographics about the pressures on the city and it is really quite staggering what we are facing. The grey tsunami and all of that" (B2).

Equally confounding was the realization that "there was no planning in place, city-wide, for this" (B2), even though Toronto has had previous aging strategies. In this regard, the staff team took stock of the city's past, present, and future role serving an aging population to "devise a coordinated approach … there are over 50,000 employees in the City of Toronto alone, so we need to make sure that we are all working on the same page" (B3). Background research consisted of mapping all the public services, programs, and agencies serving seniors operating within the boundaries of the City of Toronto. A city representative admits that, while they had intended to include the services provided by non-profit organizations, they did not have the time and resources to undertake this work. This staff member advised that through their background research they discovered that 75 percent of the recommendations to city divisions in previous aging strategies had been implemented, compared to 33 percent of recommendations to special-purpose bodies. Furthermore, there were "a lot of poorly worded and poorly developed recommendations out there" (B2) and some divisions had made recommendations that they had no power to implement. There were several frustrating moments when the policy officer contacted city divisions and special-purpose bodies about past recommendations and discovered that they had not even heard of them.

In addition to inadequate implementation of local government recommendations, it was discovered that recommendations to central governments were very rarely implemented. Because of this, it was decided that the *Toronto Seniors Strategy* would focus on "identifying what the city currently does and how the city could do things better, so it is very city-specific" (B6). The *Toronto Seniors Strategy* thus illustrates an attempt on the part of local government to realize an AFC by honing the focus on what is within their institutional jurisdiction.

The *Toronto Seniors Strategy* is defined by staff as a corporate document, as it is characterized by all parts of the corporation coming together to create a wide policy vision, agenda, and action plan. The *Toronto Seniors Strategy* had a senior management team and a technical advisory team with representation from seventeen divisions as well as from Toronto Police Services, the Toronto Transit Commission, Toronto Community Housing, and the Toronto Public Library. Several divisions that I interviewed had two representatives involved on the respective strategy tables. Each staff representative was asked to provide insight on how their existing work impacted the lives of senior citizens and to make recommendations for building on this role, sometimes in partnership with other city divisions or special-purpose bodies. Some city representatives felt that the process provided them with the opportunity to share their work and to learn about the work of other areas of local government. However, one city employee said that it was unbelievable how many divisions had not thought about this issue, and that they had a hard time pushing the city divisions and special-purpose bodies to do so, though some were better than others.

In addition to the bureaucratic working groups noted above, *Toronto Seniors Strategy* development involved an expert panel chosen because they could "speak reliably and expertly on the topic of aging" (B3). Here, a city representative notes that the "idea was to ensure a wide variety of perspectives and representatives from as many equity-seeking groups as possible as well as themes such as groups that could speak to health, transportation, safety" (B3). The expert panel was led by an expert on the province's policy work on aging and health care. This leadership was recruited strategically to make sure that the "local strategy was aligned fully with the provincial strategy" (E19), though this expert was not a representative of the Ontario Government. In this regard, both a representative from the Ontario Seniors Secretariat and a representative from the Toronto Central Local Health Integration Network joined the expert panel, though a city representative expresses frustration that "we tried so hard to get the Province and the Feds engaged" (B2) but had a lack of success engaging the federal government in particular. Furthermore, a staff member advised that, while the city is involved with the Ontario Seniors Secretariat, the purpose and power of this body within the Ontario government is unclear. The expert panel met three times and consulted frequently over email to identify and inform policy recommendations.

Participants explain that the city delineated their areas of responsibility, explaining up front what it was and what could be accomplished. Thus, the topics open for discussion in the context of the *Toronto Seniors Strategy* were delimited from the beginning by the city, based on their jurisdictional responsibilities.

In addition to the expert panel, the city engaged in a broader consultation process to inform the *Toronto Seniors Strategy*. Staff designed a workbook for data collection on both individual seniors and agencies which included a series of questions on seniors, including their ethnocultural background, their spoken languages, their ages, their occupation, their needs, and their desires. The consultation workbook was also disseminated to agencies throughout the non-profit sector. The workbook was translated into eleven different languages; 33 percent of the responses were in a language other than English. A city representative stated that they would have lost a lot of information had they not translated documents and admits that with more money for translations, they could have reached more seniors. A public consultation took place in June 2012 at the Toronto Reference Library which consisted of a large focus-group session where senior citizens and agencies serving them sat at roundtables to fill out the workbook; this was facilitated by city staff, councillors, and Toronto Seniors Forum members. The city collected 500 books at this event (City of Toronto 2013). There were also a series of town halls on the *Toronto Seniors Strategy* where city councillors and senior citizen members of the Toronto Seniors Forum gave presentations and where the workbook was disseminated.

Despite this extensive data-collection, a city representative explained to me that "there were not a lot of surprises" and "not a lot of dramatic shifts that would affect the lives of seniors that we needed to ask them about" (B6). They further advised that "there is not a fear that we were shifting anything or not taking into consideration a voice because once again, this is about how the city operates and how the city can operate better" (B6). This once again reminds us that the *Toronto Seniors Strategy* is foremost a bureaucratic tool emphasizing what local government is doing in the current context, something that was missing in previous aging strategies. However, this also suggests limitations in how the strategy enables Toronto seniors and their organizations to frame the problems that they encounter in their everyday lives in order to elicit a substantive redistributive response in the eight domains of the AFC framework.

The recommendations in the *Toronto Seniors Strategy* are organized according to the eight WHO AFC Active Aging Framework priorities. A city representative explains that although the city has its own issues and priorities, it was decided to use the WHO model because people were familiar with it. Each of the eight priority areas are broken down into sub-issues and each sub-issue is aligned with a high-level recommendation. In total, the strategy includes twenty-five recommendations and ninety-one action items. Each recommendation is then associated with: a one- to two-sentence action item; one or more city divisions or special-purpose bodies responsible for implementing the item; a timeline for completion that is short-, medium-, or long-term; and a progress measure, described typically in five words or less, that often includes reporting back on the action, the partnerships made, and counting the number of programs and people involved. Actions designated as "short-term" begin immediately and have no net cost implications to the city. Many of the short-term actions also highlight what local government is already doing; the action is thus to continue the work. "Medium-term" actions are to be implemented within two to three years, and their costs are to be raised individually by each city division or special-purpose body during the regular city budget process (City of Toronto 2013, 28). Actions labelled "long-term" can begin their implementation in "2015 and beyond" and again, their costs are referred back to local government staff in their annual budgeting (City of Toronto 2013, 28).

The following briefly describes the content of the *Toronto Seniors Strategy* report, outlined according to the eight WHO priority areas. This is meant to provide a descriptive summary, whereas the adequacy of these recommendations and actions and the operational capacities to implement them is analyzed in the chapters to come.

1. Respect and Social Inclusion

The *Toronto Seniors Strategy* proclaims a recognition that older adults are diverse and valued members of the community. To affirm this commitment, the city states that it intends to apply for WHO AFC status, conduct data analysis on older adult safety, and design a public campaign to combat ageism (City of Toronto 2013). It acknowledges that older adults are particularly vulnerable to physical, emotional, and financial abuse, and it is the role of local government to address this, primarily through the work of the Toronto Police Service. Actions in this regard include creating local community committees to address safety as well as establishing an advisory committee with multiple city and non-city stakeholders, creating public awareness campaigns, designing resource guides and enforcing officer training on the recognition and reporting of abuse, and compiling neighbourhood-based victimization data (ibid.).

To ensure that seniors access city services on an equitable basis, the Shelter, Support and Housing Administration division has committed to reviewing its staff training to "ensure the needs of homeless and at risk older adults are adequately represented" (City of Toronto 2013, 40). The Equity, Diversity and Human Rights division intends, over the medium term, to "develop, promote, implement and evaluate an eLearning tutorial for City staff" that builds on its existing *Guide to Good Practice* by including best practices on how to communicate with vulnerable adults (ibid.). To facilitate respect for older adults, several divisions have committed to fostering intergenerational connections by better advertising existing and developing new intergenerational programming. Over the long term, the Community Funding Unit intends to increase funding for non-profits engaging in intergenerational programming.

2. Civic Engagement, Volunteering, Employment

To further combat ageism, the *Toronto Seniors Strategy* states that "older Torontonians have a great deal of talent, skill, experience and wisdom to offer their city" and characterizes Toronto as a place that supports seniors "to contribute, and to feel valued and productive" (City of Toronto 2013, 43). A variety of local government organizations have committed to continuing to provide this support by including older adults in deliberative policy processes, such as in community consultations on specific planning initiatives for homeless and at-risk seniors, engaging the Toronto Seniors Forum advisory committee in the implementation of the *Toronto Seniors Strategy*, and through a Toronto Public Library older adult advisory committee. Older adult volunteerism is to be supported through the continued development of a volunteer management system within the Parks, Forestry and Recreation division and a long-term project proposed by the Social Development division to "develop peer-leadership training programs to enable older adults to help others navigate civic services and programs" (City of Toronto 2013, 48). The city also intends to facilitate employment opportunities for older adults by ensuring that existing services provided through Toronto Employment and Social Services are accessible to seniors and will "explore opportunities to customize employment services to meet the unique needs of older workers" (City of Toronto 2013, 49).

3. Social Participation

The *Toronto Seniors Strategy* recognizes the importance of accessible and affordable programs for older adults to participate in social activities and connect with others and describes broadly how it already offers workshops and programs through the Toronto Public Library, its funding partnerships with non-profits, and its support for adult day programs. The *Toronto Seniors Strategy* aims to enhance access and affordability around existing programming by locating more physical spaces for social participation, such as in the design of redeveloped long-term care homes, in neighbourhoods through existing city-planning Community Services and Facilities strategies in the context of redevelopment, and by co-locating city services in Toronto Community Housing and other city-owned buildings (City of Toronto 2013). The provincial mandate to expand funding and advertising for elderly persons' centres is the only recommendation intended to address the goal of making programs more affordable, and it is unclear what the Ontario government is doing in this area other than its new Seniors Grants Program, the funding of which is extremely modest. To improve access to city social and cultural programming, the Recreation division plans to continue its work to develop its "age-based plan for older adults" to ensure the availability and redistribution of programs across the city (City of Toronto 2013, 56). The Toronto Public Library also commits to continuing to build its collection of large print and audio book materials.

4. Community Support and Health Services

The *Toronto Seniors Strategy* delineates an important role for local government in enhancing access to health and community support services, particularly by filling gaps in access to programs for vulnerable senior citizens. The strategy highlights the referral and assessment services already undertaken by Toronto Paramedic Services, mental health intervention by the Toronto Police Service, the support for vulnerable seniors as well as health promotion and prevention by Toronto Public Health, the Homemakers and Nurses Services provided to 2,500 individuals annually, and a Hardship Fund for low-income residents to access health items (City of Toronto 2013). There are several actions around health promotion, which include continuing and expanding the community-based work of Paramedic Services; creating a group to look at how to increase the influenza vaccination of city employees working with seniors; enhancing access to affordable and culturally appropriate food through existing retail and innovative mobile-market approaches; continuing and expanding informational health workshops through the Toronto Public Library; and increasing falls prevention training programs for staff and communication strategies for seniors and their caregivers (ibid.).

In the medium term, local government intends to increase the number of seniors eligible for free dental services through Toronto Public Health, as demand and wait times are increasing. All city divisions and special-purpose bodies intend to collaborate on a suicide prevention strategy that includes older adults as one priority group (ibid.). The city's Shelter division commits to exploring how to enhance its protocol to identify and provide vulnerable populations with human services during emergency situations such as fires, floods, and winter storms where there are power outages. A city representative explains that this emphasis on emergency preparation emerged a few years back after "there was the big fire at 200 Wellesley, this was several years ago at a big TCH [Toronto Community Housing] building. We did a lot of learning because there was a lot of older folks in that social housing building and we were flying by the seat of our pants" (B20). Toronto's Office of Emergency Management has "developed a vulnerability index assessment that would be done in an emergency to identify people in need of greater assistance and triage them into other supports as needed" (B20). This does not apply, however, to vulnerable seniors living in private residences.

5. Housing

The *Toronto Seniors Strategy* recognizes the necessity of appropriate housing for all senior citizens to age in place, though the report is distinctly focused on homelessness and the needs of those who are low-income. The recommendations are to increase access to affordable housing, support housing modification and bring services into homes, and provide long-term care options both in city-run homes and in the community for those who need it. The only mention of the need to advocate for more funding from the province is on the topic of long-term care. The report highlights that the complex array of local government organizations that provide, fund, protect, and manage shelter and affordable housing have "emergency shelters, drop-ins, housing, and other supports specifically for older adults" (City of Toronto 2013, 66). This ranges from the development of 713 new affordable supportive rental units for seniors, a renovation support program for low-income homeowners, climate-change building design for emergency preparedness, the preservation and replacement of rental housing in redevelopment contexts, a new city-wide zoning bylaw that could accommodate seniors-specific housing, tax and utility rate relief programs, and the operation of ten long-term care homes (City of Toronto 2013).

To enhance access to affordable housing, the city's Affordable Housing Office commits to continue its work to "aggressively pursue a full range of partnership opportunities to create and maintain affordable housing for lower income seniors" (City of Toronto 2013, 70). This aligns with the work of the city's Housing Action Plan, and a long-term strategy to update this plan to include the housing needs of older Torontonians. To enhance independent living at home, the Affordable Housing Office will continue to deliver its renovation support program and will work with affordable housing providers to promote accessibility guidelines (City of Toronto 2013). The city's Shelter division will more actively communicate its guide to housing and support services for vulnerable seniors and will improve its data collection on homeless and "at risk" older adults and their housing needs (ibid.). Revenue Services also promises to better communicate property tax and utility relief programs for seniors (ibid.). City Planning is creating legislative and educational support for the development of secondary suites city-wide and supporting the pursuit of affordable housing through the density bonusing section of the *Planning Act*.

The Long Term Care division will, over the medium term, expand its Homemakers and Nurses Services program to older adults with chronic and acute health issues to address its long wait list for services (ibid.). The Shelter division will continue to advocate to the province to recognize the distinct needs of older adults experiencing homelessness who may have substance abuse and mental health challenges by ensuring their access to long-term care services in shelters and other community settings through the design of new supportive housing models (ibid.). In the short term, the Shelter and Long Term Care divisions are engaging in a partnership to meet the needs of homeless seniors, and this work is expected to continue. The Long Term Care division hopes to access provincial funding to hire more personal support workers for clients who have dementia or other mental health conditions, or substance abuse challenges, as well as to work with Toronto Community Housing to provide more supportive services for seniors in public housing (ibid.).

6. Transportation

The *Toronto Seniors Strategy* recognizes the importance of public transportation for seniors that "grants access to the life of the city" and is "accessible, affordable, safe and reliable" (City of Toronto 2013, 80). The strategy describes the city's current work to enhance active transportation in the form of walking and biking, as well as pedestrian safety through paving, new sidewalk installation, crossing, signage, and traffic calming. The Transportation Services division will continue to roll out longer pedestrian crossing time at intersections and develop a policy to extend times in areas with many seniors; keep track of new mobility devices to ensure that city bylaws recognize their ease of navigation through the city; review pedestrian fatalities and develop appropriate measures as needed; work with Toronto Public Health to create "slow zone" active transportation pilot projects; and include safety reviews in large planning projects (City of Toronto 2013).

To enhance the accessibility of the public transit network, the Toronto Transit Commission will change "courtesy seating" to "priority seating," language which better includes seniors; introduce some new accessible streetcars; improve its public address system and notice of repairs and maintenance; and increase the number of accessible bus stops in partnership with the city's Transportation Services division (ibid.). The *Toronto Seniors Strategy* aims to enhance transportation for older adults by increasing affordable options, improving accessibility of the public transit and pedestrian network, and advancing the safety of pedestrians. A medium-term action is for the Toronto Transit Commission to "pursue discounted or free fares for older adults during non-peak hours" (City of Toronto 2013, 83).

The Toronto Public Library has also committed to exploring partnerships with non-profits to enhance transportation to and from library facilities. A long-term goal is for the city's Community Funding unit to expand support for community agencies to increase their non-medical transportation services for seniors (City of Toronto 2013). It is particularly interesting to note that there is no mention of special Wheel Trans services and Community Bus Routes in the transportation section of the *Toronto Seniors Strategy.*

7. Outdoor Space and Buildings

The *Toronto Seniors Strategy* prioritizes accessible and safe indoor and outdoor public environments in recognition that they promote "equitable access to a high quality of life" for senior citizens (City of Toronto 2013, 89). The priority here is the reiteration that local government is currently trying to ensure that its buildings and outdoor spaces conform to the provincial AODA Act, noting that many of the actions outlined in the transportation section of the *Toronto Seniors Strategy* work to fulfill these requirements. In addition, the city intends to support better wayfinding around public buildings and spaces, and to ensure that diverse older adults feel safe (City of Toronto 2013). Transportation Services will hasten its existing plan to install public furniture at transit stops; work with its private sector partner, Astral Media, to look at how existing street furniture (which is owned by the private company) could be adapted to suit the needs of older adults; implement the *Toronto Wayfinding Strategy* to enhance navigation through age-friendly signage and mapping; increase the font size on street signs and signals; and improve the surfaces and signage of city trails and pathways (ibid.). The Recreation division has also committed to enhancing the city's tree canopy to provide more shade, and will continue its plan to provide accessible seating (benches with arm rests) under shaded areas in city parks (ibid.).

As part of its Official Plan review, City Planning will support a "universally accessible transportation system" through mixed use, walkable, safe, and transit-oriented neighbourhoods and will ensure tactile walking surfaces for the visually impaired on city infrastructure (ibid.). Over the medium term, the city's Community Funding unit intends to enhance funding for community agencies that provide snow-clearing services for seniors (ibid.). To enhance safety, the Toronto Police Service will conduct community safety audits that are based on universal (rather than senior citizen-specific) Crime Prevention through Environmental Design criteria and will "continue to provide a visible presence in public spaces" as well as offer presentations on local safety issues to seniors (City of Toronto 2013, 95). Long-term goals include the implementation of funded "safety, maintenance, and liveability upgrades" to all Toronto Community Housing seniors' buildings that includes improving communal spaces, safety cameras, elevators, entrance and exit safety, and security audits, and will develop a guidebook for seniors that promotes "safe and secure community living" (City of Toronto 2013, 96).

8. Communications and Information

In its final priority section, the *Toronto Seniors Strategy* recognizes that "clear, direct, and understandable" communication of information is crucial to the inclusion of senior citizens in city life (City of Toronto 2013, 97). This is broadly secured through a general city-wide communications directive and the 311 call-in service that informs people about Toronto services and programs. The Social Development division intends to partner with the Toronto Seniors Forum advisory group to deliver presentations that advertise to seniors the services of 311 as well as the provincial equivalent, 211 (City of Toronto 2013). The *Toronto Seniors Strategy* aims to enhance communication through further specified promotion of its services and amenities for diverse seniors and measures to remove technological barriers to the provision of information (ibid.). To enhance promotion of existing programs, the Recreation division will continue with its development of a communication plan with the intention to develop an online seniors' communication portal (ibid.). To ensure that a diverse senior audience has access to information, the City Managers Office has committed over the medium term to develop an accessible communications policy directed to city staff to meet the communications requirement of the AODA legislation (ibid.). To reduce technological barriers to information, the Toronto Public Library has a medium-term goal to create an electronic literacy program for older adults that also serves to encourage their safety online. Also over the medium term, the Social Development division is tasked with ensuring that all frontline city staff are aware of the services available for older adults so that they can act as immediate referrals (ibid.). A long-term action for the Social Development division is to identify neighbourhoods where there are high concentrations of vulnerable older adults without access to services and amenities (ibid.).

IMPLEMENTATION

The *Toronto Seniors Strategy* was passed unanimously by city council in spring 2013 under the controversial leadership of Mayor Rob Ford. Given the strategy's language around equity, fairness, and justice, and the potential cost implications of medium- and long-term actions, this timing may seem surprising. However, a member of the expert panel clarifies that "those who are generally against social services were not there" (D49) for the vote, including the mayor. The implementation of the strategy is now the responsibility of local government staff, coordinated through the city's Social Development division. The Toronto Seniors Forum was designated by city council to ensure that the *Toronto Seniors Strategy* actions are being carried out in a timely manner. The members of the forum all have jobs assigned to them and they have committees on transportation, health, and housing. These committees report to a steering committee that meets once a month.

My research on AFCs in Toronto was conducted between May and November 2014, the period when substantive actions around *Toronto Seniors Strategy* implementation were intended to be made. Specifically, the short-term actions should have been undertaken and planning underway on the medium- and long-term items. As we will see, my interviews with city councillors, city staff, senior citizen advocates, and a diverse array of non-profit organizations illustrate some successes as well as some significant challenges in actioning the *Toronto Seniors Strategy.*

Conclusion

This chapter has illustrated that the practice of age-friendly work in Toronto is extensive and highly complex, involving multiple policy domains, actors, social sectors and jurisdictions of government. Local government supports the delivery of most of the everyday services and amenities important for seniors, and the demands for this work are growing due to a history of policy devolution combined with greater population needs. Local government's response to these needs, such as long-term care and recreation programming for seniors across the new megacity, illustrates policy autonomy and discretion and should be studied to explore motivations, capacities, and outcomes. Similarly, the local non-profit role of providing community support services and long-term care to seniors is expanding, especially in the context of health care restructuring. This combination of policy devolution and expanding need seems to be resulting in a more professionalized role for both local government and non-profits in the provision of targeted emergency-oriented support for the most vulnerable seniors. The work of these actors to produce age-friendly environments is thus fundamentally affected by policy decisions made by central governments.

Toronto's age-friendly work has shifted to become more professionalized post-amalgamation and with policy devolution. While previous strategies emanated from the voices of seniors and called for improved access to services and amenities from a rights-based perspective, aging seems to have been reframed in more recent strategies to be an expensive problem for local government. The shift away from having a councillor advocate for seniors may also be indicative of a depoliticization of policy work in the area of aging as local government has taken on more service provision work. I will explore how these tensions play out in *Toronto Seniors Strategy* implementation as the policy attempts both to meet the needs of seniors from an equity perspective and to coordinate the work of local government to achieve cost efficiencies. Unlike previous aging strategies, the *Toronto Seniors Strategy* hones the focus on local bureaucracy and has a formal action-oriented process; as a result, the strategy is highly localist in its effort to realize an AFC by narrowing the focus on what is within their institutional jurisdiction. There is little emphasis in the twenty-five *Toronto Seniors Strategy* recommendations and ninety-one action items on the roles of the non-profit sector or of central governments to support a meaningful AFC, despite their importance in the production of an age-friendly environment. This raises potential red flags regarding the extent to which Toronto's AFC program acts as a place-based policy emanating from a "right to the city" perspective that will be assessed through Isin's (2008) framework in the following chapters.

CHAPTER 2

Redistributing to Senior Citizens: Improving Local Environments through AFCs in Toronto

Introduction

A core intention of the AFC approach is to improve local environments, making them more amenable to the everyday needs of senior citizens and, in doing so, to the population at large (Golant 2014; Ontario Government 2013a). This goal appears to align with Antonnen et al.'s (2012) concept of universal inclusion and the redistributive dimension of Isin's (2008) right to the city, insofar as it promotes a model of resource redistribution that meets both universal and diverse identity-based needs. However, as was highlighted in the introduction, empirical research on AFCs has identified gaps in the program's redistributive potential in actual urban contexts. While the design of the *Toronto Seniors Strategy* has been subject to similar critiques (Goar 2013), some of which I witnessed in practice in my own Toronto neighbourhood, there has been no research examining how to describe and explain any potential inadequacies.

Both the urban political economy and critical AFC literatures raise doubts about the extent to which policy can substantively improve local environments in a context of public-sector restructuring where cost-cutting is dominant. While the political economy literature might dismiss place-based policy programs as symbolic examples of austerity urbanism (Peck 2012), the critical AFC literature believes in the program's potential to promote a right to the city for senior citizens but recognizes that this cannot be realized without a fundamental understanding of the challenges in practice. This literature thus calls for further analysis that contextualizes AFC programs amid public-sector restructuring (Scharlach 2012; Buffel et al. 2012; Novec and Menec 2014). I fill this gap by basing my analysis on a "seeing like a city" approach (Magnussen 2011) that explores the everyday practices of local policy actors, including those working in the non-profit sector, that are often invisible in mainstream political science accounts (Mahon et al. 2007; Stone 2009). It is only by exploring this actual "landscape of antagonism" (Newman 2014) that we can begin to understand how public-sector restructuring works through the AFC program, including the neoliberal and perhaps more expansive political projects at its root and the challenges and opportunities that it presents.

In this chapter, I explore how AFCs promote the redistribution of services and amenities to senior citizens in local environments based on a "right to the city" model of universal inclusion. I begin with an exploration of the ideas that inform participants' understanding of the importance of AFCs as a place-based policy. I am particularly interested in examining the ways in which participants frame a place-based focus as crucial to understanding issues of access and equity for seniors, in this case in the big-city context of Toronto. I am also interested in exploring the ways in which participants might understand such policy as a more residual opportunity to responsibilize local governments, non-profits, families, and seniors to address population aging. In the second half of the chapter, I contrast these ideas with participant understandings of their actual redistributive work to improve local environments in the eight domains of the AFC framework. In this regard, I am interested in examining the ways in which AFCs in Toronto promote both universal and more targeted improvements to local environments as well as any tensions and struggles that arise during this endeavour. I conclude by discussing those themes that help explain gaps in redistribution based on a model of universal inclusion in the Toronto AFC case.

The Importance of Place-Based Policy on Aging

DIVERSITY

Participants identified a place-based focus on aging as important for public policy because it provides the best way to identify the everyday needs of senior citizens as they intersect with other aspects of their identity such as their geographic location, their gender, their income and their ethnicity. This is explained by one non-profit participant: "The system is really learning that the local is the place that should be your starting point. The local grounding should be what drives policy and political will. If we stay too high up and squash it down, we miss the permutations" (D4A). This quotation reflects an understanding shared by many participants that dominant policymaking processes, and especially those designed by central government, often fail to consider the lived experiences of diverse citizens in actual places. A local lens to government policy on aging can thus assist in understanding population diversity and is a welcome policy trend.

I found that local responses to aging were often understood as crucial to addressing the problem of those diverse seniors labelled "socially isolated." Participants understood such isolation as a uniquely urban problem: "In big cities you will see more resources, but I also find people more isolated. I do see people being much more cut off and less connected" (E27). One advocate explains that the aging experience "somehow becomes more hidden in the city because there are more people to hide behind. Because of the numbers. If you are in a small community, you tend to know the other people in the community … in a city it is easy to lose people" (D49). Several non-profit employees talked about the problem for seniors of living in apartment buildings, "concrete jungles where there are compartmentalized units and people don't have opportunities to get together, to be together and support local communities like they do in smaller settings" (D52). This invisibility was highlighted as particularly problematic for the most vulnerable: "The seniors that we work with are marginalized anyways and I think that in urban settings, they really fly under the radar. Every program that we start up, I find people in situations that no human being should be in. And I think that in a small community, it gets noticed by the community. If someone is really unkempt downtown, or psychotic or whatever, people kind of rally around that. And that is what might happen in Bradford. But down here, it becomes part of the landscape or they are just existing in a TCH [Toronto Community Housing] building and no one is knowing it" (D7). This quotation speaks to how isolation can also produce inadequate public service provision, as needs go under the radar. Councillor Ron Moeser admits that big cities are more challenged to provide personalized services and meet diverse needs because of their larger size: "Usually the bigger it gets, the more impersonal the services can get. So you have to work a lot harder to identify both the challenges and the people that need our help" (A2).

As these quotations suggest, participants contrast big cities with a nostalgic notion of small towns where family, friends, and neighbours watch out for each other. Migration patterns to and within cities result in constantly changing communities and mean that "unlike smaller localities and smaller cities where people tend to be located within communities that they have either grown up in or lived all their life in and aged into them, big cities tend to shake that up" (D52). Families are often separated, and urbanization means that in an increasing number of cases, we can no longer rely on families to provide informal care to seniors. One agency staff member speaks to the breaking up of families because of gentrification downtown: "The nuclear family is much smaller now, as seniors are now staying back here as the children are moving to the suburbs. So that becomes a difficulty when families are needed to support the parents, because they have lives many times far from here, in the suburbs" (D32). Or, if they do have family, "in the urban area a lot of those family caregivers have to work. Maybe in the rural area they might have someone to take care of them but in the urban area, many of our seniors, although they do have their family members, they might not be living with them or they work, they have to take care of their own kids. So that means that the kind of support by the family is very limited" (D38). The central theme from these interviewees was that big cities like Toronto require additional and place-specific services to address diversity, and specifically to reach socially isolated seniors who cannot access informal care.

ACCESSIBILITY

Many participants understand the policy focus on local environments as important for population aging because of physical accessibility, such as cleared sidewalks, benches, good street lighting, and lowered curbs. For some, these environmental features are more parochial and consist of minor improvements that can be dealt with locally. For others, accessibility means far more substantive changes to physical infrastructure: "It is a very important thing to add more park benches to your pathways, but this is about bigger infrastructure investments like widening sidewalks, and the maintenance and support of more crosswalks and transit and housing is a huge piece" (D53). This quotation reflects a call to universal inclusion, or an understanding that substantive AFCs require both small-scale and large-scale accessibility improvements and forms of redistribution.

Several participants believe that society requires a more encompassing and holistic understandings of accessibility:

> Accessibility is an interesting one because it is something that people pay a little bit of lip service to ... if you consider things like frailty and cognitive impairments like dementia as a disability, the numbers completely skyrocket ... Accessibility is about making spaces accessible to a broad population; it is not just about accommodating people in a wheelchair. It is a question of whether we are taking care of our society more broadly and if we are not doing that, what are the negative health and economic implications. So I think, for whatever reason, that discourse has been a bit dominated by some more traditional views of what disability is, which I think is unfortunate. (D1C)

Given that a dominant issue associated with aging is a rise in the number of seniors with chronic mental and physical health challenges, incorporating the needs of those that are frail and have cognitive impairments is crucial. A non-profit aging expert notes that "we often think about the physical things that we need to change for people, but do we think about the cognitive things that we need to help people with? So in terms of wayfinding and navigation, it is very hard to find a telephone these days if you do need help, and it is very hard to find a washroom, it is very hard to find a place where you can just ask for directions" (D1A).

This latter point speaks to the human element that is missing in professional service provision: contact with another human being who treats one like a citizen rather than a client, customer, or patient. A representative providing services for seniors reflects on this crucial component:

> We answer the phone because this generation of seniors right now are still phone people … Thursday mornings is the only time that we are on [the] answering machine. When we go to check the calls, a lot of the messages are just *click* because they want to talk to someone. So we answer the phone. We have huge pressures from our funder to not do that … They are saying, "No, we will have an answering machine." We can't have an answering machine. We have to be able to answer the phone. Because that is accessibility … But we see lots of seniors' services have *Press 1, Press 2*. Because of their budgets, and that is a huge barrier. (E27)

The Ontario government funds this organization, so the representative of this organization urges me to "expose this problem. Expose the fact that age-friendly is not always age-friendly … Services don't always think about what are the real needs of people" (E27).

I learned through my interviews that for senior citizens, accessibility problems are particularly acute in Toronto. Big cities are subject to significant change with population growth and infill as well as inflated real estate prices and gentrification pressures as city space itself becomes a commodity (Harvey 1989; Harvey 2009; Sassen 2005; Scott 2011; Hackworth 2006). This environment of change can present a challenge because "once you are in your senior years, the familiarity helps you sustain yourself on a daily basis, because you might not have dementia or Alzheimer's but you need the visual cues, the reminders" (B28).

A local focus helps to identify that seniors live in diverse environments, with different and changing physical landscapes, climates, social and physical design features as well as varying levels of services, amenities, and political representation. "With big cities, every pocket is unique. Toronto is a city of neighbourhoods, so we have to understand that the geospatial relationship is very different in different parts of the city and that this has a significant impact on how residents access services, how their community networks form" (B6). For instance, a non-profit employee explains that the needs of seniors differ in the gentrifying downtown Parkdale neighbourhood, where there are many seniors congregated in old Victorian rooming houses, from those living in high-rise apartment buildings in East and West Toronto, where broken elevators and bed bugs are an issue. This employee then contrasts these needs with those of seniors living in single-family homes in suburban Etobicoke, who often have to travel far to access different services. Big cities are diverse places that retain both sprawled and dense landscapes. There is an understanding among many participants that a mixed use and dense downtown provides better access to services and amenities for seniors within walking and transit distance than the car-dependent and sprawled suburbs: "People who live here [downtown neighbourhood] and people who live on the edges of Scarborough and Etobicoke have a very different life. And actually, statistically in Toronto, there are more seniors in the suburbs than downtown. So when they think in terms of transit or whatever, how do you plan for the aging population that is not in the downtown where things are close? There is no option. If you live in the suburbs you can use a bicycle, you can walk, you can use transit, but you will need to use a car. If you don't have access to a car, your life is diminished" (D49).

While there may be more services available in big cities, spatially they are spread out, so several participants addressed mobility challenges for seniors, including accessible and affordable public transit that facilitates access to services and amenities. As a representative from one suburban-based non-profit explains, "The number one thing that we hear from our seniors is that they have trouble accessing the services because of transportation; they say, 'I can't get there.' To a medical appointment, an adult day program, a congregate dining event which keeps them well and active" (D12). Another agency staff member explains that "as people start having difficulties walking and they use canes and walkers, transportation can be a point of difficulty. When we go on outings by TTC [Toronto Transit Commission], many of our seniors can't go into the subway system, so we rely on streetcars and busses" (D25). This also requires changing operating procedures, such as giving people more time to get on and off public transit and to sit down, as well as fewer jerky movements from vehicles so that seniors do not fall. One non-profit employee shares a story about how a bus route in their neighbourhood was suddenly changed so that seniors living in surrounding buildings had to walk too far to the stop, and how this affected their access to grocery stores and doctor's offices.

Several participants also explained the distinct challenges inner cities present to seniors, advising that fast-paced downtown contexts can be disorienting. While, in theory, downtowns should be walkable and provide specialized services, "you don't see a lot of frail elderly downtown … walkability is one problem" (E22). A senior citizen activist articulates their struggle: "I have had two hip replacements and it is so important to have enough time at crosswalks to cross the street with a cane and when you are in pain. Crossing Yonge and College was a challenge!" (D54). Potholes in streets and sidewalks is also a concern for seniors, especially those who use walkers, wheelchairs, and canes. Many participants also spoke about the challenges of retrofitting old buildings to make them accessible. In this regard, downtown housing is a challenge, especially low-rise apartment units without elevators. Several participants note the problem of needing to undo the accessibility mistakes of the past. In this way, AFCs have to be both "forward-thinking and backward-thinking" (F6).

Conventional concepts of accessibility rarely acknowledge that accessing the city requires affordable services and amenities; an issue for seniors who may live for several decades on a fixed income: "Affordability. That is probably the big thing in cities because seniors' income is pretty static. Even if they do go up, they go up by a miniscule amount. And big challenges around the fact that they have cut off getting your pension at sixty-five. That two years is going to make a big impact. Because we see lots of people who are hardly making ends meet and they are going to lose their jobs. Even without mandatory retirement people lose their jobs as they age … There are going to be lots of challenges in the cities with that. People won't have the money" (E27). Even a seemingly aspatial policy like pension reform, enacted by the Conservatives under Stephen Harper and then reversed by Liberal prime minister Justin Trudeau, can limit access to crucial services. One non-profit staff member expresses concern that AFCs gloss over economic security for seniors: "Property taxes is something local that we should consider for people that are on fixed incomes, and the other thing is utility and energy that might come up under economic security. Economic security can be touched on in a number of different ways. Free TTC [Toronto Transit Commission] for seniors, free access to recreation programs and parks, that type of stuff. There is a whole bunch of stuff that we can do to make community more accessible. And so have I seen those types of trends? I wouldn't say any more so than before the *Toronto Seniors Strategy*" (D48).

Lack of access to the city due to low income is compounded as other services such as transportation, recreation programs, and home care charge higher user fees. Several participants highlight that getting to appointments is very expensive, and this is a problem when one has different doctors across the city. Several non-profit and city employees speak to the challenges seniors confront in accessing home care, as they need more than is available in the public system and cannot afford to pay for private care. An academic expert explains that non-profit social service providers "are even charging now for some basic services just to cover their costs. People just don't have that kind of income. It is a horrible problem" (E20).

The affordability of housing is also a major problem in big cities like Toronto. Seniors can get priced out of their homes when neighbourhoods experience gentrification: "It is becoming more expensive to live in cities, and housing is more expensive and costs of repairs and property taxes and all of those things are moving more out of reach or creating more pressures for seniors aging" (D53). Councillor Kristyn Wong-Tam admits that in Toronto, "a lot of seniors who have primarily worked and lived in the downtown core are sometimes forced out of the core because the cost of living is fairly expensive and there is often times some physical barriers" (A3). This becomes a problem if seniors move out to the suburbs away from their long-time support networks, and to car-dependent environments that limit access to everyday amenities. However, a non-profit employee who has been working with seniors over several decades in a now-gentrifying downtown Toronto neighbourhood explains that they have done research on this (Janes 2008) and have found that many seniors remain in their neighbourhoods. The value of their homes has increased exponentially but they are still feeling poor because of rising property taxes. Many of these seniors have been living in these communities for decades and some want to pass their homes on to their children. Several non-profit staff members advise that they serve seniors who are living in mansions and are asset-rich and cash-poor and have little money for food and home maintenance. Many also struggle to maintain these homes, which may be "falling down around them" (D31B).

SERVICE FRAGMENTATION

While localized policymaking and service provision is favoured to meet the needs of diverse seniors, my interviews indicate a serious fragmentation between different agencies and Toronto neighbourhoods that affects access. The level of services in big cities like Toronto can be confusing, as they are provided by different sectors and agencies and seniors are expected to go out on their own to locate them. Coordination between different forms of support is thus a challenge, as is highlighted by one non-profit employee: "I think that access in big cities is unique because you are going to have lots of services, but if it is not a city that connects things well, then how do you navigate and access?" (D1A).

A major issue is that many services for seniors are provided by the non-profit sector, but the role of the sector varies by community. A staff member from an umbrella organization discusses their struggles: "We serve the whole city of Toronto, and part of our challenge when we refer clients is the catchment area. So even in the same city, it makes a huge difference living south of Bloor or north of Bloor" (D31A). Some agencies provide services in one area but know that neighbouring areas are underserviced: "If we would be more far-reaching, if we could go farther, well, that certainly would be more people that we could monitor to make sure they are okay" (D20). Several non-profits admit that seniors commute to their programs because they cannot find anything similar in their own communities. An employee from a suburban non-profit that provides transportation to medical appointments for seniors discusses their challenge that "40 percent of our rides for seniors were outside of our catchment area … that is where the specialist is or that is where the diagnostic is taking place" (D12).

Even within neighbourhoods, there is diversity from block to block that can result in differential access. A city staff member explains that "you can have fabulous stuff going on in an apartment building with supportive neighbours and people helping you age in place or on a city block where people take care of one another. Or, you can be in an area where nobody knows each other, nobody talks to each other, and that kind of stuff has to be looked at and taken into consideration when you are planning" (B16A). Whether a neighbourhood is age-friendly can thus be very ad hoc, and speaks to additional inequities that can exist when there is an expectation on the part of governments that informal care in the community can support seniors to age in place. One non-profit employee explains this eloquently: "What you can get will depend on where you live. So it depends on where you sit on the equity side. Are we comfortable living in a society where if you live in this geographic area, you may be able to get way more support for the particular problems that you have than if you live in another geographic area? Certainly we have tremendous variability" (D1B).

There is an understanding among participants that public policy can create, exacerbate, and address service fragmentation. One advocate explains how important public policy, and particularly urban planning, can be for the creation of community facilities and infrastructures to support aging in place: "You can have neighbourhoods in the downtown but it is extremely difficult to have neighbourhoods in the suburbs. You can, but it takes a lot of work. A lot depends on the infrastructure there. This area [downtown neighbourhood] is a planned community … it makes a big difference when you plan mixed housing, when you plan having shops and services. So if you plan, this is where the city comes in. And the province comes in because it dictates what is allowed to be done because of the *Planning Act*. It is the plan that makes it possible for people to have community" (D49). This speaks to continued challenges associated with amalgamation in the megacity of Toronto as they relate to inequities in service planning and availability between different parts of the city, particularly in formerly suburban municipalities. A city representative explains that "we are still feeling the effects of what amalgamation did, or the effects of amalgamation where we are one big city of Toronto but in Scarborough, there is very little, in the west there is very little and there are huge issues there" (B16A). In addition to inequities in service availability, there are different service models in the former municipalities, particularly in recreation and library services, that offer seniors different types and levels of programming as well as different degrees of involvement in decision-making. Another legacy of amalgamation is inequity around snow-clearing, which is provided in one of the former municipalities by the city but on an ad hoc basis by community agencies elsewhere.

The provincial regionalization of health care is another policy domain with considerable spatial fragmentation in Toronto. There are five different regional health boundaries within the city, which means that there are different eligibilities for home care through the provincial Community Care Access Centres (CCACs). One city employee reflects that "It is insane; it is not the same all the way around depending on where you live and what you can access. It can be very different if you happen to live on the border or the edge of the boundaries" (B16A). Another city staff member advises that "we in the big city have to deal with multiple levels and sectors or divisions or catchments of government and services" (B25). As services and amenities become more localized, accessing them is more and more dependent on location. While governments continue to fund localized service programs, there appears to be less oversight over geographic access. This affects a senior's right to services. The question is whether governments see this oversight as their responsibility and whether AFCs represent a coherent effort to fill gaps in access and improve coordination or exacerbate fragmentation.

The discussion in this first half of the chapter illustrates that, while a place-based focus on aging helps to understand diverse, personal, and everyday needs of seniors, it is important to refrain from seeing these as individual issues of social isolation that require only more targeted services. Several participants reflect on the point made by Councillor Ron Moeser that "there are a lot of similar needs, no matter whether it is downtown or Scarborough. But the actual programs themselves may be tailored to where they live" (A2). As such, one non-profit participant advises that "it is extremely important to understand the aging population in a global point of view as well as the local perspective. This is because we have to have global standardization but, at the same time, we have to have local uniqueness and flexibility" (D38). Achieving an age-friendly environment requires a redistributive model of inclusion (Antonnen et al. 2012a) that includes universal policy informed by everyday experiences of access as well as niche projects to meet localized needs. The next section of the chapter contrasts the need for a place-based policy that promotes a redistributive model of universal inclusion with participant understandings of their actual work in the eight domains of the AFC framework in the Toronto case. The purpose is to highlight gaps, tensions, and opportunities in building an AFC in Toronto.

Redistribution in Local Environment

1. RESPECT AND SOCIAL INCLUSION

Participants recognize that although local government has made some effort to meet the needs of diverse seniors in Toronto by enhancing inclusion, there is still work to do. A non-profit participant noted that "the *Toronto Seniors Strategy* presented a lot of data, but I am not sure that it got down to the level of specific community needs" (D1A); that is, examining how specific characteristics such as age, gender, living alone, income, and geographic location affect the needs of seniors in local environments. An AFC practice rooted in more democratic engagement and community-based research in which seniors identify their challenges, needs, and desires is difficult in a context where emergency needs are so great and there are limited resources. Local government participants frame social inclusion as a process of focusing on and targeting the needs of the most vulnerable seniors, specifically addressing service fragmentation. For instance, as was highlighted in chapter 1, the increased prevalence of aging in place has driven the development of the SPIDER protocol, which brings together all the first-responder divisions to support vulnerable adults who struggle with mental health and addiction challenges. Despite these efforts, a city employee describes this work as "one of the patchworks in a patchwork quilt. Unfortunately, we are not phenomenally organized around services to this sector of vulnerable adults and it is still very patchy" (B16A).

The topic of elder abuse illustrates this lack of systemic response. There is only one non-profit agency in Toronto that supports seniors who have been abused, and a staff representative admits that they cannot come close to meeting needs, given that only two of the five employees doing this work are full-time. A major problem is that "no level of government will own that issue in the community" and as such "there is no systemic response or ability" (D31B). This means that elder abuse is "all booted off to the chief of police to deal with" (D31B). Several non-profit participants reflect on a pre-amalgamation history when they worked with the former Metropolitan Toronto Public Health department to prevent elder abuse; this work was discontinued because it was not mandated by the province. An elder abuse expert advises that "a lot of times the city is driven by their legislated requirements, so over the years we have seen shrinkages in funding envelopes" (D31B). In the case of elder abuse, only the police are mandated by the province to respond. This is evidenced by the *Toronto Seniors Strategy* recommendation to train police to sensitize them to elder abuse, though one non-profit expert found this odd because training has been ongoing for years. I learned that the police had an elder abuse coordinator, but due to restructuring and reorganization, this role was replaced by a "vulnerable persons" coordinator who covers elder abuse as well as other issues relating to disability, homelessness, and mental health. It is interesting to note the switch from naming seniors in the job title, which undermines preventative understanding of how abuse is an age-related issue.

Elder abuse often relates to the expectation that family will provide eldercare and this dynamic presents a challenge for police, as one non-profit staff member explains:

> Often it is the adult child who is being abusive, and the last thing that the senior wants is their son or daughter getting in trouble with the law. Even if they are getting hurt, even if they are being taken advantage of financially and they have no money and are at risk of eviction ... Many officers that I train will say that they get called into a home in the middle of the night and somebody has been trying to provide care with somebody with dementia, they are worn out – "I can see it, they lashed out, what do I do? Arrest the family member and cart them off like I am supposed to? Then I leave the person with dementia by themselves, I take that person to an emergency room, they are not going to be thrilled that they are there. The family member is going to be released within 24 hours back into the situation." (D31B)

The policy emphasis by governments, and especially the provincial government, to encourage aging in the home is critiqued by several participants as a serious challenge for families. Some people need around the clock care and this puts a lot of pressure on family caregivers, unless you happen to be rich and can afford hiring someone to live in. Several participants tell me stories about how governments are training families to provide care: "We had one case where a woman was told that she had to take her husband home from the hospital, but he was in a coma. They said, 'You're a nurse.' She was eighty-two years old. It was ridiculous" (E27).

This participant advises that "they are doing that because they are trying to stretch the dollars" (E27). This is a clear infringement on the rights of seniors to adequate care. There is only one small legal clinic covering the entire province of Ontario that focuses on legal rights for low-income seniors, illustrating a concerning lack of access to justice. Furthermore, a representative explained that despite the fact that we have an aging population, funding is not available to expand the legal aid program.

There is greater reliance on informal care where cost cutting is the primary motivation:

> One of the things that we are not saying enough of is "How do we sustain the people that look after the people?" ... The greatest workforce that keeps an aging population healthy are their family. Are there tax breaks, service breaks, incentives to cohort people and make houses more amenable and accessible? So as much as we should focus on the patient, we should really focus on the people that keep them whole, the freebies. And why aren't people taking people home? It is because they are saying, "Oh my god, I have to take mom home but I have to work, otherwise I will lose my home; I will lose everything that I have." (D4A)

Several participants note that it continues to be the informal work of women that constitutes the "freebie":

> It means that this is going to be families, and what does that really mean? It means that it is going to be the female members of the family. Daughters, daughters-in-law, female grandchildren ... the squeeze is on the women ... Many people are forced to leave the workforce and that negatively impacts on our future jobs, on our future salaries and our pension ... The government isn't jumping up and saying, "Oh, we recognize all of the work that you wonderful women are doing caring for your family," because we, the government, have abdicated on our responsibility or we have failed in our responsibility or don't really care because the voices aren't loud enough and they are not screaming hard enough for us to actually want to do something about it. (B27)

An AFC approach that glosses over the increasing reliance on family care is inadequate to address the diverse needs of senior citizens in a context of urbanization (Golant 2014). The *Toronto Seniors Strategy* does not directly recognize elder abuse as a systemic issue that requires a coordinated intergovernmental response.

In the absence of such a public response, one non-profit employee reflects on funding they have received from the federal government for what is understood as a more local approach to the issue: activating communities by training them to watch out for elder abuse. These programs are targeted to ethno-cultural groups least able to afford private care for seniors and thus more reliant on informal care. This project is about "training a cadre of volunteers" and "developing peer leaders" (D31B) to engage in elder abuse prevention. While "each community is working in different ways, in culturally appropriate ways, to bring forward the issues of elder abuse" (D31B), these do not appear to be conversations that inform policy upwards to develop a holistic governmental response that also includes public investment in home care and day programs, supportive housing, and long-term care for seniors whose families who need it.

With respect to meeting different needs, Toronto has recently, in the aftermath of an Ombudsman exposé in which a city bylaw officer cut down a tree in the yard of a women with Alzheimer's, begun to confront the need to learn how to serve people with diminished capacity through the *Duty to Care* protocol. However, despite this protocol, I find efforts to train staff lagging. A city participant admits that staff "sort of have to be jacks of all trades. That is why the training piece is so relevant and we don't even get any money for that. Which is unfortunate, because it wouldn't really cost all that much, but it would be so helpful to our staff" (B15A). Several city staff members talked about relying on volunteers and relationships with ethno-cultural non-profit organizations to meet the diverse needs of seniors. A *Toronto Seniors Strategy* that claims to enhance equity and inclusion requires investing in training and translation to support staff to meet the needs of an increasingly diverse population. This includes hiring staff with particular language skills, or at least paying translators rather than relying on volunteers.

Several participants spoke about the need to improve local government services to ensure the inclusion of LGBTQ+ seniors. An agency of the City of Toronto that supports LGBTQ+ residents had representation on the *Toronto Seniors Strategy*, though a staff participant notes that the needs of these seniors are not placed centrally in the final report. In contrast, the 1999 Toronto Seniors' Taskforce report recommended that local government focus specifically on LGBTQ+ seniors, calling for the promotion of a diversity lens to all services and a movement to outreach and track population needs (City of Toronto 1999). This seems an impossible task in a context where there is only one staff member in one agency representing Toronto's LGBTQ+ senior citizen community. The intention of this agency is to outreach to other senior organizations across Toronto to alert them to the distinct needs of LGBTQ+ seniors. This outreach and training is especially important in the context of long-term care homes because of "the idea of going back into the closet, which is a real concern and huge fear about going back into institutions and having to hide and not being able to live with your partner that you may have lived with for thirty years. Or do that comfortably" (D33). This community agency has hired a person to create training programs to go into long-term care homes, as currently there are only three in Toronto that have a distinct LGBTQ+-friendly designation and two of these homes are run by local government. This illustrates that the practice of AFCs as it relates to respect and social inclusion occurs in long-term care homes, and these institutions should not be ignored in the policy discourse.

Finally, intergenerational programming was cited by several participants as an innovative way to build respect and enhance social inclusion. Several city employees talk about conflict between youth and seniors: "We see this sort of generally, and it is one of our challenges and our opportunities, is that you see tension between youth and seniors in a space. It is about breaking down the barriers and looking at how we can bridge those gaps through program opportunities and synergies" (B15B). The talk of synergies relates to another priority of intergenerational programming: to address service competition for funding attention from diverse population groups. Several city staff members advise that local government must consider that it has a seniors strategy, a newcomer strategy, and a youth strategy, with each requiring more funds, thus synergies between these strategies must be sought. Unfortunately, participants from both the local government and non-profit sectors admit that they struggle to justify investments for seniors compared to newcomers and youth, because it does not give you the same bang for your buck (Biggs 2008). For instance, I learned through my interviews that Toronto's Youth Strategy has received money to hire two youth officers to support implementation while, at the time of my interviews, the *Toronto Seniors Strategy* had received no specific human or financial resources.

2. CIVIC ENGAGEMENT, VOLUNTEERING, EMPLOYMENT

Civic engagement by senior citizens in Toronto is encouraged formally through the Toronto Seniors Forum advisory group. As was highlighted in chapter 1, the forum was involved in the development of the *Toronto Seniors Strategy* and are supposed to "check in" on its implementation. However, there is no formal mechanism for group members to inform the strategy's implementation. Furthermore, the expectation that members will travel across Toronto to reach out to seniors by giving presentations on the *Toronto Seniors Strategy* undercuts this policy role. There is a co-production agenda at work here that emphasizes citizens taking on more of the service and coordination role of government (Martinson and Minkler 2006; Newman and Clarke 2009) that is challenging activism on the part of the group. While some members of the forum are fine with this, others expressed frustration that they lacked a political purpose.

Engaging equity-seeking groups in a formal and regular process of participation takes significant resources on the part of local government. Several participants spoke about wanting to engage seniors formally in programming, but admitted that this is a challenge where services like libraries and community centres have over one hundred branches over a large geographic area and only one senior citizen specialist. There is also a conflict between the rhetoric of civic engagement and expectation to maintain or limit budgets.

Many participants believe that population aging presents an important opportunity to recruit more volunteers for service co-production. In a context where we continually need additional support services for seniors such as meals on wheels, friendly visiting, and accessible transportation, governments are worried that there are fewer volunteers than there used to be (Senate 2009). A city representative advises that "a lot of our volunteers are seniors and there has been a long history there. The nature of that may be changing, as people are working later and they are more active and engaged" (B15B). Those seniors that have time on their hands appear to be more interested in sharing their knowledge and expertise in other ways. The expectation that privileged seniors will locate, outreach, and provide charity to more vulnerable seniors is unlikely to come to fruition and cannot be relied upon to realize AFCs (Winterton 2016).

This trend of sporadic and decreased volunteering is also onerous on non-profit organizations. Non-profits require resources to screen and train volunteers, as seniors are particularly vulnerable to various forms of abuse. Furthermore, these volunteers may be the first to respond to a senior facing a crisis. A senior citizens' advocate explained that volunteering is also a challenge for advocacy-oriented non-profits:

> We also can't use volunteers in the sense of a gift shop where you teach them how to use the till and they are set. If you came here to volunteer, someone would have to mentor you a long time to show you how things work, how to respond. We are not a service provider but we still deal with people who call us up who are suicidal. You can't simply say, "I'm sorry, but we're not a service provider, call 911, goodbye." People will say "I just lost my housing, my husband just died," whatever, and we are supposed to put them in touch with people, and you can't have any old volunteer do that. You need skill sets. So while we have a lot of skilled people, it is not all that easy to find good volunteers. Let's say if we got a student volunteer, who would be in here every day to mentor them? Because they can't be in all on their own. So this is time that someone has to take to mentor this volunteer. (D49)

Several participants suggest that volunteering with seniors should be long-term, because relations of trust and familiarity are so important. There is an inherent conflict here relating to the expectation that youth will volunteer to help seniors. For instance, one city employee asks: "Why don't we have more intergenerational kinds of things? We have got all these kids in school who need to do forty hours of volunteering or community service or whatever; why are they not somehow linked with older people who are trying to stay home?" (B16A) while another advises that "it is a lot of resources to manage this influx of students that are kind of fly by night. Are we actually building an intrinsic value in students to help or are we just pushing a curriculum agenda that is then a burden on non-profits?" (B6).

There is also a greater need to recognize that many poorer seniors are having to keep working later in life, limiting their ability to volunteer.

This is a problem because those working (which includes care work such as grandparenting) may not be represented in policy development. The lack of representation of such seniors in the development of the *Toronto Seniors Strategy* could be the reason why employment is not a significant dimension of the report. A city representative explains that the *Toronto Seniors Strategy* is not very strong in the area of employment because, although it is a component of the WHO framework, it was not identified in city consultations as a big issue of concern because of an assumption that only privileged seniors are concerned about employment: "An active and more capable older adult might be more interested in employment opportunities. Whereas what we are focusing on are the more vulnerable, isolated older adults" (B6). This may relate in part to who was consulted, not always the most vulnerable and isolated seniors, and the types of questions asked, given that vulnerable seniors might have little choice but to keep working.

3. SOCIAL PARTICIPATION

A significant finding in this research has been the extent to which the Toronto Public Library has been actively engaged in encouraging the social participation of senior citizens. One advocate explains her surprise in this regard: "The Toronto Public Library can take kudos for being the ones that are most active in dealing with these various issues … But if you were standing on high, you probably wouldn't think that the library would be highest on the priority of what you need to deal with. It is an example of 'OK, this is the turf and this is what I have to work with so I am certainly going to try to get in there and do, in every possible terms of the definition of what a library can do'" (D29). The library has hired a specialist to coordinate this role across the city and the statement above illustrates the important contribution that paid staff can make. The library offers many workshops and activities, particularly focusing on health promotion, financial sustainability, and technology.

City divisions providing social programs for seniors admit that they are only able to provide them because their staff have built great partnerships with various experts, non-profits, and universities. Building more public libraries and community centers with programming for seniors is not on the table. To address this lack of public provision, city staff members talk about building awareness of what other services are being offered in the community privately, and whether the city can attract more seniors to these programs. However, there is no formal process for this, so it is left up to frontline staff to reach out to partners. While this can result in interesting local partnerships, it contributes to fragmentation and inequities in service provision across the city. One solution proposed in the *Toronto Seniors Strategy* is to engage in a more formal process to "create a map that consolidates services to see what our service coverage is" (B3) and perhaps fund community agencies to fill in the gaps in these geographies. While it is encouraging that local government wants to understand service gaps, this response falls short of enhancing participation by providing more services as a right of citizenship.

There are also challenges to getting seniors involved in social activities that are affordable. Both non-profits and the city have initiated user fees for programming. The city's previous seniors' strategy – The Toronto Seniors Assembly report (City of Toronto 2002) complains that this is exclusionary for those who cannot pay and therefore should be provided as a right. A non-profit employee admits that "we have user fees and can't give a lot of stuff for free and things like that. But we do what we can" (D21), though Smith (2013) warns that this can further marginalize low-income participants.

This lack of investment in expanding social participation has created competition for programming. A member of the Toronto Seniors Forum explains that "renting a space in libraries and community centers is very competitive, especially on weekends, not only among senior groups but also between seniors and youth groups" (C4). This is identified as a challenge for small ethno-cultural agencies providing niche services and programs for seniors in their language of origin: "the ethno-cultural groups feel that they need to have a place to go to speak their language. It is not always about bringing a broader group together to speak English because some feel like outsiders. So for that, the community rooms and the recreation rooms that Parks and Rec manage are not enough" (C2).

Local government and non-profits are expected to be innovative in their programming to meet personalized needs but these niche projects need public resources. Speaking about their existing partnerships, a city representative explains that "there are all kinds of possibilities there and I guess success begets success, it grows exponentially. The issue is money. Always" (B26A). Similarly, another municipal staff member advises that "there is an opportunity where we can transfer learning and share learning. But there is not enough resources, there are never enough resources" (B19). My interviews with representatives from other levels of government frame big-city partnerships between local governments and non-profit agencies and the private sector as a replacement for public resources, but this appears to be an impossible expectation. What is clear from my interviews is that more resources are needed to meet demand, particularly if we are concerned about the social isolation of seniors.

4. COMMUNITY SUPPORT AND HEALTH SERVICES

The elephant in the room for AFCs in Toronto is both past and current projects of public-sector restructuring in the domain of health care, which produces complex intergovernmental and intersectoral relations. Participants understand local government as responsible for the social determinants of health, or the amenities and services that promote healthy living in local environments, while the province is responsible for medical health care delivery. Most participants outside local government, and even some within local government, advise that the city plays a small role in primary health care provision. My findings suggest, however, that a bifurcation between local government as enabler of health promotion and the province as health care provider is over-simplistic. Instead, I find local government filling significant gaps in primary health care, such as dental services for low-income citizens, and providing more emergency-oriented services such as ambulances and long-term care. This work challenges local government's ability to invest significantly in the social determinants of health.

The Association of Municipalities of Ontario has written a report (2011) reflecting its concerns that the provincial mandate of municipal investment in long-term care homes for seniors with increasingly complex health challenges is limiting their ability to invest in health promotion. Past restructuring in the health care sector, undertaken by the province under Premier Mike Harris's Conservative government, consisted of funding reductions to hospitals and a move to privatize long-term care. The province issued a competitive call for providers to supply long-term care beds, but failed to designate the type of beds needed, precipitating a situation where private providers offered light care while non-profit and local government providers increasingly delivered acute care (United Way of Greater Toronto 2001). In this context, some non-profits sold beds and transitioned to private retirement and long-term care. A non-profit representative explains that "all of this means more demands on municipal homes. But the city needs municipal homes, because where else would vulnerable people go?" (D3). A failure on the part of the province to keep track of the location of beds across Ontario has also meant that Toronto has lost beds, putting more pressure on the city's long-term care homes. A city employee explains that this loss of beds has been a problem in downtown Toronto where land is expensive and that there is no response from the province other than sending seniors to long-term care in the suburbs. This employee explains that downtown seniors "need an urban strategy that recognizes the cost to produce long-term care beds in the downtown. Their worry is that they don't want to be segregated and they want to be part of a community. The idea being aging in place, place being not only where you live but the neighbours and the broader community in which you live" (B17). The commodification of land is infringing on the rights of seniors to access care in this case.

Despite its emphasis on active aging to prevent entry to long-term care homes and hospitals, the AFC model can encompass investments in long-term care. In fact, in the Toronto case, AFCs were first introduced by the city's Long Term Care division and they have been redeveloping facilities using the AFC as a model with a daycare on the ground floor, intergenerational programming, adult day programs, a courtyard, and community space. This illustrates flexibility around the AFC concept as it can be used to complement and improve more medicalized institutional provision. A city staff member from the Long Term Care division explains that aging "shines a brighter light on us and also gives us the opportunity to be more proactive and to show all of the living that goes on in our homes … Long term care isn't really sexy. But it is also the reality for all of us. Not everyone has kids and family that can care for them" (B19).

Several participants are suspicious that a narrow project of public-sector restructuring prioritizing cost cutting is happening again today by stealth, through localization in the field of health care. There is concern that the responsibility for seniors' care is being shifted by the province, through its policy goal of aging in place and its discourse of health promotion, away from those hospitals and long-term care homes and towards the local government and non-profit domain of home care, social services, and public health. Local governments and non-profits are at once expected to prevent seniors from using costly public systems through active aging supports and, at the same time, to care for seniors once they exit these systems. In this context, they are struggling to deliver health services and waitlists for affordable services are getting longer. Because of these conditions more rationing happens, and the focus becomes targeting emergency services to the most vulnerable seniors. Several non-profit participants explain that even with some focus on home care by the province, funding is for people who are acute and not for preventative community support like meals on wheels. This targeting is being reconstituted as health promotion because it prevents seniors from ending up in, or back in, hospital and long-term care homes.

The province is operating from an assumption that local actors will form partnerships and devise innovative pilot projects to target vulnerable seniors. An example of this is the Toronto Paramedic Services project, introduced in chapter 1, where paramedics notify non-profits when they have contacts with seniors and/or take them to the hospital. This program emerged because the province told agencies that they had to know when their clients went to hospital so that they could support people when they were discharged. When probing further about funding for this program, a city employee explained that "it has actually been a grassroots thing, so it is through each individual community support agency that has come and enrolled their clients. But as a collective, we have petitioned and been able to get funding for a larger platform that will have more capacity and functionality" (B25). While such a project may address local service fragmentation, it struggles to do so with ad hoc funding support.

Several participants with institutional memory advised that the city has limited certain aspects of its preventative health care role, as was discussed earlier in the realm of elder abuse: "Years ago, when I first started here, public health nurses used to go visit seniors, and that is all gone. I think that this is what they should be doing again because it is the outreach in the community that they should be doing before things fall apart. They make the connections to people. But that is a challenge, because why was that discontinued? Because of money" (E27). This has limited the relationship between local government and non-profits in this policy realm: "We used to work hand in glove with public health nurses and go out and do door knocks where people were very isolated … that kind of thing has fallen away because it is not a mandated, legislated program" (D31B). This aspect of health promotion appears to have been recategorized by the city as primary health care, and thus under the legislative jurisdiction of the province: "Seniors became not a priority population for the city … Our understanding is that the city is really trying to get out of seniors' services because they see that as a provincial responsibility. And actually we … work very little with the city" (D32). We see tensions here where the province is framing the responsibility for seniors as a municipal issue and the city is resisting by framing seniors as a provincial issue.

The city's public health work has shifted to focus on falls prevention to reduce health care "burdens": "Five to ten years ago, our focus was almost exclusively on children and youth … given the huge burden that falls among the elderly cause, we do have a much larger emphasis now on what we call 'prevention' in the adult years. I would say that there is a lot more appetite now, a lot more interest, in really looking at keeping adults healthy so that they enter their senior years more healthy" (B16B). This work mainly includes informational sessions on healthy eating, encouraging medical visits, and the training of professional and family caregivers. Prevention is thus framed as the responsibility of individual citizens and caregivers (Orsini 2007). A former city councillor expresses the view that "the approach of public health to seniors has been a loss to seniors to a great degree," advising that programming such as falls prevention "really doesn't do all that much … It is kind of like elder abuse. The money that has been spent, millions on elder abuse, and I don't know because nobody has come up with a solution as to how to handle it" (A4). Falls and abuse, as well as social isolation, are complex problems that have to do with inadequate and inaccessible infrastructure, a lack of social services, and a residual reliance on self and informal care, despite the assumption that these are behavioural issues that information and training can fix.

In addition to falls prevention, the city's Public Health department has recently decided that they needed to do more work on vulnerable adults, with a staff member advising that "people are not doing this work in public health. They got out of this business many years ago and we are getting back into it" (B16A). However, this is not community prevention work but rather targeting supports to the most vulnerable seniors with addictions and mental health challenges. The city is increasingly providing care for those with very acute challenges because there is nowhere else for them to go, but staff are struggling to keep pace as this group is growing. A city representative expressed frustration in trying to make this work a holistic intergovernmental response instead of a targeted service issue. "[Our service team] are still hidden. This is an operation and so we are mired in operations, trying to get our heads up enough to do some other work to talk about this, to do some advocacy to say 'It is not so much about the services but the systemic gaps and we have to keep thinking this way.' But I don't think that we have enough power to have a voice that is heard" (B16A).

It is, in fact, the non-profit sector that increasingly provides services to the most vulnerable seniors aging in place. This reflects a fundamental change in the context of health care restructuring (DeSantis 2013), explained clearly in the following passage:

> the responsibility is growing as hospitals are very expensive. You can see that when you get a call from the hospital that they are discharging a patient, and they are under enormous pressure to discharge patients because they have only so many days. That is the connection. So the health system, it is great that it is free and socialized, but it is collapsing. There are not enough family doctors, there are not enough specialists, there are not enough beds in hospitals, so there is pressure. I have seen them discharge patients just because they are breathing, basically. And I had that, that the client was in shock and needed more attention. One of the challenges is that the health system could perceive us as the dumper, you just go fix it. Delegating responsibility. (D31A)

Non-profit provision is framed as solving the social problems of seniors, but these are often not quality of life issues but issues of hospital usage. One staff member highlights this clearly: "Any funds that are coming in the system now, which are quite limited, are being targeted to very specific sections of the population of seniors. So they are focusing on high-risk seniors. So they will tell you about the pyramid and the top 1 to 4 percent, so that is where the funding is going. But then, in that little pyramid, they have another grouping of individuals that are mid-course in that pyramid and it gets bigger, it is 7 to 10 percent of the 'at risk'" (D31B).

Non-profits are increasingly providing medicalized services to "high-risk" users. Several agencies spoke to me about the increasingly complex needs of the "clients" they are asked to serve. The great majority of non-profit participants admit that they are not provided with adequate funding to meet the increasingly complex needs of seniors: "At some point, something has got to give. Yes, we understand that it is trying to save the system money and we are trying to do more with less, and we have done that. But again, there is a certain point where you have to say 'No, we can't do that.' We have a responsibility to our employees to make sure that they are working in a safe environment and that they are not getting hurt taking care of a client who is much heavier in their care needs now" (D12). These interviews highlight the fact that the gaps in the health care system are so large that non-profits are attempting to meet increasingly universal needs. O'Conner (2004) worries that this will affect the capacity of the sector to "provide local accountability through membership and boards, develop skills among volunteers, supplement services by filling cracks left by government programs in innovative ways, and build on local knowledge" (208). This is a problem because these attributes of the community sector are listed as crucial in the design and implementation of AFCs.

5. HOUSING

Adequate housing is a major social determinant of health and is crucial to achieving an age-friendly environment. However, my interviews reflect troubling inadequacies in housing needs for senior citizens in Toronto. A major challenge is the need for services at the intersection of housing and health care. A city housing employee argues that a proper housing response must reflect a continuum of care that understands all housing needs from care in private homes and supportive housing with built-in services to long-term care homes, hospitals, transitional housing for recovering seniors, and end-of-life palliative care. There is considerable confusion as to what level of government has responsibility for seniors' housing. Several participants from the non-profit sector believe that "it is a role of the municipal government to create better access to supportive housing, assisted living, all of these variations of housing solutions. They have the ability to provide funding for and encourage new builds" (D47B). However, a housing expert explains that for cities, "the problem is that they don't have the tools and it isn't entirely in their jurisdiction to resolve. So, typically, municipalities are saying 'I am responsible for zoning bylaws and municipal standards but I am not the one that provides the care.' And so how do you solve something that isn't really yours?" (E26).

Several participants note that the private sector is beginning to provide retirement residences with different care options, but they are unaffordable to many seniors. At $4,000 to $5,000 a month in Toronto, these options are increasingly only for the wealthy, meaning that we have a two-tier care system: "It is the public response that addresses the need of the 15 to 20 percent that are not capable of affording and accessing what would be a private system for seniors. That is where the role is for government" (B17). This is a large section of the population, and participants agree that this group will expand as the cost of housing in Toronto continues to increase at unprecedented rates. A housing expert explains that building affordable supportive housing models is a challenge in big cities with high land prices: "I have run into a couple of interesting models of seniors' care that operate in a more affordable range, but it is all in small towns because they can make the numbers work. So we can build in places like Apsley, Ontario [2,479 residents], but the numbers just don't work in big cities" (E26). Furthermore, a city staff member stated that there are almost 25,000 seniors on the waitlist for affordable housing and that "a senior today could just as easily be waiting for a long-term care bed before they would get a social housing unit" (B17). While local government has enabled the development of 2,000 new affordable housing units for seniors in the last few years, a city representative admits that "those are 80 percent of the CMHC [Canada Mortgage and Housing Corporation] average market rent, so they still don't provide deep affordability and they are stop-start programs depending on federal and provincial funding levels. So they are helpful, but they are extremely modest" (B17).

The intersection of housing and health supports are particularly challenging for seniors with low incomes, as is explained by a housing expert: "When it comes down to, let's call it 'care light' or for people who are low-income, there is nothing there, or it is very limited, or it is haphazard, or it has been pulled together from a variety of resources" (E26). Toronto's social housing provider, Toronto Community Housing, is not technically supportive housing because it is primarily a landlord rather than a health service provider, but there is demand that it struggles to meet because of intergovernmental technicalities and policy silos. A city staff member admits that they "would love to get our hands on that [provincially supportive housing] funding because we could do so much more" (B2). Instead, non-profits are funded by the province to develop innovative projects in particular buildings that target the most "high-risk'" users of the health care system. A city-owned building might act as a hub and the non-profit provides around-the-clock care to the 5 percent of "high users" who need more care than the government provides. This use of existing infrastructure is seen as leveraging resources relative to providing new supportive housing. However, a housing expert disagrees with this stated effectiveness, advising that it creates even more service fragmentation and confusion: "You can have a building, and TCH [Toronto Community Housing] is a good example, where individual tenants will have different organizations that they are working with and you end up with ten different organizations providing services in the same building. Talk about ineffective. There may be reasons for some of that, but maybe there is a better way of doing it. The whole thing needs to be remapped" (E26).

As in the health care sector, non-profits are situated as stepping in to address gaps in housing for seniors. Several non-profits already provide housing and/or offer supportive housing and assisted living in existing social housing buildings. One expert recommends transferring full ownership for social housing to non-profit organizations: "The one thing that Canada misses and does not have a strong sector in is what I call 'mission-oriented affordable housing.' There is tons of it in BC, but in Ontario they are still, 'We are government, we know best, and we will keep you under our thumb.' In other countries, that is how things have been happening. It really is the merger of the business world and the mission piece" (E26). This would represent a transfer not to small agencies but to large organizations that can compete with private providers, requiring the non-profit sector to take on core service provision once considered to be the domain of the state rather than simply providing niche services.

In addition to problems in social housing, I find local government under-resourced to meet the emergency needs of senior citizens through shelter provision. A city representative admits that "we don't have adequate resources. We are still trying to cope with the number of people that we have in the emergency shelter system in general" (B20), as they have many aging citizens permanently living in city shelters. This staff member goes on to explain that because Toronto has many seniors in shelters that the long-term care system is not in a position to admit – in part because long-term care has not traditionally embraced a harm-reduction approach in its work – the city's largest men's shelter, Seaton House, is running a long-term care facility on the budget appropriate to a smaller hostel. Because of this, Seaton House is not in fact an emergency shelter but permanent housing for these seniors. One of the recommendations in the *Toronto Seniors Strategy* is for the city's Shelter division to continue meeting this need through a partnership with the city's Long Term Care division in the redevelopment of Seaton House in order "to access additional funds to specialize in meeting the needs of people that may have different behavioural issues and substance abuse issues and things like that" (B20). While this plan reflects an effort by local government to do what they can to meet needs, there are concerns as to whether this service partnership is good for seniors and thus age-friendly. Councillor Kristyn Wong-Tam, whose ward includes Seaton House, reflects frustration about this form of last-resort service provision:

> In my visits to the shelters, I am seeing a much older population than I think existed before. They don't belong in shelters because there are younger people who also come to these shelters – aggressive adult men – and I think it is a mistake to bring that population together in a volatile situation. You've got seniors in their sixties living in shelters because there is no affordable housing for them and then you've got these aggressive young guys in their thirties and forties who intimidate the senior homeless men and women. They steal from them and they bully them. This is something that we have to deal with in the City of Toronto. (A3)

Local government could be supported by other levels of government to create more hubs of care that include services to homes, but also different facilities that meet needs as a full continuum of care. One senior citizens' advocate believes that "cities would accept the challenge if there were dollars available from the government to start building some of these things" (F6), and my interviews with staff suggests that this is the case.

As seniors age at home, there is also a need to invest in accessibility features in their residences. Here too, public support in Toronto is inadequate. A city employee reflects on having to cut a tax renovation credit, the management of which was rescaled from the federal to the provincial government, who then transferred responsibility to local government and made the program discretionary. Toronto decided to maintain the credit to means-tested homeowners and has "had to restrict it to avoid a public expectation that the government is in a position to help and assist" (B17). This employee relates this struggle to serve seniors to public-sector restructuring that has moved away from universalism to programs that are targeted and capped. Reflecting the need for a more universal program, they explain that they have "over 500 applications waiting for processing and I have four staff. Just this past week, I suspended until 2016 a senior's capacity to apply into the program" (B17).

6. TRANSPORTATION

Past restructuring has increased the local government's role in public transit, providing it through the Toronto Transit Commission (TTC), as they are now fully responsible for covering both operating and capital costs with very little support from the province (Joy and Vogel 2015; Golden and Slack 2006; Horak 2012). My interviews indicate that this restructuring has been and will likely continue to be a strain on seniors, with the most vulnerable suffering the most. When I asked whether there are adequate resources to support transit for seniors, I received the following response: "The answer is a very glaring no. A hugely problematic no … the TTC is broadly seen as the worst-funded transit system in North America and possibly even the Western world. In terms of government ability to provide the funding needed for us to do the job for everybody, seniors and everybody else who rides it, the answer is no … everybody knows that the TTC is painfully underfunded" (B22).

Despite the population aging and need increasing, local government has cut back Wheel Trans, its accessible transit service, due to lack of funding. Funding cuts were followed by the introduction of stricter eligibility criteria that limited access for frail seniors with chronic health issues (City of Toronto 2002). A city representative admits that "one of the issues that we, as an organization with TTC and not just Wheel Trans, are all struggling with right now is that we are at that point where Wheel Trans as a stand-alone service, as an accessible service, is at the breaking point" (B24). Wheel Trans is working to meet increased demand through improved booking via their website and touchtone phone, but actual pick-up service has not been enhanced or upgraded. A representative admits that "we cannot continue to bring on additional staffing because of the cost. We have just added some additional bodies this year and possibly for next year, but each time the justification becomes more and more difficult" (B24).

Despite the need for enhanced Wheel Trans services, one employee explains that "because we are funded by the city, we will not get money to get more buses, so we have to find other methods of transporting these people, whether it is taxi or other contracted services. Our main goal is to transition a lot of these people onto the conventional TTC" (B24). TTC is supposed to be made fully accessible through the provincial *Accessibility for Ontarians with Disabilities Act* (AODA) by 2025. Staff admit that this transition will not be easy for citizens with mobility restrictions but that they will have to accept it, kicking and screaming. Rather than valuing diversity and personalized services and enhancing equity and inclusion, vulnerable seniors are being asked to go without an essential service to save the system. The *Toronto Seniors Strategy* report includes no recommendations or actions to invest in or improve Wheel Trans services.

A city representative admits that the TTC struggles to serve the "in-between group" of frail seniors "for whom getting to a bus or a street car service is tough but for whose mobility difficulties are not severe enough that they are eligible for Wheel Trans" (B22). Many non-profit participants expressed frustration about TTC services for this "in-between" group. In addition to malfunctioning escalators or non-existent elevators, one agency talks about challenges with the pace of transit: "My biggest pet peeve is the patience of the drivers. Twice, when I am walking off with a group of seniors, you see a line of older adults coming off and the driver closes the doors and twice I have had people stuck on the subway … I have to stand at the door so the door doesn't close. It is ridiculous. It makes me angry but can you imagine what it makes them feel like? Pushed around and stuff" (D21). A city staff member situates the five Community Bus Routes, highlighted in chapter 1 as a standalone service that connects seniors to venues of interest, as an illustration of how to meet the needs of the "in-between" group. The fact that there are only five routes in such a big city points to the fragmented access to services. Furthermore, a staff member admits that the service is "not very efficient in terms of the productivity that we get per hour … our conclusion is that this is not the best use of the precious dollars that we get" (B22).

While a medium-term action outlined in the *Toronto Seniors Strategy* is to "pursue discounted or free fares for older adults during non-peak hours" (City of Toronto 2013, 83), several city staff members clarify that there is no chance of this happening until larger multijurisdictional issues around transportation funding are resolved. Illustrating the depth of the problem, one staff member admits that conventional TTC services are struggling to meet provincial accessibility requirements to serve diverse needs: "Because of city cutbacks in funding, including capital, we no longer have enough funding to complete all of the station retrofits with all of the elevators and all of the other accessibility features by 2025 … we are pretty twisted in knots because we want to make that deadline theoretically and legislatively we have to make that deadline. The money isn't there. Just to give you some small measuring stick, we are short the money to do seventeen stations right now, only seventeen, and that money is $240 million dollars, so that is a lot of money" (B22). We see here that local government cannot afford niche services nor improve universal services to enhance accessibility for the aging population. If these issues are left unaddressed, it is quite likely that some seniors may simply decide to stay home because travelling on the TTC is too daunting; ironic given the concern among governments to promote active aging.

I also observed that accessibility improvements are sometimes framed as a problem by a city employee who notes that "from a purely business perspective, from a pure productivity and efficiency perspective, this will reduce our productivity and push our costs up" (B22). This employee explains that accessibility features in vehicles reduce seating capacity and thus revenue, and that slower service makes public transit less competitive as compared to private automobiles. Enhancing equity costs money, and this clashes with a "city-as-business" philosophy where departments like the TTC are measured on cost recovery: "The one and only thing that we seem to be evaluated on at the end of the year is 'What is your subsidy requirement?' and 'How is your financial performance?' When it comes to budget time, everybody forgets about the other noble objectives that people expect of us and they ask, 'How much money do you need this year?'" (B22). A city representative reflects frustration with policy strategies that place demands on these services without working out the cost implications: "It is so easy for either the public or these expert panels to say 'Why don't you just do this?' and 'Why don't you just do that?' We say, 'Happy to do it, but there are costs implications on capital, operating practices ... that will somehow have to manifest in our budget.' People don't seem to make that connection" (B22). Bureaucrats are expected to deal with these funding deficiencies and to find more efficiencies, and they are frustrated. "We go to City Council every year and we beg and we grovel and we get down on our knees and beg for more money and they may or may not throw a few crumbs at us ... you could debate whether that shortage of funding, the desperate shortage of funding, is because the city cannot afford to give more or whether they don't understand the critical need for it. I'm not sure" (B22).

Because of underfunding, local government has begun to look to the non-profit sector to support the mobility needs of vulnerable seniors. For example, the library is "investigating a transportation initiative ... to find partners in the local community to assist older adults to get to the library to attend programs" (B26B), though a representative admits that if they had more resources, they would put money towards the transportation initiative themselves. Furthermore, even getting non-profits to do this has been a struggle, given that "there is a hierarchy of needs for older adult transportation, getting them to health care and getting them to other things" (B26B). Increasingly, non-profit organizations are providing core transit services for seniors because the public system is inadequate. "If somebody is living with a mental health challenge, for instance, a Wheel Trans complication can really throw them off. That is why we have vans at all our programs, to be honest, so that we can provide a lot of transportation. Wheel Trans can be more cumbersome sometimes. And even accessing it, many of our clients don't have phones, so a big part of our support staff is booking Wheel Trans for people" (D7).

Larger agencies have developed a computer program that allows them to share transportation services if someone who may not be located within their catchment area needs a ride. When I probed further about how this program was funded, a non-profit employee explained that while the program was grassroots in its development, the province is now providing funding for the database, and sometimes for a coordinator. The employee advised that one of their "ultimate goals in the next few years is to work that into one big system. We will turn it into one good transportation system" (D27). Rather than innovating to improve an essential public service, this model is fragmented and sporadically funded. Public provision for universal services complements the work of the non-profit sector, freeing them up to meet more niche community needs. This requires greater public investments in public transportation but does not appear to be on the table with the *Toronto Seniors Strategy*.

7. OUTDOOR SPACE AND BUILDINGS

The AFC program puts pressure on local government to play a bigger role in ensuring accessibility in a context of aging infrastructure that has experienced years of underinvestment and where there is no increase in funding. The instigator of the *Toronto Seniors Strategy*, Councillor Josh Matlow, explains: "I think it is a challenge because our cities are not ready. And I think that this means that there needs to be more infrastructure dollars, which in many cities like Toronto just don't exist. Toronto's already got billions of dollars of debt and backlogs on everything from social housing and a transit system that is at least a generation if not more behind where it should be. It is still working on repairing and replacing its water mains, etcetera. So all of a sudden, if you say that you need to change everything to make it accessible to seniors, well, that is a tall order. So this will be a huge challenge for cities" (A1). While there is an assumption on the part of some participants that big cities have a large tax base from which to raise funds to invest in infrastructure, Toronto faces difficulty in innovating when it is so focused on addressing social and infrastructure crises: "We have huge challenges with respect to the kinds of services that we want to maintain for the general population. Budgets are tight, and when you look at issues such as infrastructure, housing, transit, they are all huge files that are competing for scarce dollars … programs that are uniquely targeted for people who are aging have to compete for the scarce dollars that are available for all these other big files" (B20). Furthermore, Toronto is growing, and this creates additional pressure: "The city's infrastructure has barely been able to keep up with the existing pressure of population and employment growth. There is the significant challenge of upgrading our infrastructure to make it accessible and age-friendly and just sustainable in terms of repair and maintenance and meeting the growth of the city" (B23).

The province appears to see their role as stewarding accessibility via the AODA, but their desire to build an inclusive province is left wanting without financial support. A city representative advises that there are divisions where implementation will not occur unless there are dedicated, stable resources. Furthermore, a non-profit representative explains that the province is "requiring mandatory training and we are like, 'OK, now we have to figure out how to do that, because training costs money.' So there is disconnect. Great idea, but on the ground not so good; we have to comply with the legislation" (D12).

One city employee working on accessibility improvements complains that "we are creating new tools, such as standards that the higher orders of government are not creating, to support implementation of their own legislation and requirements" (B23). In particular, this person is talking about the extensive research they undertook making a new accessibility improvement – tactile walking surfaces for those with visual impairments – which they are now sharing with other municipalities both across Canada and internationally. There is a sense of unfairness about being required by the province to provide goods and services and to innovate without adequate funding: "We are not a company, we can't charge each of these municipalities for the work that we have done, and I don't think that we would necessarily want to as it is a public good" (B23). Interestingly, this person also complains that because "the province likes to say, 'We don't get into the local detail'" (B23), they neglected to require a universal standard of accessibility for this tactile walking surface and this makes travel between cities difficult for those with visual impairments. Here, local government staff would have welcomed some leadership and foresight on the part of the province.

On the topic of outdoor spaces, a city staff member reflects on tensions between efficiency and equity. An example is the new pedestrian four-way stop "scrambles" at busy intersections such as Yonge and Dundas, which benefit pedestrians who spill out onto the street but which are disorienting to seniors. The staff member says that they are trying to advocate for a slower average walk speed, but that "there is such political pressure to coordinate our signals to alleviate traffic congestion" (B23). Because this pressure includes reducing the number of traffic stops to speed vehicular travel, the result is fewer pedestrian crossings and longer distances between intersections, making walking more difficult for those with mobility restrictions. The staff member notes that for real accessibility, "there are some traffic industry rules of thumb that may need to change. These are not city-specific, these are national and they are provincial" (B23). To be "age-friendly" requires change in multiple policy domains at multiple levels of government where access and equity are paramount.

8. COMMUNICATIONS AND INFORMATION

Again illustrating the clash between efficiency and equity, new communication technologies have presented a challenge for local government. A staff member explains that while the city gets criticized for not being quicker to adapt to new technology such as cellphone applications, these present a real problem of access for those with physical and cognitive as well as affordability challenges. The staff member shares an interesting story on this topic: "I was meeting with a woman who is blind recently and she is on a fixed income and I asked her whether she was using any of the latest technologies about navigating streets. She said, 'You have to pay to play and I don't have a smart phone'" (B23). The staff member advises that "we are trying to be an inclusive city where you plan for everyone and so there are numerous trends that make this a challenge for us as we balance things" (B23). However, developing a city-wide process for achieving this balance through an equity lens appears to be a challenge. Another city representative admits that the *Toronto Seniors Strategy* recommendation to develop an accessible communications policy had yet to have gotten off the ground at the time of my interviews.[15]

Attempting to enhance communication by making all frontline staff aware of services for seniors has also been a challenge. This is a huge undertaking, given the number of staff in such a large city. Given limited resources and state capacity, they decided to target staff working with the most vulnerable seniors. This is also reflected in the city's strategy to target neighbourhoods where the most vulnerable seniors are located. The *Toronto Seniors Strategy* has, as one of its recommendations, the identification of neighbourhood improvement areas that are community and resident-based and where there are many seniors residing with inadequate access to services. This includes identifying problem environments and targeting to make them more ideal, with funding to community development and non-profit agencies. This builds on the city's "priority neighbourhood" approach, which focuses on areas of concentrated poverty in Toronto's inner suburbs to understand access to services and amenities and

---

1 The City of Toronto adopted a corporate accessibility policy on 26 June 2018. Further research is needed to examine how this policy meets the needs of senior citizens in the city.

target service responses (United Way Toronto 2005). Non-profits providing services in these areas were prioritized for funding in the past and neighbourhood action tables that brought different local players together were developed. However, seniors are not concentrated in one area of the city, and this strategy created inequities in financial and human resources. A non-profit employee working at an agency in a seemingly wealthy neighbourhood advised that "there are a lot of wealthy boomers but there are also a lot of boomers that are low-income. Those are the country club type of boomers, and you won't see a lot of them at a little community center. We are the ones that the people that come from the subsidized housing go to. You know how hard it is to get funding here? … All around us is subsidized housing. And these people are living at or right above or below the poverty line. These are our seniors" (D21). While the localized neighbourhood focus is intended to address diversity, it can also fail to adequately conceptualize diversity within the neighbourhood, which leads to more fragmentation and inequity (Walks 2001). Age-friendly investment is needed for city-wide provision, as well as neighbourhood-specific initiatives in each area. However, there are no formal neighbourhood-based governance and planning structures in the amalgamated City of Toronto.

Conclusion

In this chapter, I have examined the claim that AFCs improve environments for senior citizens, and in so doing improve local services and amenities for the population at large. I contrast how participants understand the importance of policy focusing on local environments to support senior citizens with the actual roles and capacities to make redistributive improvements through the eight domains of the AFC framework in Toronto. I find that participants believe that place matters in seniors' quality of life and is an important lens to understand their needs for both universal and niche services and amenities. As such, they applaud the AFC movement for being grounded in everyday environments. I find that place is a particularly important lens because the scale of the problem of inadequate access for seniors to age-friendly services and amenities in Toronto is significant. While there may be more supportive opportunities available in the big city, participants talk at length about the social isolation of seniors due to physically and/or cognitively inaccessible services, amenities and programs that are unaffordable, and the administrative and spatial fragmentation of available supports. Participants clearly voice a need for a redistributive policy based on a model of universal inclusion.

The interviews begin to offer insight into why local environments in Toronto remain problematic despite the apparent government commitment to enable age-friendly cities. I find challenges rooted in the hegemonic concept of individual responsibility for self-care. There was considerable concern for socially isolated seniors who struggle to care for themselves in big cities because they are unable to avail the informal care of family and friends which is thought to be more available in small towns. The understanding underlying this thinking is that if an individual cannot care for themselves, their family, then friends and neighbours, then non-profit community agencies are expected to step in to provide support. The more "local" the better, reflecting the normalization of individualized, familial, and communitarian forms of care. Many participants hark back to an idyllic village where people cared for the elderly and seek to recreate this through the AFC program emphasis on volunteerism, non-profit provision, and local government programming.

This thinking allows the AFC concept to be used to incite more do-it-yourself urbanism and neighbourhood betterment by active citizens or armies of volunteers (Szreter and Ishkanian 2012; Laforest 2013a; Taylor 2013; Hardill and Baines 2011) that is framed against a public approach to enhance redistribution and equity. The public-sector steps in only as a provider of last resort in this framing (Antonnen et al. 2012a), and again, the more local the provision, the better. Non-profits and local governments are expected to replace the care that is not being provided adequately by the individual, family, and neighbours, and the formal redistributive care being provided inadequately by central governments. These gaps are significant and needs far exceed such a residual approach on the part of the state. While AFCs are intended to support the establishment of healthy environments through investments in the social determinants of health, in practice they are more about localized pilot projects targeting vulnerable seniors and neighbourhoods rather than significant investments in income support, housing, transportation, and home care. The localization and projectization of this strategy risks exacerbating inequity in access if a local community does not have an active group of seniors and non-governmental organizations to push for and deliver AFC projects (Scharlach 2012). Pilot projects with ad hoc funding and an over-reliance on non-profit provision create service fragmentation and inequity in local environments.

This is a welfare strategy based on subsidiarity and residualism where the state only steps in emergency situations to target "high-risk" users and neighbourhoods (Antonnen et al. 2012a). The "local" is used as a strategy on the part of the province to save money by using community agencies to target "costly" senior citizens. Local government departments and non-profit organizations are scrambling to provide emergency supports. A major finding in this chapter is the extent to which non-profits are increasingly expected to offer essential services in the areas of transportation, housing, and health care. The following chapters will explore the extent to which this service professionalization is using up resources that could be spent on more democratic processes to recognize diverse needs, invest in the preventative determinants of health, and inform policy at other levels of government.

This chapter begins to highlight that targeted social services cannot replace health care as a cost-saving measure but rather must exist as a right of citizenship along a continuum from prevention-oriented social programs to emergency support. The social determinants of health cross jurisdictional boundaries and have been the subject of underinvestment for years through a narrow politics of public-sector restructuring, resulting in serious gaps in local environments. These gaps materialize as crumbling infrastructure that is inaccessible, and isolated seniors who are sick for lack of income, mental health support, and access to social supports, housing, and transportation. Part of this underinvestment has involved transferring policy responsibility for large infrastructure domains in the realms of health care, housing, and transportation to local governments and non-profit organizations through a rhetoric of localization but without commensurate financial supports and policy capacity, indicating that inadequate "rights of the city" are an issue. Local governments and non-profits are supposed to at once address the problems with a top-down universalised system of senior care that fails to incorporate difference and voice as well as the problems of inequitable access and fragmentation that a more localized approach has produced. Non-profits and local governments are thus asked to be both "local" and "universal." While this offers interesting opportunities for a model of universal inclusion, my research suggests that local actors struggle to meet diverse needs and engage in the mass service delivery required in the realms of health care, transit, and housing. Staff advise that building more affordable and accessible housing and transportation for senior citizens is unlikely in a context where "universal" transit and social housing systems face serious underinvestment.

While place-based policy can support a focus on how problems occur in everyday life and identify diverse needs on this basis, my findings suggest that Toronto's AFC strategy is too highly localized and cannot meet the needs of seniors without financial assistance and policy change by central governments. The "seeing like a city" approach is being taken too far in practice by ignoring any form of "seeing like a state" and its associated emphasis on the politics of redistribution. The failure to take a multi-scalar approach to seeing like a city simply replaces a single-scale methodological nationalism with a single-scale new localism. This is due to the dominance of anti-statism and cost cutting as part of a narrow political project in which local government and non-profit provision is understood as a replacement for rather than a complement to wider forms of public redistribution. Place-based policy requires governments at all scales to provide investment in the core social and physical infrastructures crucial to healthy environments. The following two chapters offer a more detailed exploration of the two obstacles to producing age-friendly environments highlighted in this chapter: 1) the way in which individual seniors are recognized and 2) the rights of local policy actors to support them. Examining the themes of recognition and the rights of the city will allow me to explore the second and third claims that AFCs promote a positive aging identity and empower local policy actors.

CHAPTER 3

Recognizing Senior Citizens: Promoting a Positive Aging Identity through AFCs in Toronto

Introduction

The AFC program claims to challenge societal ageism by promoting the development of a positive aging identity. Central to this identity is the recognition that seniors are not passive bodies characterized by mental and physical health problems but active citizens who continue to contribute to society (Kalache 2016; Golant 2014; Ontario Government 2013a; Barusch 2013; Gonzoles and Morrow-Howell 2009; Plouffe and Kalach 2010; Halvorsen and Emerman 2013). Buffel et al. (2012) explain that this notion of active citizenship has been central to policy work on aging by the United Nations and the WHO for almost three decades. The authors advise that "the notion of 'active' refers to the idea that older people should be able to continue to participate in social, cultural, spiritual, economic and civic matters, i.e. not just the ability to participate in the labour market or to be physically active" (Buffel et al. 2012, 599). The AFC model reflects a more recent understanding that local environments characterized by age-friendly social services and physical infrastructures can foster active citizenship for seniors (Kalache 2016; Buffel et al. 2012).

The previous chapter has highlighted that there are considerable gaps in the extent to which Toronto's local environment is age-friendly and that this will likely remain the case even with the presence of the *Toronto*

Seniors Strategy. Programs of cost cutting through policy rescaling as well as efforts on the part of the local state to keep taxes and spending low are indeed compromising the realization of substantive AFCs in Toronto, as was identified as a general problem with the program in AFC literature (Buffel and Phillipson 2016) and a broader problem with place-based policy in geography literature (Peck 2012). Yet, these findings also suggest that gaps in substantive AFCs relate to the very ways in which senior citizens are being recognized: as a problem to be managed in a society that values individual self-care and productivity. This raises a more fundamental question as to whether the AFC approach inherently promotes a positive aging identity. This chapter explores this question through an examination of the ways in which seniors are being recognized as citizens through the AFC program in Toronto.

Isin et al. (2008) define "citizenship" as the norms and behaviours that characterize the relations between people in a political community, particularly how individuals are recognized as worthy and thus the extent to which they belong in the collective and have their needs deemed suitable for a redistributive public response. For Isin (2008), it is in the space of the city that these citizenship relations take place and affect life experiences most viscerally. These relations can be expansive, based on intrinsic understandings of human worth and rooted in principles of empathy and solidarity, and practices that build mutual understandings of experiences, desires, and needs (Antonnen et al. 2012a). Isin et al. (2008) characterize an expansive form of citizenship as follows: "citizenship involves the art of being with others, negotiating different situations and identities, and articulating ourselves as distinct yet similar to others in everyday lives, and asking questions of justice. Through these social struggles, we develop a sense of our rights as others' obligations and others' rights as our obligations" (7). Citizenship relations can also be reductive, based on instrumental understandings of human worth that ignore or even shame different experiences and needs and seek to change people to make them fit particular standards (Antonnen et al. 2012a; Antonnen et al. 2012b). A right to the city would reflect expansive citizen relations and actively challenge narrow ones.

In this chapter, I apply this citizenship lens to AFCs in Toronto to make better sense of gaps in the program and to assess the claim that AFCs promote a positive aging identity. I identify key themes in the ways that local actors undertaking age-friendly work recognize senior citizens as an identity group and population aging as a policy issue. Through these themes, I explore how the life experiences, wants, and needs of seniors are recognized and how seniors and their agencies define the challenges they face in local environments. The conclusion to this chapter reflects the larger purpose of this examination: to offer greater insight into the problems and prospects for AFCs as a right to the city for seniors.

Recognizing Senior Citizen Wants and Needs

SENIOR CITIZEN DIVERSITY

There was a clear recognition among research participants that seniors are a heterogeneous group, as age intersects with several diversity considerations. A non-profit participant explains: "Seniors are the most diverse population. So as life is going on, you can find people on the whole spectrum at any level. So, physical, there are seniors who are healthy and active and there are seniors who are very compromised. And at the same time financially. So some are very good at planning retirement or those years that they won't be able to work; other people just find themselves without any resources. Socially as well, there are people who are very well-connected and there are people who are very isolated. So basically, in any issue that you see, you will find people across the continuum" (D31A). Toronto seniors are particularly diverse in age range, physical and mental health, income, language, and race/ethnicity.

In defining "older adults," the City of Toronto recognizes that such terms are fraught, not only because the period commences at a different age range for different policy programs but also because the term "old" is socially constructed and is considered by some, and many seniors themselves, to be discriminatory as it denotes passivity and dependency (City of Toronto 2013). That said, in its effort to understand its older adult population, the city focuses on citizens over the numerical age of fifty-five to "provide a broad overview of the demographic diversity of older Torontonians" (City of Toronto 2013, 7). A non-profit participant explains why this is important: "When we are talking about aging, there are the aging fifty-five to seventy-year-olds, the seventy to eighty-five-year-olds, and the eighty-five to hundred-year-olds. Aging for each of those people within a community has different service needs. While we are getting better at it, we don't always recognize these unique needs across those different groups within a large city and locally we need different solutions" (D1A). According to the 2011 census, there are 680,945 Torontonians over the age of fifty-five; this number is expected to double to 1.2 million by 2041, with those aged between fifty-five and sixty-four and those aged eighty and above representing the groups with the fastest pace of population growth in the city (City of Toronto 2013). The number of older adults has increased in all but one Toronto neighbourhood, but especially noteworthy is the degree of change in the city's car-dependent and service-poor outer suburbs of Scarborough and Etobicoke (City of Toronto 2013). As was highlighted in the previous chapter, there is thus particular concern about the social isolation of senior citizens in these suburban environments.

With aging comes more health challenges, and 40 percent of Torontonians over the age of seventy-five describe their health as fair or poor (City of Toronto 2013). As one non-profit employee explains, "chronic health conditions are more prevalent in older adults, and these adults are living longer. This means an increase in disability years" (D1B). As we live longer, we live with more complex chronic physical and mental health challenges and this can affect our access to services and amenities (Abrahamson 2015). Several city representatives reflect concerns with the growing incidence of dementia and the necessity for cities and non-profits to adapt their services and programming accordingly. One city employee emphasizes the diversity of needs within the long-term care setting where more seniors are coming in with dementia who may live for a very long time, as well as people who have acute physical challenges but sharp minds.

Another surprising statistic in the Toronto case is that 72 percent of senior citizens over the age of sixty-five are women (City of Toronto 2013), illustrating the need to take a gender lens to AFC policy. Modlich (2011) explains that women tend to live longer, have lower incomes than men and thus inadequate pensions, provide more informal care over the life-course and into older age, and are the majority of formal care providers in jobs that are undervalued and underpaid. Calasanti (2008) clarifies that in retirement, many women continue to perform domestic and social functions that ease their spouses' transition into retirement.

A policy expert advises that increasingly, it is older single women who are living in poverty and at risk of homelessness and require affordable and supportive housing that meet their needs. This remains an issue that has been inadequately examined and addressed by public policy and academic research (Darab and Hartman 2013). While women are likely to face more challenges to age in place given these realities, neither the WHO AFC movement nor the *Toronto Seniors Strategy* include a gender-based analysis (Modlich 2011).

Another non-profit participant has concerns that policy ignores societal changes around marriage and family structure, noting that policy makers "are looking at families with 2.2 kids. It is wrong. They are still looking at that traditional family model and it is gone, gone in my boomer generation. We need to call attention to who is making policy and what their assumptions are" (D55). This is a serious omission, as 44 percent of Toronto's senior citizens over the age of eighty-five are living alone, not with family or a spouse (City of Toronto 2013). A non-profit participant explains that "we underestimate the number of seniors who are on their own or who don't have family or who aren't able to, as their cognition changes, communicate and access information ... While many seniors are able to advocate for themselves, many can't" (D1A). Golant (2014) reflects concern that the AFC movement makes an underlying assumption that senior citizens have access to informal family care and therefore fails to incorporate the necessary supports for caregivers, who will be the seniors of the future. The *Toronto Seniors Strategy* does not speak to or provide formal actions to address the needs of informal family caregivers.

What makes Toronto unique is its history and present characterization as a city of immigration. Sixty-eight percent of Toronto residents above age fifty-five immigrated to Canada, 40,340 of whom arrived in the country within the past ten years and are more likely to be members of racialized groups, experience poverty, and be non-English- or French-speaking (City of Toronto 2013). Several participants advise that the needs of foreign-born seniors might be quite exceptional because they may need familiarity cues such as their own language spoken, their festivals celebrated, and their food preferences provided. As such, local government and non-profit services must adapt their programming. A city representative explains how important this is in a long-term care home setting: "We have to value people and respect them and we benefit from this diversity, but it does present some challenges when you have got people with different cultures, language needs, and food specifications … when you have everyone living in one home sharing dining and sharing programs, there are definitely some challenges" (B19).

Several participants spoke about newcomer seniors struggling to access health and community support services in Toronto. A particular challenge is those who have been sponsored through the federal government's family-class system and have limited knowledge of Canada's health care sector. A non-profit staff member explains that there are also many seniors who have been in Canada for a long time but who have little knowledge of English or of government programs because they have remained embedded in ethnic enclaves. A policy expert cautioned that this lack of integration is particularly problematic because "these are often patients who are higher users of our health care system … the fact that so many more have trouble communicating affects their ability to be aware of services, to access services. And then, even if they do access services, the question is whether the services are being delivered in an accessible way" (E19). A further systemic challenge is the federal government's sponsorship scheme itself, according to which newcomers have no access to the Canada Pension Plan and, if they have been here for less than ten years, no access to Old Age Security or benefits and services through the Ontario Health Insurance Program. A policy expert explains the consequences of this: "We will fund their hospital care but not their long-term care or community care, which is a huge issue, and we see this locally in Toronto where we have a huge local immigrant population. What happens is these people become homeless, which is a whole other costly issue, or they end up staying in a hospital for a long time where either they die or they go back home with some kind of support" (E19).

A particular issue that affects integration among newcomer seniors is grandparenting. Several participants note that some seniors are sponsored to come to Canada to help raise their grandchildren and as such, can be isolated from opportunities to learn English and to socialize with others. Councillor Kristyn Wong Tam reflects at length about how seniors are contributing through childcare, which is likely correlated in part to the high costs of childcare in Toronto. Councillor Wong Tam is concerned that many seniors providing childcare feel that they cannot say no, advising that "in many ways, the services that grandparents are offering in terms of childcare provision is not appreciated or understood" and these seniors "are now being asked to take on additional responsibilities" that "have now become part of this underground economy" (A3). This issue is unaddressed in the *Toronto Seniors Strategy*.

The *Toronto Seniors Strategy* highlights that many senior citizens in Toronto have low incomes and are struggling to make ends meet (City of Toronto 2013). A city staff member reminds me that "aging isn't just a correlation with increased risk of medical problems, there is also that relation with income and income distribution ... it affects the ability to take care of yourself, the ability to finance your life, your food, your housing, everything else" (B25). While workforce participation for those over age sixty-five has increased since the province of Ontario ended mandatory retirement in 2006, unemployment has also risen dramatically (City of Toronto 2013). A non-profit employee offers a personal reflection on this situation: "I have no industrial pension. I am going to be sixty-five and I will get $1,200 a month, but that doesn't even cover my rent. I am dying in the saddle here. I never married, I don't have the significant other, I am a woman – lower salaries all the way along, worked in the arts ... It is very different to wake up in the morning and go, 'I have $60,000 coming in, what am I going to do today?' and waking up in the morning and going, 'I have $14,000 coming in, I have to find a job, but I can't find one.' In the Age-Friendly Community, there is also employment, it is keeping people employed" (D55). However, as was highlighted in the previous chapter, the *Toronto Seniors Strategy* is not very strong in the area of employment. This is perhaps due to an assumption on the part of city staff that only privileged seniors are interested in employment opportunities.

Income precarity among senior citizens is reflected in homelessness trends in Toronto and, in particular, the finding, outlined in the *Toronto Seniors Strategy*, that one-fifth of those using the city's homelessness support services are over the age of fifty (City of Toronto 2013). A city employee explains that according to a Street Needs Assessment, the number of respondents over the age of sixty-one doubled from 5 percent to 10 percent between 2009 and 2013. It is also important to understand the ways in which different dimensions of inequity experienced through the life-course affects the biological aging process. A city representative explains that those that have experienced homelessness for longer periods "are aging and presenting as older adults much younger in their lives. We are looking at people who might be in their forties and fifties who might be presenting with needs that you may see in folks in the general population who are in their seventies, eighties, nineties" (B20). This person goes on to note that "with respect to criteria around services for this group, they may not be sixty-five plus, but they may have the same needs as folks that are sixty-five plus. So how do we create programs and policy that is going to meet their needs, without making age a barrier?" (B20).

An academic expert expressed frustration that on the topic of aging and AFCs, "the homeless older adult has been particularly ignored in all of this. We did the very first study on older homeless in Canada and I can tell you, the resources were zilch. And they are still pretty zilch … We interviewed tons of agencies and we interviewed a bunch of homeless older adults in two cities, Calgary and Toronto. Not happy. Their health care is appalling" (E20). This academic goes on to explain that "there is a massive problem with the communication between the gerontologists and the homelessness people. They don't talk to each other, and they don't want to" (E20). For example, the celebration of park benches with handles on them to enhance accessibility as having an added bonus of reducing rough sleeping among those experiencing homelessness is used as a metaphor because, increasingly, it is senior citizens who are becoming homeless. A non-profit participant reflects on this: "The City of Toronto has had the aging strategy. I was involved in it. It is all over the place and there are contradictions between different departments. For example, the parks department is setting up benches, replacing benches so that they have handles so people can get up. Well, a side effect of that is that the homeless, the old fellows, lose a place to sleep. I wonder what the real reason was to change this" (D35).

Another senior citizen advocate explains the importance of understanding the different experiences of homelessness, noting that she has had to explain to government "that they have to consider not just the homeless seniors but the near-homeless seniors. The ones who are couch- surfing, so they don't show up in the statistics because they are living with their daughter, their sister, whoever. They are not homeless and living and begging on the street but they are still precarious" (D49). This is illustrative of a much broader systemic problem, especially given the finding that this group of vulnerable seniors appears to be growing, with one non-profit employee admitting that they are "dealing with more and more people that are on that poverty line" (D21). A city staff member explains that there are currently 25,000 seniors on the wait list for rent-geared-to-income housing in Toronto who are currently paying such a large percentage of their income on housing that they often use food banks to survive.

Precariously housed seniors may struggle with mental health challenges and issues such as hoarding and addiction and may be living in public or non-profit shelters or apartment housing. A non-profit employee explains their frustration around inadequacies in supporting this group:

> Mental health related issues are, I know, not being dealt with. There is this assumption that seniors don't have mental health issues. They might have dementia but they don't have mental health issues. They might have had them when they were younger but somehow, they suddenly disappear when you reach a certain age. So there is a huge gap there both provincially and city-wide. Again, the city would say, "We are not a mental health funder" … So it is very concerning because it is not going to go away, so everyone just kind of has their hands in front of their eyes. I think partially because it is such a huge issue, if you take your hands away from your eyes, and you open them, it is very scary. (D31B)

In summary, a non-profit employee states that governments that promote age-friendliness "need to be aware of and incorporate the complexities of those with mental health and addiction and histories of homelessness and trauma" (D7). As the previous chapter has outlined, this is being recognized in the Toronto case through the SPIDER protocol as well as through the work of Toronto Public Health, though staff admit that this work remains fragmented.

The incredible diversity of Toronto's senior population requires that services and amenities be designed and delivered in such a way as to mitigate barriers to access on the basis of identity. This requires that policymakers understand and respond to biological and social similarities based on old age, such as health challenges and the loss of loved ones, as well as differences produced through an array of socially structured inequality characteristics (Abrahamson 2015). The *Toronto Seniors Strategy* and the interviews highlight that senior diversity is being recognized to some extent, yet this discussion and the findings from the previous chapter suggest significant gaps in efforts to meet these needs. As we will see, a core reason for this is the way in which the increased social diversity brought about by population aging is being recognized as a problem or even a crisis. The remaining themes in this chapter seek to characterize this "problem" and the ways that it is being "managed" through AFCs.

AGING AS A CRISIS

While several participants admit that population aging is a positive demographic occurrence because it indicates improvements in societal health, more people living longer is overwhelmingly seen as negative because it will result in more reliance on government to provide care. My findings illustrate that population aging is considered a problem because it increases societal difference as it brings new experiences, particularly needs. The metaphor of a "tidal wave" or "tsunami" of need about to drown us all is prevalent in the rhetoric used by several participants. This drowning metaphor relates to our capacity as a society to meet the needs of a more "hard-to-serve" population, with several participants questioning who will provide this care and who will pay for it. A city employee explains that aging is "a challenge because of the 'inverted pyramid,' which means that we will have less tax dollars to offer services" (B6). Redistribution is considered infeasible in this context of increasing need, as young people will be unable to support the old and this will create a fiscal crisis for the state. This reflects an increasingly prevalent argument that our social welfare systems cannot survive the onslaught of diversity (Antonnen et al. 2012a).

A major concern among participants is the so-called "burden" senior citizens present to the public health care system, which risks being "bankrupted" by their needs. The "horrible expression that you hear about the 'bed blockers'" (D8) refers to seniors who end up staying in hospital beds for long periods of time because inadequate care is available for them at home and there is no space available in an appropriate long-term care home, transitional housing, or palliative care facility. According to this rhetoric, the senior is understood as a burdensome body, taking up space and resources. Often ignored in this discourse is the decades-long project of hospital restructuring and cuts to beds in the acute sector in Ontario that has caused this drastic shortage of supports, as was outlined in the previous chapters.

Equally underexamined is the problem that there is an inadequate system of public long-term care homes and home care to support seniors both before and after their hospital stays. Challenging investment in the former is a discourse that associates living in a long-term care home with "bad aging" because the individual is understood as dependent, passive, and segregated from society or community. I detected a normalized critique of welfare state policy, which participants align with a statist past that characterized all seniors as sick and poor and with a paternalistic approach that segregated seniors in institutional environments because they were considered no longer able to participate in everyday life on their own. While this approach was based on an image of senior citizens as worthy and deserving of a collective public response, it was also based on stereotyping and resulted in paternalistic programs that failed to recognize diverse needs. Alternatively, aging at home is associated with "good aging" because there seniors are considered independent, active, and included in society and community. Aging at home, with some home and community supports, is central to the emphasis on the need for "systems change" in the health care sector.

The AFC movement is a key component of this systems change, as it is meant to facilitate independent aging at home. In this way, AFCs cannot be separated from health care restructuring because they are part of the discourse focussing on the promotion of the social determinants of health (Kalache 2016; Orsini 2007). Local policy actors are supposed to do their part through the AFC program to prevent health crises and save health care dollars by enhancing the fit between seniors and their environments and understanding them as active contributors. This rhetoric may help explain why the provincial enablement of AFCs has not been complemented with funding to long-term care in the Toronto case, despite the fact that this is clearly needed, as the previous chapter has outlined. Yet, the AFC process in Toronto has also created a space for the city's Long Term Care division to showcase their needs and to advocate to the province for additional support to address growing diversity.

ELIMINATING AGEISM

A core policy goal of the AFC approach and the *Toronto Seniors Strategy* more specifically is to eliminate discrimination based on age. Yet I found the concept of "ageism" to be complex and contested in the interviews, as well as in the literature. Discrimination on the basis of age was explained as a lack of exposure to seniors and inadequate recognition of their place in society. For this reason, participants talk about the need for local government to build public awareness about population aging and create programs that focus on "helping younger people to understand and accept that older people are still people, and they don't like to be treated as invalids or that they don't know anything" (D30B). Many participants understand ageism as the knowledges, ideas, and practices that equate aging with vulnerability, or the notion that seniors are inherently frail, needy, dependent, sick, and mentally unfit. Ageism is treating seniors like patients, as though they are nothing more than their health problem, and results in a paternalistic approach whereby we talk over people because we believe that they are passive and have lost their capacity to make rational decisions.

I learned from non-profit and city service providers that some older adults resist being called seniors and being part of seniors programming because they feel segregated. A member of the Toronto Seniors Forum says, "I don't know why, but there is some kind of stigma against even using the word 'senior.' People don't like to be labeled as being elderly and I think that this is something that we have to challenge and overcome ... I think it was Shakespeare that wrote about how when you reach a certain age you are 'sans teeth, sans eyes, sans this, sans everything.' Well, that is not the case anymore" (C6). Green (2012) claims that the active aging discourse is fundamental to a positive identity because it breaks the link between aging and dependency. Green (2012) compares an active "third age" to a dependent "fourth age," and argues that AFCs should focus prevention activities and investments on the third age group to prevent an early descent to the fourth. A non-profit participant explains that "we do know what the fountain of youth is or the solution to aging, and that is remaining physically active and mentally engaged" (D1B). As such, we see a policy shift from a focus on organizations such as long-term care homes, public supportive housing, and hospitals, that are seen to promote dependency, to localized programs that target changing the behaviours of citizens to prevent risks to themselves and to social systems (Newman and Clarke 2009; Orsini 2007; Kemshall 2002).

> The change in thought is so necessary so that new generations really enjoy the same quality of life. We need to say in twenty

> years, "back then we were innovative and we knew that we had to switch from crisis care to chronic care and we had tax incentives for people to go to gyms, for instance." This doesn't exist yet. There is no tax credit for older people to go to the gym or if you have a tax incentive where you save more money if you stop smoking cigarettes. There is no tax saving if you lose weight when you are fifteen pounds overweight. We have to mandate health and preventative medicine; otherwise you and your kids won't have health care. (D55)

Public policies that incentivize activation focus on behavioural solutions through the life-course to reduce risk. An academic expert explains: "Develop yoga and cross-training for strength and flexibility early in life … Eat well and reduce processed foods and the sugars and salts and all of that, eat more fresh stuff, don't smoke and drink moderately, keep stress down and floss your teeth … Invest in our health through our life in a positive way and bring others with us and build strong support systems" (F4). A senior citizens' advocate goes on to note that "We know that exercise and nutrition are critical. Frequently, this is an information thing we need to get out" (F6). We see an emphasis on information campaigns encouraging people to change their behaviours as a crucial program component of AFCs. There is a somewhat paternalistic assumption here that people are clueless about how to live well and simply need better information to improve their lifestyles. This can distract from a focus on how social determinants of health such as adequate income, affordable housing, access to nutritious and affordable food in one's neighbourhood, and public recreation facilities are essential to such healthy living.

These findings raise a concern highlighted by Biggs (2001) as to whether the active aging discourse fundamentally challenges or more deeply engrains societal ageism. Biggs (2001) argues that, in a capitalist system, humans are valued for their productive capacity, and older adults who no longer contribute as labourers and have care needs are considered dependent and an economic burden. A non-profit participant explains this succinctly: "I think that the main challenge, from the system perspective, is a population that is not productive in a capitalist system. It is perceived as taking money away rather than seeing services as something that they deserve" (D31A). Biggs (2001) explains that there is very little room for a positive aging identity in the narrow neoliberal political project, because individuals who require care and cannot work are considered useless unless they have funds to purchase services in the private "silver industries." Attempting to combat ageism by arguing that seniors continue to contribute as "citizen-consumers" (Clarke et al. 2007) leaves out those who cannot participate in the market. Care is valued primarily as an investment to produce independent and productive labourers, as the social investment model which favours the young as future economic contributors suggests (Saint-Martin 2007; Chen 2008). Biggs and Carr (2015) argue that in a context where citizenship is based on economic contribution, investing in children as future contributors is perhaps more easily justifiable than investing in older adults, and therefore the bulk of mainstream policy literature on population aging focuses on the continuing economic contribution of older adults. Biggs (2001) illustrates how old age has been reconstructed away from economically unproductive, burdensome, and dependent to active, productive, and thrifty.

This is a discourse that fundamentally assumes that being young is a normal and good human state while being old is an abnormal and bad human state (Chen 2008). Where treating all old people as vulnerable is ageist, the solution is to treat old people as we do young people. Aging becomes socially acceptable because we pretend that it does not exist. This amounts to what Biggs (2008) calls a "new form of ageism" that erases any consciousness about the uniqueness of later life and seeks to "impose the priorities of one part of the life course on others" (119). Seniors may feel the need to prove that they are like the young – independent and healthy economic contributors – because this is valued as ideal in our society.

Stemming from the fear of aging related to the heightened burden of care comes the policy idea that we should not feed dependency through institutionalization but encourage seniors to be more independent and to age in place in their communities. The ideal citizen is supposed to be independent and responsible for their care (Clarke et al. 2014; Newman and Clarke 2009). In the current socio-political context, we are seeing at once a narrowing of collective notions of citizenship rooted in universal inclusion as well as an increasing responsibility for individual citizens (Clarke et al. 2014). The concept of equality is reoriented to emphasize choice, responsiveness, and flexibility, and accessibility and fairness is to be earned through individual economic contribution by responsible agents (Newman and Clarke 2009). This form of activation is supposed to address the exclusion of seniors by including them in the mainstream and preventing them from making unreasonable demands on public systems, especially hospital and long-term care homes (Biggs 2001). The dominant discourse is that ageism is a form of social exclusion and therefore changes need to be made to bring seniors into existing social institutions, rather than understanding that ageism is at the root of these institutions and it is these institutions that need to change.

Underlying ageism is a socially constructed notion of the autonomous citizen as the best citizen, and of dependency as failure rather than as a natural part of life for every individual. If vulnerability and dependence are seen as abnormal, the solution is activating seniors to normalize them. There is a not-so-subtle undertone here that frames aging as a problem that must be overcome. The image of the "silver tsunami" drowning us all is based on a negative notion that old people are needy, dependent, and a drain on society. Older individuals are increasingly cast as burdensome to the "rest of us," and especially to the young, whose generation they are anticipated to bankrupt. The aging body is thus considered a risk not only to oneself but also to others (Kemshall 2002).

This "active aging" discourse can distract from the fact that many seniors have mental and physical health challenges or may be passive due to a lack of access to affordable transit and housing and to home care. The emphasis in this discourse on savings in health care can distract from needed investment in the social determinants of health. Furthermore, the seemingly positive identity risks blaming individuals for not activating themselves enough and thereby causing society larger health care payments. As Orsini (2007) notes, there is an underlying victim-blaming to this new emphasis. A senior citizens' advocate expressively links the discourse to an underlying ageism: "And then if you get sick, there is the assumption that you didn't do the right thing; that it is your fault. You are responsible for the fact that you have got this aging thing happening to you and you are supposed to be youthful" (D49). However, this critique of active aging was rare among participants, many of whom felt that it represented a progressive public response that empowers seniors and tackles ageism, as it focuses on their assets rather than their vulnerabilities.

VOLUNTEERISM

A major component of the active aging framework is volunteerism. Talking about volunteering, late Councillor Ron Moeser states that "it is not always that seniors are a burden, as they are a wonderful resource for the community as well" (A2). The knowledge and time that seniors can contribute to society through voluntary endeavours are considered "valuable assets" and are lauded as an opportunity for cities and non-profit organizations alike. A senior citizen advocate explains that "as the population is aging, we realize that there is a new cohort that has different kinds of resources and different kinds of contributions to make to society that was not being considered before … [that contribution is] knowledge" (C2). There is an undertone here that previous aging cohorts, the oldest of the old or the aforementioned "fourth age" (Green 2012) had little knowledge to contribute, perhaps because they were considered frailer and more dependent. This is contrasted with the new cohort of "third age" baby boomers who are considered active and thus worthy of investment.

While volunteering can offer additional opportunities to socialize and share stories and emotions that build empathy and solidarity, several participants noted that it can become problematic if policy expects seniors to prove their worth by volunteering. The issue here is choice and opportunity, as one academic expert cautions: "I try to be careful what I say about productive or successful aging. So to be a successful ager, you need to be volunteering and doing community work. I don't think that at all. But I do think that there are people who are older who, given the right opportunity, would like to share more with the community, give more … There is a huge challenge for people to stay connected meaningfully as the opportunities just aren't there now" (D2). The capacity to volunteer depends in large part on the societal systems that allow it (Rochester et al. 2010). There is recognition among several participants that it costs money to be active, and that volunteerism in particular is expensive: "They have got to afford to volunteer … You still have to get somewhere, you use the TTC [Toronto Transit Commission], you drive, or you cab and it costs" (E27). This is a problem because "those on fixed incomes are often those that are in need of the kind of emotional support that is required through volunteerism … So how do you get them engaged in non-profit activities?" (F6). Inadequate government recognition of the need to support volunteering can further divide the "third" and "fourth" ages and stigmatize the most marginalized seniors as burdensome because of their seeming lack of contribution (Martinson and Minkler 2006; Minkler and Holstein 2008).

Increasingly popular is the rhetoric of using seniors as an untapped resource to provide care in a context of fiscal restraint (Martinson and Minkler 2006; Janes 2008; Minkler and Holstein 2008). There is an assumption that volunteerism among seniors can act as a replacement for public programs. For instance, Gonzales and Morrow-Howell (2009) claim that "communities and civic society are likely to need the ongoing productive engagement of the older population" who will continue to produce social goods and services through paid and unpaid work because "the current economic situation only fuels the need for a more involved citizenry to meet economic and social needs of communities" (51–2). A provincial representative frames population aging as an opportunity for local government and non-profit organizations to tap social capital, supporting seniors to advertise and even deliver services in order to help fill gaps in dwindling public programs. An academic aging expert clearly makes this link: "I think that volunteerism among older people themselves is an enormous resource. On the downside, you don't want to over-rely on baby boomers and older adults to have to replace services that are probably better provided by governments, all levels of governments. I will just throw in that caveat" (F4). Provencher et al (2014) equate active aging to the UK's "Big Society" approach (Szreter and Ishkanian 2012), which offloads service responsibility onto geographic communities and citizens without actually understanding capacities. Seniors, who are themselves affected by cuts in social care and health care, are being asked to replace public service provision through their own free labour (Biggs 2001; Martinson and Minkler 2006; Janes,2008; Minkler and Martinson 2007). This cycle of cuts and offloading of public responsibility is illustrated in an article by Du and Xie (2015), who argue that older adult volunteerism can reduce the workload of community service staff and provide care for older and more vulnerable seniors. The *Toronto Seniors Strategy* aims to do just that, as it includes an action to coordinate independent seniors to reach out to dependent seniors and also has its senior citizens' advisory committee, the Toronto Seniors Forum, acting as a city spokesperson by giving presentations on local government services to seniors' organizations.

In this framing, the AFC model is not just a neutral framework meant to support seniors but a project that seeks to activate communities of seniors to help themselves and others. Rather than a public-sector strategy, I learned from an academic expert that the original AFC concept was more localized in nature, intended to get small groups of seniors engaging in volunteer work to improve their local environments through niche projects such as sidewalk repair, putting a bench outside, or alerting local businesses to elder abuse. This academic expert advised that the AFC model is more accurately described as an age-friendly neighbourhood approach rather than a municipal policy strategy.

This approach is an issue with respect to action on bigger improvements in quality of life for senior citizens such as accessible and affordable housing and transportation, which are key elements in the AFC framework. An academic expert admits that it has been difficult to make the leap from improving confidence among a small group of seniors to achieving larger impacts to seniors beyond this group. The highly localized, ad hoc, and informal nature of this approach raises questions as to whether the originators were actually expecting these kinds of outcomes. This is challenged by one academic participant: "Opportunities are always related to money and finances, and if you don't have any of that, how many volunteers are you going to get out [to] change transportation? Who is going to go out and build houses for old people? Nobody. Those things aren't going to happen" (E20). Speaking to volunteerism more broadly, Rochester et al. (2010) note that "the expectations that volunteers and volunteer-involving organizations will be ready and able to replace the shrinking state in many areas of activity are challenging at best and unrealistic at worst" (xv). An academic expert reflects frustration about this unrealistic expectation: "Ugh. You know what, volunteerism is really good for you. But there is only so much a volunteer can do, number one, and number two, it is not consistent. It is project here, piece there; not great" (E20).

This discussion highlights the serious gap in the way AFCs are conceptualized as small groups of seniors getting together to brainstorm and fix a local issue, and the expectation that this is going to substantially impact quality of life for senior citizens. Substantive change needs the state. In this regard, much more discussion and guidance is needed, perhaps on the part of the WHO, to identify the kinds of intergovernmental politics, administration, and revenue tools needed to actualize AFCs. Linking the AFC movement to the work being done to advocate for and develop a

United Nations Convention on the Rights of Older People is one way to orient the AFC agenda on the role of the state.

The dominant active aging discourse tends to valorize a more conservative "helping" vision of volunteerism that tends to ignore more activist political organizations (Martinson and Minkler 2006). Seniors may also have knowledge of a past when the state offered more collective redistribution and can support building on this legacy of state support through activism and policy advocacy, acting as a complement rather than a replacement for public programs. One agency representative talked to me about a recent visit to their local member of provincial parliament (MPP) to advocate for a Bill of Rights for Older Adults in Ontario. This person explained the importance of this legislation for the realization of AFCs:

> We see [a] Bill of Rights for people who are in care homes and residences but nothing that uniquely addresses all of the needs and interests of older adults living in the community … it is unfortunate that there is nothing unique in terms of laws or policies governing the rights of older Ontarians. So that if there is a problem, they can actually say, "OK, you have violated my rights, or not considered who I am as an aging person with my various vulnerabilities." They have to fall or go back to laws that govern the rest of society and those are not really tailored uniquely to the experience of the older adult. (D25)

This person was surprised that their MPP was unaware of the existence of this legislation despite the province's alleged support for aging in place and AFCs.

Some participants talk about the need for local government to create forums with senior citizen members. An academic expert notes that this is particularly important for cities, which are not always very strong policy thinkers: "Probably a lot of the equity-seeking groups have been better on research and articulation on policy, especially women's groups. The seniors' groups less so, but I think that this is the coming thing. Those that have retired from policy positions and want to bring a policy lens to seniors' issues. That may be visible very soon" (E22). Yet, as was identified in chapter 1, Toronto has a history of organized and activist senior citizens working with a local councillor advocate. This gave seniors policy leverage, and such a formalized relationship has not been re-established with the *Toronto Seniors Strategy.* Instead, the city's current seniors' advisory group, the Toronto Seniors Forum, is struggling to have a distinct policy voice.

My findings suggest that the Toronto Seniors Forum is being used by the city through a co-production framework (Martinson and Minkler 2006; Newman and Clarke 2009) as a way to advertise the *Toronto Seniors Strategy* via community presentations. I learned from some members that there is no formal political process or meaningful two-way engagement for this work that includes obtaining feedback from seniors to local government to enhance the recognition of diverse needs. Further illustrating the co-production agenda, one member explains a recent project where they obtained federal funding to train a diverse seniors group in a lower-income Toronto neighbourhood to volunteer, to learn about local government programs, and to govern themselves as an organization. Another member critiques this work, noting that it is not systematic or clearly structured. I also found that the forum's political activism is challenged during their monthly meetings, as precious time is devoted to presentations from city councillors. This was protested by a member who advised that "we cannot cope with this and do our other business" (C20). The concern was that information provided by the councillors is not being used strategically by the forum to take to communities to encourage advocacy. The forum also struggles to engage the bureaucratic elements of the city's administrative structure substantively. As one member explains, "occasionally we meet with the head of a department and get some information, but we figured that we have to do that in a more consolidated fashion" (C6). Another member expresses their frustration: "There is not a lot of talk about what we should know, how we should be up to date, and how we should be the ones asking them, 'How come you do this?'"(C2).

The forum is asked to outreach to vulnerable seniors, recruit seniors, advertise city policy and services, and inform city policy to ensure that city services meet the needs of older adults, by sitting on committees that can meet up to four times a month. This includes a lot of travel all over the city, which is physically draining. This begs the question whether we are taking active aging too far and expecting voluntary groups of seniors to replace government both through policy work and service co-production (Minkler and Martinson 2007; Winterton 2016). It is no wonder that forum members require that potential applicants have basic internet skills and advise that they not have full-time jobs. Several senior organizations I spoke to also believed that members could not be employed full-time and do good advocacy work: "We have had several people who have come and want to be a part of our group but they are employed, so their ability to come to meetings and to work with other people is very limited" (D30B). This also speaks to care work: "You can't be babysitting your grandchildren all day and then do this. Or working in any real way. Then you can only do bits and pieces … it is really hard to have an outside life and do much here" (D49). This raises the question as to whose voices are being listened to, as more seniors are having to continue working to make ends meet (Moody 2008). This is a particular dilemma with the Toronto Seniors Forum because they are supposed to represent more vulnerable seniors, who very well may still be working and/or providing child-care, and do not always have easy access to a computer. The active aging approach thus raises serious concerns when it fails to conceptualize different abilities to "activate" oneself, given the vulnerabilities that do come with age intersected with other forms of socialized inequity (Abrahamson, 2015).

AGE-FRIENDLY FOR ALL

A core theme that challenges a recognition of senior citizen diversity through AFCs is the debate as to whether cities should be supporting "age-friendly" or "senior-friendly" environments. A core premise of the WHO's AFC approach is the emphasis on creating local environments that are inclusive to people of all ages and abilities. In this way, I found that the "age-friendly for all" discourse reflects concerns about community cohesion (Newman and Clarke 2009) between age cohorts. "Age-friendly" is preferred politically because focusing on seniors specifically is seen as unfair to other population groups: "Age-friendly as good for everyone is important, because not everyone buys into the message of special treatment for older adults" (D1B). A "senior-friendly" space is understood as exclusionary, while an "age-friendly" one is good for all because it is inclusive, as a city staff member explains: "I will stick to the term 'age-friendliness' because it is more inclusive than a 'senior-friendly' city" (B11). One participant framed "age-friendly" as a savvy branding strategy in a context of ageism: "Sometimes it is very difficult to sell the idea of doing things for older people. You put a picture of a young person on a newspaper and suddenly there is money going to that, but putting a picture of an older adult on a paper doesn't tend to get the same type of emotional play and it is less successful. So, part of my argument is what is good for old people is good for everybody" (D1B). Other participants see special treatment for seniors as ageist because it segregates and singles them out based on their vulnerability. Hence some argue that "age-friendly for all" is a good strategy because it treats seniors the same as "everybody else," or as those that are understood as young and active.

Biggs and Carr (2015) worry that the policy rhetoric of similarity "eclipses the specific needs of a particular age group and reinvents a 'universal urbanite,'" thus allowing local policymakers to claim that any investment they make is age-friendly (105). In particular, the authors explain that the "age-friendly for all" concept is the reason physical accessibility improvements are a dominant focus for AFCs (Biggs and Carr 2015). This is done through the field of universal design: "There is a whole school of universal design that says that a city, its schools, its parks, and benches shouldn't be designed for seniors but should be designed for everybody. What is good for seniors is also good for all. The whole thing is that the age-friendly city is not dedicated or predicated on easier living for seniors, it is age-friendly for everybody" (D55). Interview participants justify a focus on seniors as being age-friendly for all because of the emphasis on physical accessibility for multiple population groups. Councillor Matlow explains: "If you create an environment that is accessible and respectful for seniors, it is good for moms and dads pushing strollers, a middle-aged person who is in a wheelchair, it is good for anybody who wants an accessible city" (A1). Focusing on one aspect of the aging experience, physical accessibility, is justified because it can provide a good base from which to make people-based improvements that are necessary for the population at large. While making accessibility improvements is certainly important, Biggs and Carr (2015) are concerned that the need for differentiated social services and the affordability of services and supports for seniors risks going under the radar in the "age-friendly for all" discourse.

Alternatively, several participants argued that everyone buys into the concept of a senior-friendly city because we all experience aging and will need specialized services someday. Rather than framing seniors as a special-interest group, this perspective understands aging as the "great equalizer": "And if I want to put on my rose-coloured glasses, I can say something like an aging population is that catalyst for forcing that kind of discussion … an aging population is in your face all of the time. You can't ignore it. It is not just 'the bloody immigrant is causing issues once again.' No, it is all of us. So that is how I think this might happen" (D29). A policy expert advises that there is a political strategy underlying this approach: "The issue is thinking about how to make this an opportunity and I think this is where a number of politicians have gathered that it is also a 'no lose' issue, talking about making this world a better place for the older adult population … because when you talk about refugee health or the needs of diverse people, you have those who don't think that this is a beneficial way to be spending tax dollars or leaders' time, for example. With seniors, the fact is that we will all get there someday; there is a huge selfish motivation" (E19). However, only the luckiest of us will get to an old age and while we will all need services, some of us might need more intensive "different" services than others based on biological luck intersected with societal systems of inequity (Abrahamson 2015). In this way, aging is not necessarily a great equalizer, as there is much diversity within this population group.

TARGETING

As the previous chapters have highlighted, local policy actors cannot ignore senior citizen diversity because the needs are so acute, so in a context of limited public resources they are focused on recognizing those that are most "costly." I found that a dominant response is to subdivide the population according to the risk or potential risk the individual presents to themselves and society in the form of larger health care costs. This reflects a broader trend in social policy (Newman and Clarke 2009).

Three groups of seniors were recognized by participants. The first group of seniors are considered the "ideal" low-risk group of citizens that "are just fine and … don't need any assistance" (D31B). These are the active individuals deemed healthy, wealthy, independent, and responsible for their own care and the care of spouses, neighbours, and grandchildren. A city employee explains: "If you are healthy and independently wealthy, you are not going to worry about what Public Health are doing, or about whether EMS [Emergency Medical Services, now Toronto Paramedic Services] is going to charge you for an ambulance, or to get a ride to a doctor's appointment, or if you are going to need someone to come in to help you clean your apartment through our Homemakers and Nurses program – and guess what, you have to be means-tested" (B19). My interviews also reflect concern about a second group of senior citizens who are "at risk" of becoming socially isolated, whom one city participant calls the "in-between group" (B22). These are the seniors who are dealing with the challenges of aging combined with low income, and struggle to afford transit, housing, food, home-care supports, recreation activities, and health care that allow them to age in place. This staff member advises that these seniors "will tell you clearly, 'I want some assistance ... to help me maintain my wellness. To make it more possible for me to join Parks and Rec programming, for example, because it is getting expensive.' Being able to have one class a year under their policy is nice, but not enough to maintain your wellness ... It all costs money, but in the end, if we don't spend it somehow wisely, it is just going to cost us so much more" (D31B). Finally, the vulnerable "risky" group of senior citizens is very poor, unhealthy, may be experiencing homelessness, has no access to informal care and, rather than being labelled the most in need, are labelled the greatest potential burden to society. A city staff member advises that "the city is trying to figure out how to serve the most vulnerable, or really the most high-needs residents, clients, tenants. Everyone is trying to figure out how to serve them better because they fundamentally, and it is the wrong way to go about it, but because they cost so much money" (B2). Another city employee who works with this group admits that "while I wish that we could be a society that could only concentrate on what we might be calling 'good aging,' I don't think that we have a hope in hell of doing that and it is only going to get worse" (B16A).

There is concern in the AFC literature as to who should be targeted through the program. Golant (2014) worries that in a context of budget constraint, AFCs will end up being more about targeting the most vulnerable seniors. As such, the AFC strategy risks ignoring those investments that focus on the quality of life of seniors who are healthy, but may need a bit of assistance to prevent them from falling into the "risky" category because they do not meet means-tested requirements for dwindling public programs but cannot afford private provision (Golant 2014). The bigger question is where this risk comes from. Orsini and Smith (2007) argue that such a targeting approach allows the state to claim that they are doing something about social ills without addressing root socio-economic contributors. Several participants that work with the most vulnerable seniors criticize this strategy (Antonnen et al. 2012a) because we are not dealing with the underlying problems: "I can be pretty dismal about it because as our city continues to become divided by rich and poor and the elimination of the middle class, the determinants of health really determine whether or not you are going to be healthy and able to age healthfully" (B16A). Another city representative advises that increasingly, even the middle class is unable to use support services, meaning that the "in-between group" is growing:

> It is tough enough to get into retirement homes for long-term care. When you find that you have a need, you realize that you should have gone two or ten years ago because now there is a waiting list and who knows how long it will take to get in in large cities such as Toronto. The costs are enormous … it is a very small percentage of the population that has that kind of money. For-profit places are gearing to this population … Good for you if you can do it, but what about the rest of us? You have the quote unquote "middle class" that is getting squeezed more and more and is getting smaller. There are going to be lots of us, many of us who can't afford these types of things. Where do we go and who is going to look after us? (B27)

We see here the need to focus on vulnerability in old age as a problem that is socially produced through inadequate infrastructures. Rather than understanding systems change as targeting individual seniors according to their risk to society, a city representative explains that "we need a broader systems-based response for seniors. I think that the opportunity is there because frankly, the system is not responsive and is broken and I think that everyone will acknowledge that" (B17). The AFC movement is not inherently promoting this systems-based response in Toronto, and this is rooted in the way in which population aging is recognized as an individual rather than a societal problem (Joy 2018).

Conclusion

My findings problematize the claim that AFCs fundamentally promote a positive aging identity and challenge societal ageism. Population aging is recognized as increasing diversity and bringing experiences into local environments that necessitate new and different service and infrastructure investments. However, this diversity is often recognized as problematic to the extent that it is seen to increase costs that will bombard what is left of our social welfare systems. AFCs are situated as a solution to the "aging problem" because they activate seniors and thereby prevent their dependency on costly public programs. In addition, these active seniors can fill gaps in dwindling public programs through volunteerism. Seniors are harnessed to do their part to contribute to society in a context of austerity that is seen as being driven not by political and economic conditions but by their own aging. This activation is formulated as both empowering and anti-ageist. However, seniors have different abilities to activate themselves due to both biological and socially structured factors. The role of local policy actors is often to target service delivery to particularly vulnerable or "costly" seniors to save money in the health care system.

In the dominant discourse, aging is recognized as an individual and societal problem because vulnerability, needs, and dependency are considered negative human conditions, whereas independence is considered normal and good. There is an underlying assumption here that the worthiest citizen is young and contributes economically as producer and consumer, is responsible and does not burden others through their dependency (Newman and Clarke 2009). In this discourse, public programs that recognize the vulnerabilities that come with age are believed to segregate seniors and encourage their dependency while limiting their voice and empowerment. The institutions associated with the welfare state, such as hospitals and long-term care homes, can be understood as the remnants of an ageist past where seniors were considered dependent and are thus framed as paternalistic and disempowering. While powerlessness and voicelessness were a problem with welfare state institutions (Clarke 2004), the problem was not with vulnerability inherently but rather with its depiction as a negative state. The issue was, and still is, that dependency and vulnerability is seen as shameful – during the welfare state it merited segregation and today it is made invisible, or made private rather than public (Clarke 2004).

Dependency and vulnerability on the basis of age is both biological and socially constructed (Abrahamson 2015) and in both respects is deserving of a collective response to ensure that it does not reduce quality of life. These experiences should not be shamed but, instead, more fully understood, so that seniors can age with dignity no matter the situation that they are faced with. Discrimination on the basis of age is failing to understand these experiences in an embodied sense and assuming that people are fundamentally the same in the way that they live their lives and the way that they access services and amenities. Here we see the "age-friendly for all" approach that seeks not to change seniors but to hide their difference (Cruickshank 2008; Biggs and Carr 2015; Calasanti 2008). We need to understand differential access in an environment that is structured to meet the needs of those that are young and ignores the impact of policy decisions on senior citizens. There is a risk with this rhetoric about senior citizens that we do not put money into public organizations (Newman and Clarke 2009) such as substantive social and physical infrastructure programs because we are trying to activate people to do it themselves. The dominant "prevention" discourse risks ignoring the right to essential services and amenities such as affordable and accessible housing, transportation, social and health services, recreation, and nutrition throughout the life-course, and an attendant focus on economic development and income security. It is based on a fundamentally narrow concept of citizenship. Aligning the AFC movement with the movement to develop a United Nations Convention on the Rights of Older People offers an opportunity to broaden this concept of citizenship and the rights that accompany it.

One can have needs and be vulnerable and still have a voice; they are not mutually exclusive. Vulnerability can lead to empowerment, to citizenship claims to recognize embodied needs and redistribute differently on this basis (Isin et al. 2008; Clarke et al. 2014). Rather than being a burden, public recognition of the need for care can create well-paid and stable jobs in fields that maintain independence and dignity for senior citizens and can provide care options to their loved ones. Biggs (2008) argues that progressive projects recognize age as difference in a context increasingly claiming that there is none. This requires understanding difference through new forms of research, democratic and deliberative policymaking, and investments in services and infrastructures. The following chapter examines the extent to which the AFC program empowers local governments and non-profit organizations to do this via the rights of the city in the Toronto case.

CHAPTER 4

Rights of the City: Empowering Local Policy Actors through AFCs in Toronto

Introduction

In this chapter, I explore the final claim that AFCs empower local policy actors to support senior citizens to age in place. AFCs can be understood as part of a broader movement, known as "new localism," which emphasizes the local as the most natural site to address major policy issues in a context of global urbanization where the national scale is being decentered (Brenner 2009; Clarke 2004). Local governance is assumed to be crucial for democratic, economic, and social renewal because local government, private sector, and non-profit partners operate in close proximity in local communities to engage in problem-solving that includes citizens (Katz and Bradley 2013; Barber 2013). As such, we are witnessing a transfer of public responsibility to local policy actors and an increase in place-based policymaking to address complex policy challenges (Horak 2013; Bradford 2007). I situate AFCs as an example of policy that valorizes the local as a "new" space to address the needs and demands for services and amenities associated with population aging. As the local addresses population aging, policy actors from local government and the non-profit sector are increasingly called to support senior citizens. It is thus crucial to understand whether these actors have the capacity, in the form of legal authority, financial tools, and bureaucratic processes, to undertake this role.

While critical studies acknowledge that AFCs are not living up to their hype as major projects, few explore how this relates to the capacities of the actors expected to undertake this work in actual "landscapes of antagonism" where they are administratively restricted (Newman 2014). In a more conceptual article, Biggs and Carr (2015) allude to institutional problems with the program, arguing that AFCs rarely incorporate formal "legislative and legal commitments and a set of universal norms" (101). While these scholars, among others, call for AFCs based on a right to the city for senior citizens (Biggs and Carr 2015; Buffel et al. 2012; Buffel and Phillipson 2016), the rights of the city itself are rarely examined. This chapter fills this gap by offering further insight into the challenges confronting Toronto's age-friendly city movement.

Isin (2008) advises that achieving a right to the city requires that local governments gain resources, legislative tools, and the administrative freedom to recognize difference and engage in redistribution. Some of these new rights are within the political jurisdiction of local government while others require engagement by central governments. Given my "seeing like a city" (Magnussen 2011) perspective, I argue that it is also crucial to understand the rights of the non-profit sector as they provide crucial services and policy advocacy in urban spaces. Clavel (2010) argues that a "progressive city" requires an independent coalition of non-profit social movement organizations working in partnership with, and able to push, a capable local government.

This chapter is organized into three sections: the rights of local government, the rights of non-profit organizations, and the relationships between local government and non-profit organizations. I begin each section with a more discursive analysis of how participants understand the role of local government, non-profit organizations, and the relations between them, in supporting seniors. Clarke et al. (2014) explain that state decentering through localism "may indeed be mobilized for very different political purposes" (148–9), making it crucial to understand the values, interests, and motivations behind framing specific scales as the most suitable settings for particular social, political, and economic activities. I am particularly interested in how these understandings might illustrate a more expansive role for these actors in supporting seniors, or one that is more residual, responsibilizing actors without offering additional policy support. I then contrast these discursive findings with a more material examination of how interview participants understand the institutional mechanisms at their disposal to enable a right to the city. I examine the extent to which AFC practice in Toronto illustrates meaningful institutional change that includes new norms and formalized sanctions and incentives (Lowndes 2002; Lowndes 2009) to support age-friendly work. This encompasses the institutional frameworks that operate between departments and agencies within local government as well as between "levels" of government, allowing for an understanding of the overlapping governmental relations.

The Rights of Local Government

THE INCREASED RELEVANCE OF LOCAL GOVERNMENT

There is an understanding among participants that local governments are "on the frontlines" (E16) with respect to population aging and ensuring that seniors age in place: "With the number of services required, the role of municipalities being called upon to play is expanding, and it makes sense because cities are becoming so much more relevant to our growth and economy and education and children and all of these things … those innovative pieces need to come together, and this can be fantastic" (D53). A senior citizens' advocate explains that local governments "are the primary providers of services, particularly the services that are there that keep people active. Educational services, leisure, social interaction, health prevention or promotion" (D30A). We see again this emphasis on "systems change" in which local policy actors are understood to deliver services that ensure active citizenship to prevent future demand for remedial services managed and coordinated at other scales of governance.

Many participants reflect "new localist" thinking that central governments will no longer have the capacity to invest in the welfare state, thus local policy actors will have to figure this out and become resilient: "Bottom line is that the types of services that we provide here in Canada, and having an opportunity to be able to take advantage of services like we do in this country, really taps resources and so we need to really look at strategies to optimize the use of those resources. You can only really do that when there is a larger opportunity to really talk and work together" (D52). Several participants speak to the unique capacity of local governments to pinpoint gaps in access to services and identify the partners needed to help fill them. There is a predisposition to blame the aging population for resource constraints, whereas the last three decades of narrow projects of public-sector restructuring that have prioritized funding cuts in key areas of the AFC checklist are rarely mentioned by participants (See Shields and Evans 1998; McKeen and Porter 2003; Rice and Prince 2000; McBride and Whiteside 2011; Banting and Myles 2013).

My interviews indicate that local government is particularly valourized because its geographic proximity to citizens is believed to provide personalized policy that meets diverse needs (Clarke et al. 2014; Newman and Clarke 2009). According to a city representative, local governments "have local intelligence and knowledge of what is happening on the ground that other levels of government might not necessarily have. We take a micro-level approach at addressing issues" (B3). Local government is considered to be closer to "ordinary citizens" (Newman and Clarke 2009), as is highlighted by a non-profit participant: "I think that they have a vital role. A vital role because they are the hands-on. They are the ones who are right there. These are the constituents that they are serving" (D20). This framing is interesting because these are also the constituents of other levels of government. Local governments are understood as more trustworthy because people have more direct access to city hall, calling local politicians and staff directly when they see a problem. Federal and provincial governments are understood as more artificial, while municipal government is cast as operating in the "the organic location of 'real' or 'popular' politics" (Clarke et al. 2014, 139): "The local government is a very responsive and immediate order of government. Federal and provincial governments tend to be much more removed" (D53). Here, a city staff member explains that "more community infrastructure work gets done at the local government level that affects citizens, whereas the type of policy work done at the provincial and federal levels are so vague and broad, paralyzed by ideological positions [so] that the work that is most tangible for seniors is left to the delivery agents, like local government and NGOs" (B23).

A city representative identifies rescaling policy responsibility as "an opportunity for cities because we are often, from a lack of leadership at the provincial and federal levels and from so much downloading, taking a leadership role on these issues" (B2). As in the new localism literature (Katz and Bradley 2013; Barber 2013), this is the time for cities to shine, to be active rather than passive players who can show other levels of government their inherently pragmatic, innovative, and creative problem-solving nature. The potential for innovative service and research partnerships among local government departments, non-profit organizations, and universities to provide personalized services to seniors in a large urban center is lauded as a major opportunity. Several city staff members advise that there are many potential partners who are willing to run programs in city facilities, creating opportunities for innovation. Representatives from other levels of government speak about small-scale innovative community-based projects such as exercise, cooking, and gardening classes, as well as intergenerational and transportation projects. Some participants allude to the city as a test site for innovative pilot projects in the realm of service provision for seniors, though this is a trend that can exacerbate service fragmentation.

Despite these expectations placed on local governments, I find considerable skepticism about the extent to which governments are taking the AFC movement seriously: "We are led to believe that this is the strategic plan for the province or the city but in reality, it is an arms-length report and yes, the province or the city commissioned that report and it came out with many recommendations but we never have a sense of it. There is too much false hope built into it. Is there money attached? Is there an implementation plan?" (D3). One year into the implementation of the *Toronto Senior Strategy*, several participants evoked the imagery of another government report that "will just sit. It will just collect dust like too many reports before it" (D8). For many operating outside the city, the *Toronto Seniors Strategy* is criticized for being a symbolic gesture that simply reframes what the city already does, distracting from a more fulsome commitment to investment in existing and new programming. An academic policy expert explains: "They are running around doing a lot of hot air about it … I look around and say, 'What has happened?' I don't see anything. Is there something? Did I miss something? I think that AFCs is a wonderful catch-all for doing nothing. It is for doing nothing and just doing what you were doing anyway, but you can reframe it and say, 'Look what we are doing, we have park benches with handles on them!' Whatever" (E20).

My findings indicate a lack of trust in government generally, with several participants reflecting anti-political and anti-statist sentiments to explain gaps in AFC initiatives. As was highlighted in chapter 1, since amalgamation, Toronto has made several attempts to instigate a seniors' strategy; this is attributed by some to politicians who wanted to rebrand the issue as their own rather than arising from real recognition of the needs of seniors. There is also cynicism around populist forms of political capital as it relates to pandering to seniors because "older adults are the most active voting bloc … So if you want a quick win, then you want to get older people onside. They are active, they have time, and they will vote. So that's what a number of politicians have said. I'm asking, 'Why do you care so much all of a sudden?' and they are saying 'Seniors vote!' That is the number one priority" (E19). There is also the complaint that the public sector is not forward-thinking and tends to be reactive and short-termist because of election cycles. This often takes the form of meetings and committees of experts that sit around and talk but rarely take policy action. Some participants note that even when action is decided upon by politicians it is rarely substantive, because public bureaucracies are by design not set up to advocate for radical change. AFCs are thought to require "a whole different kind of individual rather than the traditional bureaucrat. The time for bureaucrats is long over. You have to care and be looking for meaning in your work" (D55). However, the previous chapters have illustrated that city staff appear to be the ones driving the concern and focus on vulnerable seniors and, in many cases, are acting to provide supports in a context of intense need and fiscal constraints. Rather than dismissing local actors as uncaring and not innovative, it is thus crucial that we better understand the policy challenges faced by them.

The *Toronto Seniors Strategy* is considered a "living document" (City of Toronto 2013) that is supposed to become more comprehensive over the years. It does present a first effort to engage in age-friendly planning across local government bureaucracy, unlike previous aging strategies. However, the question is whether the city is creating the supportive institutional framework to ensure that the *Toronto Seniors Strategy* remains a living document.

STRUGGLES TO EMBED THE INTENT

My interviews indicate that there is movement to recognize the distinct needs of seniors through the *Toronto Seniors Strategy*, though with varying degrees of formalization that does not equate to Biggs and Carr's (2015) concept of "universal norms." A staff member involved in coordinating the *Toronto Seniors Strategy* characterizes their role as an effort to "embed the intent" (B6) for staff to consider seniors in programming decisions. Some local government organizations have identified seniors as a priority group and have designed special seniors' programming and have advisory groups to understand and plan for new needs. Furthermore, city organizations that engage in day to day work with seniors felt more appreciated and understood through the *Toronto Seniors Strategy* process. They saw their role as advocating for the vulnerable and providing insight to other city organizations. However, I also found some organizations resistant to admitting that they serve seniors. One staff member expressed frustration that resistant city organizations "are not going to have a nurse all of the time and you won't necessarily have a nurse at all; you actually have to develop the capacity of your own staff to deal with this, because it is going to be everybody's business and it is the tsunami that is coming in" (B16A). The staff member goes on to note that "it isn't going to be any one service in a city that is charged with dealing with this, but it is going to be a coordinated effort with a lot of work at trying to make some reforms where there are systemic gaps" (B16A). There is a debate within the local bureaucracy as to whether AFCs are about better service provision to individuals on an as-needed basis or a holistic and coordinated response to address both niche and more general needs through a model of universal inclusion (Antonnen et al. 2012a). This debate makes it difficult to establish new bureaucratic norms (Lowndes 2009; Biggs and Carr 2015) to consider seniors in all policy planning.

My interviews with city staff indicate that certain organizations see identity-based "embodied" service and infrastructure planning as discriminatory because their work should benefit all population groups, so they claim to plan in the "public interest" instead. For instance, one employee explained to me that the city is unable to consider specific identity groups in decisions regarding its zoning of land use, as this is discriminatory. Here, positive discrimination based on age is seen as taking away from other population groups. As such, policy should disembody and strip away identity to focus on "the public," or make things "age-friendly for all," or else policymaking becomes too complex. Central to this is the liberal public-sector philosophy of procedural universalism (Antonnen et al. 2012b) in which focusing on the difference of a particular group is considered unfair. On this topic, Newman and Clarke (2009) note that "liberal values ... offer a relatively narrow politics of the public sphere – one that has trouble acknowledging new claims for voice and justice" (112). This approach sees existing urban spaces and policies as neutral, and fails to understand how they have been built by and thus tend to benefit working-age residents (Biggs and Carr 2015), and specifically able-bodied, middle- to upper-class, white, cisgender men, and are thus discriminatory for those who do not share these characteristics (Antonnen et al. 2012b; Clarke and Newman 2012). This discussion also speaks to the need to understand hard infrastructure as social and political in nature because it is accessed by people of varying intersecting identities. One city employee explains that "policies focusing on space affect peoples' lives, and seniors are people ... sometimes you really have to lay this out for certain divisions" (B6). At the same time, engaging in such equity-oriented planning is difficult in a narrow public-sector restructuring context where planning has been deregulated by the province, development application review timelines have been sped up, and staff positions have been eliminated (Frisken 2007). This is exacerbated by service offloading by the province, as local government is increasingly reliant on the property-tax dollars that private development will bring to pay for new responsibilities in areas such as transit and social housing.

In this context, city staff working on the *Toronto Seniors Strategy* admit that their role to "embed the intent" to focus on seniors is a work in progress. Councillor Kristyn Wong Tam admits that "with all of the best intentions when that [*Toronto Seniors Strategy*] subcommittee began to meet, there was no real lens over seniors that are under-housed or homeless" (A3), which is odd given the stated focus of the strategy on the city's most vulnerable seniors. And even with a lens, Councillor Wong Tam admits that monitoring and enforcement seem to pose a significant problem in planning for many vulnerable groups in the city: "It doesn't just go with trying to be an age-friendly city. It is also the same with access and equity for racial minorities, the same thing about gender. Are city services delivered to women and girls in an accessible way and are all institutional barriers removed? I would have to say that we have some very lofty motherhood statements and we have some policies that say, 'This is what we should do,' but as far as I can tell, the benchmarks are always very poor" (A3). The *Toronto Seniors Strategy* does not incorporate an official age-based lens that applies to all city programming, complete with incentives and resource support to engage in research and policy work and sanctions for non-compliance (Lowndes 2009). Councillor Wong Tam's statement clarifies that such a lens should be intersectional to capture the diversity of the aging experience.

CITIES HAVE A THIN POLICY LEVEL

Another challenge to cross-city alignment through the *Toronto Seniors Strategy* relates to the unique service-providing role of local government, as is explained by this academic policy expert: "It is a big disadvantage of municipalities that there is a thin policy level and it challenges silos. You have got all these truck-drivers and nurses and so the policy level can be very thin. And it is this policy level that they need to coordinate, but often a thin level compared to the hideously thick level of the federal government. There is a nice concreteness to municipal politics but it does make the policy planning more difficult" (E22). Different local government organizations do related work but have different mandates, operating languages, budgets, and front-line bureaucrats to manage. Even where divisions have identified seniors as a priority group, management struggle to get front-line staff to work with seniors as well as to design programming for them. This coordination is made even more complex in a context of amalgamation and social and physical infrastructure rescaling, where size and responsibility have dramatically increased. Management staff admit that while a *Toronto Seniors Strategy* action may appear relatively minor, its implementation is a considerable task that involves changing the institutional norms and incentives of thousands of people across the city's massive bureaucratic and geographic landscape. This becomes all the more challenging when training is unfunded and where seniors are considered less "valuable" service clients as compared to youth and newcomers. Because of these challenges, many *Toronto Seniors Strategy* actions are focused on targeting staff that work with the most vulnerable seniors, which once again realigns the preventative intent of AFCs to focus on the most potentially "costly" seniors.

UNFUNDED POLICY

A major challenge to ensuring that the *Toronto Seniors Strategy* continues to evolve is an absence of the administrative and financial tools necessary to implement and enforce it. First and foremost, no specific budget was committed for *Toronto Seniors Strategy* implementation. A city representative explains that the strategy "is definitely just a start. This strategy was adopted with no resources. So that means that it cannot be comprehensive" (B6). This person notes that "I think that what we could accomplish versus what we will be able to accomplish will be quite different. And that's just system integration within the city that we are talking about, let alone broader contextual issues that we could be promoting" (B6).

This lack of resource commitment is a major reason why some local government organizations were reluctant to come up with recommendations that would see their work and service demand increase. A city representative admits that making recommendations was difficult because the process was not funded. Hence, the *Toronto Seniors Strategy* reiterates what the city is doing already and many staff members in different divisions admit that they have not been able to move on medium- and long-term actions that require additional funding. Even training for frontline staff to recognize the unique needs of seniors is not being prioritized, let alone money for new redistributive projects. Staff are continuously asked to do more with less, and are therefore reluctant to commit to new actions through the *Toronto Seniors Strategy* even if they have, in theory, "embedded the intent" to recognize seniors.

In addition to the lack of a formal budget, I learned that the *Toronto Seniors Strategy* has very limited human-resource support. A city representative notes that three employees worked on the strategy and drove the process, but not full-time and with other projects on the go. At the time of my interviews, there was only one staff member charged with coordinating the implementation of the *Toronto Seniors Strategy*. That person was in "operational management" and this was only one project among many in their portfolio, because there was no new funding to hire a seniors-specific policy expert. A city representative admits that having dedicated staff would maintain the profile of the *Toronto Seniors Strategy* but, given new priorities, staff keep getting pulled into other things. While staff coordinating the *Toronto Seniors Strategy* can invite other local government organizations to sit at the policymaking and implementation table, if they fail to show up there is nothing they can do. This is a particular problem in Toronto, with so many special-purpose bodies that have different accountability structures in which they report to a board and the board must support the recommendations in order for them to be actioned (Mette Kjaer 2009). While staff are required to report back to council on the *Toronto Seniors Strategy*, the enforcement mechanisms or formal sanctions (Lowndes 2009) built into the strategy are minimal and so a large responsibility lies on the backs of overworked staff. While Toronto may be unique in having a social-planning infrastructure, it is inadequately resourced and not given legislative authority to make substantive policy change. City employees complain that they are constantly asked to maintain and improve their programming at the same time as they are required by council to cut their budgets and freeze hiring. Staff are continually asked to do more with less, and many complain that they are unable to meet existing needs, let alone develop new redistributive programming for senior citizens.

LIMITED POLITICAL LEADERSHIP

At the time of my interviews, the politicians who led the development of the *Toronto Seniors Strategy* did not appear to be pushing to obtain the financial and bureaucratic resources needed to implement the strategy. This has led many non-city participants to complain about political expediency surrounding the strategy. One city councillor, Josh Matlow, brought forth the motion to develop the *Toronto Seniors Strategy*, suggesting that no politician would say no to seniors, illustrating that he believed that he did have the political coalition in place to move forward. However, this motion was also passed because the strategy was cost neutral, with future investment budgeted incrementally, year by year, taken out of different funding pots. This allowed some councillors to say "Yes" to seniors symbolically, while saying "No" substantively. Councillor Kristyn Wong-Tam complains that this is a common occurrence on Toronto council: "That is something that continues to evade city council. There is this perception that 'If we adopt the report, we have done something.' Which I find completely asinine, because that report is the beginning of a lot more work. This is clearly *not* the end of the work. It is just the beginning and a strategic plan to do the work, but I don't believe that this is every councillor's perception" (A3).

This approach was considered pragmatic by Councillor Matlow, so that the *Toronto Seniors Strategy* could get passed during the Rob Ford era of austerity: "I think this is why this process was a bit more successful. I think strategically, with the state of council that we have now, the goal was just to get the strategy through, especially if it costs nothing to implement, at least in its first year. This is why council had no problems in passing it. I think it passed unanimously by those who were present" (E19). Councillor Matlow's approach is critiqued by several other participants. A senior citizens' advocate involved in *Toronto Seniors Strategy* development complained that "they watered the whole thing down to get a unanimous vote" (D49). In addition to the lack of budget, the vague, long-term timeline for implementation is criticized: "For the long-term goals, we wanted a number on this, so whether it could be done in ten years. And they just have 2015 and beyond. So, in other words 'someday,' as in 'never-never land.' So the long-term actions were watered down to happen god only knows when … So already, just in the planning, it is not as concrete as it should be" (D49). Furthermore, this political strategy does not seem to have been shared with the city staff members leading the *Toronto Seniors Strategy* and expected to implement it. One employee explains their work in preparation for deliberation on the report in council thus: "Do you know how much work I did behind the scenes to cost out every recommendation? I had a spreadsheet that associated a cost to every recommendation in case I got a question, and nobody asked. Which is crazy, because if you have a new program, it will cost money; it can't be resource neutral. But nobody asked it! For the youth strategy, that was the first thing they asked" (B2).

Challenges in realizing a substantive *Toronto Seniors Strategy* relate to Toronto's divided politics, which is a particular legacy of amalgamation because of which suburban councillors, who tend to be more right-wing and do not support redistributing social services and recognizing identity-based groups, drown out the voices of progressives (Joy and Vogel 2015; Frisken 2007). Councillor Matlow's strategy for the *Toronto Seniors Strategy* is also representative of a critique that Toronto's left-leaning city councillors favour a facilitative and pragmatic rather than conflictual leadership style (Lexler 2015). While the rhetoric is there to enhance access and equity in city service provision, these councillors do not appear to have a holistic policy vision, leadership, or an action agenda linked to the everyday struggles of city inhabitants, including seniors (Rebick 2014). It may be the case that this is more difficult in Toronto because the Ontario government does not allow municipal governments to operate with political parties, which might otherwise provide a more natural coalition and policy coherence (Lightbody 1999). Furthermore, amalgamation reduced the number of city councillors by half and increased the size of wards, creating a complexity of responsibilities for politicians that may make it difficult to follow through on policy visions and maintain close relationships with local constituents (Thomlinson 2000).

UPSIDE-DOWN FEDERALISM

An academic policy expert argues that intergovernmentalism presents a particular challenge in Canada around realizing AFCs because the system of federalism is "basically upside down" (E16). The institutional tools and resources to actualize effective and innovative AFCs are not available at the level of local government, where they are needed. There are systemic problems around using the property tax for redistribution, as the province has engaged in restructuring projects that have transferred social and physical infrastructure responsibility onto local governments (Golden and Slack 2006; Horak 2012). Toronto is reliant on the property tax as its core source of revenue because it is restricted by the province from enacting a sales or income tax. The property tax was intended to fund property-related services like road construction and garbage collection, and cannot adequately support social infrastructure as it does not increase automatically with economic growth. This presents a challenge, because citizens are particularly sensitive to property tax increases, especially as their costs may increase without a gain in income simply because the value of their home increases. This is especially problematic in a big city like Toronto where real estate prices have risen dramatically over the last several decades. This situation creates a particular paradox for AFCs, as seniors on fixed incomes who are house-rich and cash-poor likely do not want to see property taxes increased. Seniors get a property tax discount in Toronto; however, as a municipal policy expert asks: "How does this balance out if we have an aging population who are property owners and have their property taxes halved to help support them to stay in their homes? Then municipalities are reducing their bottom line to help plough the snow in front of people's homes or run the transit at off-peak hours to accommodate their needs" (D53). Some seniors may even vote against their own interests in investment in local social and physical infrastructure improvements, in part because of rules of municipal finance dictated by the province.

Toronto was given more taxing authority through the *City of Toronto Act* and has taxing room that it does not use, such as a vehicle registration tax and taxes on alcohol, entertainment, and tobacco (Joy and Vogel 2015). As such, Toronto could raise revenue to fund some components of the *Toronto Seniors Strategy* through other forms of taxation. However, a city staff member explains that these taxes would barely cover the research needed on the innovations to support population aging and accessibility. This employee recommends that other levels of government claiming to support AFCs provide the city with funding transfers to engage in these improvements.

The big-ticket items required to build an expansive AFC, such as substantive investment in housing, transportation, and health care, all require intergovernmental financial support as Toronto struggles to pay for building, improving, and maintaining large infrastructure items. A municipal policy expert explains that "there is a greater role for the other levels of government to play when we start talking about how we are going to pay for all of this. Both the provincial and federal levels of government have talked about the need for age-friendly communities, but when you look at the list of what an age-friendly community needs to be, 90 percent of responsibilities fall onto municipalities. But again, the funding formula has not changed in decades and municipalities are primarily funding things through property taxes" (D53). While provincial representatives advise that the *Toronto Seniors Strategy* focuses on what is within the municipal jurisdiction, these policy domains have become more substantive through restructuring and this context of past political choice is under-assessed by the province. The majority of interview participants from both the government and non-profit sectors agree that the resources and capacities of the city are not taken into account by other levels of government in their promotion of AFCs. A senior citizens' advocate provided the following response: "I am laughing because no, it is not taken into account. You may hear the rhetoric that 'They know the local needs.' And they may indeed know the local needs, but the issue is that they don't have the resources and you are not going to move on that, so either at the provincial level try to meet the needs or put the money into the local level. But the responsibility and the resources fall in two different places" (D29). This advocate goes on to explain that "I kind of see cities at the bottom of the food chain in terms of local, provincial, and national governments. They have far less resources" (D29).

What became glaringly obvious from my interviews is that provincial and federal representatives never mentioned the infrastructure crisis in cities highlighted in chapter 2, nor how this affects AFCs. This reflects a troubling lack of acknowledgement and understanding of local capacities to initiate and sustain meaningful AFCs. Provincial representatives allude instead to AFC strategies being motivated by the crisis in population aging, wherein all levels of government will face greater needs but have fewer resources due to a smaller tax base. The last three decades of narrow projects of public-sector restructuring and tax cuts are ignored in this rhetoric. This crisis is framed as an opportunity for local governments and non-profits to shine and show their important preventative work in the area of the social determinants of health, while other levels of government act as enablers by convening partners and sharing information. However, one city employee doubts whether this is a meaningful partnership: "You would have thought that the feds and province would be much more interested because they have so many more dollars and so many more issues, for example, health and aging. That they would be doing more, but they are not" (B2). Once again, linking the AFC movement to the push for a United Nations Convention on the Rights of Older People offers a platform to push for such a meaningful partnership.

Both the federal and the provincial government claim to be supporting municipalities and non-profits to develop AFCs, though this is primarily through small, one-time project-based grant programs. A municipal expert explains that "it is a very surface approach to addressing some of those needs by saying that the municipalities should be doing x, y and z, and that they have grants of up to $10,000 to help you organize that. It is not realistic. Maybe it is a starting point to do that" (D53). Instead, the federal government as well as the province have developed how-to guides and encourage local governments to voluntarily adopt AFCs, but a city representative complains that "they are just giving us reading. I didn't find that terribly helpful" (B2). My interviews with federal officials confirmed their position that AFCs are a local and provincial issue and their role is to coordinate best practices and provide advice. The province is reluctant to formalize AFCs through legislation, preferring to put the onus on local governments and non-profits to deliver services, devise age-friendly policy, and create new administrative infrastructures to see this through. My interviews with representatives at other levels of government indicated that they hope that partnerships between local governments and non-profits, as well as with local businesses and universities, will replace the need for substantive funding on their part. There appears to be a lack of concern about capacity issues in big cities, on the basis that they have more non-governmental partners to help them meet the needs of seniors. There is a risk here that if local governments fail to develop AFCs, they are blamed by other levels of government for not undertaking their role to know and meet local needs.

In the absence of sustainable and substantive support from other levels of government, the *Toronto Seniors Strategy* focuses only on those items within the jurisdiction of the municipality. While this reflects the city's concern to align their "age-friendly" work internally, it is also a response to past strategies that focused on advocating to the province on big-ticket items like housing. These strategies were deemed failures because recommendations that extended beyond the city's jurisdictional boundaries were never implemented and there was little monitoring and accountability. As Councillor Josh Matlow explains: "the main challenge or reason that a lot of the ideas and recommendations in the past had not been seen to fruition was that, believe it or not, governments don't always get along. The City of Toronto might say 'we want to do a, b, and c,' but they need permission from the province. But the province doesn't want to focus on that at the time or doesn't want to cut a check for that, and it just doesn't happen" (A1). One city representative explains that a premise of the *Toronto Seniors Strategy* was to focus on what the city can do and be held responsible for, and thus it did not strive to inform other levels of government. This is problematic, because several participants advise that the recommendations that came forward from older adults themselves had to do with areas of jurisdiction that the city has little direct control over. In the context of public consultations, staff had "to say sometimes, 'We are not responsible for that,' and, as much as we don't want to say, 'We are not responsible, so we won't talk about it,' the exercise is putting it in a parking lot or something so we can focus on what we can do" (B6). It is difficult for outsiders to understand who is ultimately charged with coordinating the various elements of the AFC checklist and where to direct their advocacy efforts.

A meaningful AFC requires "a larger vision for figuring out how cities can operate better" (D53). This means that other levels of government must step in to support AFCs either by enhancing municipal taxing authority to pay for the items that seniors need in their day to day lives or via funding transfers for infrastructure supports. A city representative suggests that what is really needed are long-term, age-friendly, infrastructure programs supported by the federal and provincial governments, with an emphasis on increasing corporate taxes because private companies are benefiting from infrastructure development in cities. An academic policy expert explains that AFCs offer the "potential for one of these intergovernmental frameworks that would identify a very clear policy division of labour" (E16). This participant sees the development of a systematic intergovernmental policy framework as a natural evolution, as current research work across governments and organizations on AFCs will eventually result in greater commitment from the federal and provincial levels of government. However, other participants worry that an evolved federalism will never occur if governments are "acting strapped" (E20) and refuse to work together to improve the lives of senior citizens through meaningful investment. In this environment, local governments are expected to support both prevention and emergency services, provide core social and physical infrastructure, and address deficiencies through niche programming, undertake the governance work to bring the fragmented service landscape together, conduct research on diverse seniors, and engage in AFC policy development. As was highlighted in chapter 2, the inability of local government to do all of this work has resulted in a considerable role for non-profit organizations, at least in the Toronto case. The following sections explore the capacity of the non-profit sector to undertake this work.

The Rights of Non-profit Organizations

THE INCREASING RELEVANCE OF NON-PROFIT ORGANIZATIONS

Like local government, non-profits are understood to be "on the front-lines" of population aging in Toronto: "So much of the response to population aging has been done by the non-profit sector. Grassroots organizations trying to respond to local need" (D1A). Scharlach et al. (2014) note that "community social organizations are of increasing importance in the context of increasing population diversity and declining roles of families, religious institutions, and governments in the postmodern state" (183) and my interviews confirm this. Non-profits are contrasted with governments for knowing "the populations that they work with … governments might think they do, but they don't as well" (D8). Non-profits are valued for responding to needs innovatively, not "one size fits all" but in a way that meets diverse needs. I find that non-profit care work is often contrasted with government provision, particularly in the realm of home care: "Big government has got things like the CCAC [Community Care Access Centres] … they have got things like 'Your service is from 10:25 to 10:35 and sorry, I know you are bleeding, but you don't apply and will have to call a different department'… It is very bureaucratic. I sympathize with them, but my volunteers can flex" (D35).

This grassroots nature and proximity to citizens is understood to mean that non-profits care about their clients; they watch out for them and retain a human touch. I found in my interviews that non-profits often positioned themselves as an "extended family" for urban seniors who lack access to informal care. Several non-profit staff members spoke to me about their role checking in on people and finding people who are living alone. An agency employee reflects on this work: "But just being able to play that role of truly assisting people with no one is amazing. It is truly amazing, and I think that we need to see more of this everywhere. In order to keep these people safe, it has to be hands-on, it can't be mass. It does have to be, say, about having a lunch group where you meet the people and you get to know them. And as you are calling them weekly, that weekly call saying what time we are picking them up is acting as, 'Are you ok?' Sometimes the family is maybe speaking with them only on the weekend and they don't know if there is a fall or a problem" (D20). It is also non-profits that provide targeted emergency services to seniors: "We have crisis people who help relocate people who are on the verge of eviction and we get them into nursing homes … We put on the bedbug suits and go in and pack up apartments" (D20). In this way, non-profits are considered to go the extra mile to do the hands-on work that no one else is going to do. "We had an instance this week. We have restaurant trips usually, and we went to pick up one of our seniors in the building and she wasn't there. We were quite concerned and called the superintendent to look in the building, in the apartment, and she wasn't there. This woman has no family, so we started calling hospitals now and found out that she was in a hospital. And this is TCH [Toronto Community Housing] and there really should be a form of obligation because there are seniors in these buildings, but there isn't really" (D20).

My interviews suggest that non-profits are valued for "getting things done," which is contrasted with government: "I think that we are pretty good at implementation, and the tactics. And oftentimes the policy-makers are good with the strategy and the policy, but they just don't have the experience with the tactics and the implementation. And that is where the conflict comes up sometimes" (D12). There are several reasons highlighted for this prowess in implementation. The first is that non-profits are considered closer to "ordinary citizens": "It is the community agencies that are more on the ground. They are more flexible. We can turn around in no time … We are constantly doing acrobatics here, left and center, but it is the non-profit sector that listens" (D35). Second, the non-profit sector knows how to work with other local partners: "We are able to work with other initiatives and other agencies quickly … It's because we have been operating for so long with limited resources that we have learned how to creatively work with local agencies" (D47A). This speaks to the third reason non-profits are considered ideal implementers: they lack resources. Many participants believe that non-profits know how to respond to challenges, do more with less, and create value for money: "The role of the non-profit service sector is incredibly creative and efficient, and the taxpayer will get a fantastic bang for their buck investing in the non-profit sector" (D35). Innovation in the sector is understood to be driven by the adversity of limited resources: "Let the non-profit organizations, who are the ones that can afford sometimes, often because they are forced to with tight budgets, to do some really neat things … I do know that the non-profits can innovate. They often have limited funding and that can stretch them to say, 'OK, can I do that one job with two part-time people or how can I work that?" (D54).

A CHANGING FUNDING CLIMATE

My interviews indicate that non-profit funding, particularly public-sector funding limits and the shift from core organizational funding to project-based contract funding (Evans and Shields 2010; Richmond and Shields 2004), presents a barrier to informing policy development in the realm of AFCs. A participant who represents a sizeable and well-known non-profit agency advises that "everyone is stretched as an organization … So as much as I would love in my role to spearhead a specific age-friendly project, there is just not the time and the resources" (D8). Several city representatives note that despite the *Toronto Seniors Strategy*, there will be no additional funding for non-profits serving seniors. City funding is unique in that it is an evergreen contract that is relatively stable year to year, though this is only the case for service- providing agencies and not for policy-oriented groups. A volunteer from a policy-oriented agency explains their funding struggles thus: "Once upon a time, there used to be various government agencies that provided core funding. That disappeared and everybody fights for the little pots. If we apply for funding, we have to apply for a project. So, let's say that we get a project. You have to spend money to hire someone to run the project and there goes most of your money. Because you glean your core funding from the project, and you are lucky to come out ahead. It is not usually worth the fuss and the paperwork and the time" (D49).

As was outlined in chapter 2, restructuring in the health care sector has meant that non-profit service agencies are expected to serve seniors with more acute and complex health challenges. While the province claims to support community agencies, a non-profit employee advises that "in terms of the funding support, it is still very limited. Especially when compared to funding given to other service sectors, it is still very, very, very small. But the home first and community first relies very much on the community agencies to provide the service. Otherwise, it wouldn't be concrete or effective" (D38). My findings are similar to that of Scharlach (2012) who notes that non-profit work often takes the form of pilot projects aimed at meeting niche needs, but these programs are frequently funded for only one round, with the assumption that private funding will replace public support. One non-profit participant explains that "[this] speaks to the sustainability of programs that have been implemented through previous funding. As the population continues to age and that aging population continues to increase, there needs to be sustainability to keep the programs going, and that seems to be the piece that is continuously forgotten. They ask us to look for further efficiencies to offset and we can only look so much in our own house as a non-profit" (D12).

Non-profit organizations are framed as innovative and, in an environment of constant policy churn (Casey 2012) which challenges sustainability, there is pressure to develop something new and creative to keep seniors living at home. One agency employee explains that they are increasingly resisting new government funding proposals that focus on short-term pilot projects: "We are actually at a point where we might actually say no. Which I think is a trend with other agencies, where they have to say no … we go to our board and say, 'Here is our proposal.' And they go, 'But what is the liability and the impact on our budget and what is this and this?' All good questions. And we say, 'Well, that could be a problem two years from now.' That is not in our nature. Most not-for-profit home care want to say, 'Yes, we'll do that, we will look after that senior, don't worry about it.' So to say no means that wow, this is a huge decision by a board to say that we can't" (D12). Government funders do not seem to recognize that these agencies are now providing essential services for seniors, not just filling gaps in public programming. As such, these agencies have less capacity to undertake new and creative initiatives, especially when they are inadequately funded.

Several participants talk about the importance of non-profits engaging in research on their client needs. I found that predominantly, research was valued for helping to build cases to prove non-profit worth to government: "At the end of the day, research buys money, it gets you the money, it brings in the money. You need to have evidence to make a case, and without the research and the resources to conduct the research, it is challenging" (D8). Rather than engendering more trust between government and the non-profit sector, the current context illustrates more pressure on non-profits to prove their worth, particularly as they take on more and more public service delivery work. One agency explains that the non-profit sector is "getting a lot more pressure to do it in a way that is efficient and effective. Not just because it feels good or there is a nice story, but you have got to back it up with metrics. And I think that the whole accountability, deliverables, milestones, those are all really good things" (D7). This is a feature of managerialism meant to keep delivery agents in line and tackle accountability challenges (Newman and Clarke 2009). As such, "the level of scrutiny and demands on the non-profit sector have gone up exponentially" (D31B).

Accountability is understood as efficiency, and the non-profit sector in particular is getting increasing pressure to prove that their programming achieves results and that they offer a good return on investment (Dowling and Harvie 2014; Joy and Shields 2013; Joy and Shields 2018). Such measurement includes the extent to which targeted service provision saves money by preventing demands on so-called "remedial services," also known as the social value created (Dowling and Harvie 2014; Joy and Shields 2018). Increasingly, the emphasis is on quantitatively proving that programming reduces health care costs, and some agencies like this because it means that government is finally acknowledging their worth to "the system." However, one non-profit employee questions whether we are using the right metrics:

> One of our outcomes, as an example, is the percent of people that go home. This is a wonderful outcome, but this is where the funders and the providers have to get more granular, because I can send someone home who is isolated and not thriving who will be back in the system in six weeks. The funders and the non-profits and any provider have to get together and say, "This is not good enough, this is not a good enough metric." How do you know that the outcome is one that you are as happy and healthy as you can be given your situation, that you are thriving to the extent that you can? Not only that we sent you home and we can now tick off the box. (D4A).

This illustrates pressure to direct accountability to the funders over and above the community served (Shields 2014; Wells 2008). While several non-profits agree that evaluating the outcomes of their work is important, they want measures to be devised in partnership and resources to do this (Lum et al. 2016). An agency employee echoes this concern: "All of us in the community support services are desperately lacking the resources and time to do that, and that would go a long way, it really would" (D8).

Government fragmentation in policy and funding in the field of population aging creates instability within the non-profit sector. A city staff member admits that sometimes the three levels of government are not in sync and have different focuses, and that this is difficult for the non-profit sector. Several non-profit participants express frustration at having to adapt to the needs of provincial funders while "their policy doesn't necessarily fit the perspectives of what is happening in the community" (D27). Different levels of government and funders are not moving to integrate their funding to the non-profit sector based on grounded needs and problems with service gaps and fragmentation, illustrating an overt power imbalance (Evans and Shields 2010; Milbourne 2013). Non-profits are subject to multiple state contractual regimes where no one grasps the population needs for seniors holistically. At the same time, agencies are expected to meet the distinct needs of communities innovatively and staff may have to work overtime to search for grants, prepare reports, deliver services, engage seniors, and prove their worth through outcome measurements. They operate in an incessant state of temporariness and instability (Shields 2014). Rather than a real partnership to improve policy, non-profits feel that "we send all of these reports in and we never quite know what happens with them, we just hope to get them in by the deadline and it goes into this big beast and we don't get any feedback" (D31B).

There is a serious gap between the demands placed on non-profits and their capacity to engage in AFC programs: "There is some capacity. It is important capacity. I would like to see them have more capacity but they certainly can't take on the big role in really making any city or community age friendly. And the assumption that you can offload, from a federal, provincial, and local government perspective, that you can offload onto the non-profit sector, I think that this is not fair and it is not the reality of it" (E24). Decontextualized assumptions of capacity where cost-cutting is a dominant motivation is a reality that I have uncovered through my interviews, and this reality needs to be better understood by AFC promoters. Non-profit services require stable government support in the form of core organizational funding and evergreen contracts (Shields 2014) for both service and advocacy agencies, especially as they are lauded for their ability to provide personalized services to senior citizens. This support must be fundamentally driven by a more universal norm of care (Biggs and Carr 2015), as one academic participant emphasizes: "We could provide more financial support, but it is more than financial support but like, 'This is a good service, we should have more of it, and we should really care about it.' And I don't think we have. You wouldn't believe what goes on. We don't take care of anybody. They are struggling. They don't have money, they really don't have two cents to rub together, yet they are out there and one person might get paid out of some [federal] New Horizons Grant to try and help" (E20).

THE ECONOMIZATION OF THE NON-PROFIT SECTOR

As non-profits are made to compete with private providers in the services they deliver, they are expected to operate more and more like private businesses (Milbourne 2013). In a climate where value for money is prioritized, the delivery agent matters less and less, and governments increasingly go with whoever can save them more money (Laforest 2013a). A representative from a large non-profit agency explained to me that the major issue with community services right now is that they reach seniors and are coordinated, and whether this is done by a non-profit or for-profit doesn't much matter: "If non-profits can organize well around what the real needs are for an aging population, they will do well. The last couple of years actually has proven that they are not well positioned to deal with that, and it is the for-profit providers who are much better positioned" (D1C). This understanding is highlighted by Laforest (2013a) who advises that the new market orientation of service delivery has blurred the boundaries between the state, the private sector, and the non-profit sector. A non-profit participant advises that "there is no difference between a for-profit and non-profit except whose pocket the money goes into. Profit- making goes into stockholders and, in a non-profit, the money goes back into the organization to keep the wheels turning for programming. The idea is to make money but the old school doesn't think of a non-profit like that, and those people will have to disappear" (D55). There is a risk here that what is actually produced in terms of services to seniors matters less and less as the focus is on making money.

Non-profits may gain a competitive edge in this funding climate if they show that they can become self-sufficient through private fundraising and entrepreneurial pursuits, and obtain free staff through volunteerism (Taylor 2013; Casey 2012; Rochester et al. 2010; Milbourne 2013). My interviews showcase a drive to bring more private charity into the non-profit sector to enhance its entrepreneurial nature and fill funding gaps: "the community sector, the non-profit sector, attracts the rest of the community. I have on my board executive directors, lawyers, accountants, businesspeople. People that would never dream of working for the government or volunteering for the government. That affects the rest of the community. All of a sudden, they realize that there are people in this city that are older people that have mental health issues and have nowhere to go" (D35). The result is that decisions as to who has access to public services are increasingly being made by unelected boards. In a context where we have seen decades of cuts to public programs and charitable tax deductions increase (Elson 2011; Laforest 2013b), this privatization of welfare is occurring instead of the provision of services as a right of citizenship. Some agencies laud having business professionals on their board to provide accountability because there is an assumption that non-profits are not businesslike enough: "Rotman [Business School] has a whole school of governance for nonprofit board members. If you really want to see policy change, throw all non-profit board members through this course … All of the non-profits have boards, and boards have a fiduciary responsibility of making sure that this non-profit does what it is supposed to do and grows where it is supposed to grow. And if those board members are Mom and Pop, who are just there to say they sit on a board, you have got a stalemate" (D4A). This reality exists in tension with the current valorization of civic engagement in AFCs, especially as I find that some agencies have removed senior citizens from their boards. This is not about community members debating whether to apply for funding, but management teams who can make quick decisions about service grants. At the same time, a senior citizen advocate notes that "if they are really going to drive the agenda, they have to have people who are there from in the community. There are barriers and pushback from the rest of the board who don't think that the person can contribute. What we need is a mix of people" (F6). However, several interviews illustrate that financial expertise is valued above experience when making policy decisions, because non-profits have to survive in a competitive funding environment (Milbourne 2013).

Innovation in the sector is framed as "marketization" and non-profits are reframed as "social enterprises," as markets are considered the seeds of innovation (Kendall 2008): "non-profits need to find innovative ways of thinking and financing, funding … they just keep complaining 'There is no money, there is no money.' Well, money is not the big issue" (D55). According to this non-profit participant, the solution lies in "strategic partnerships that over time could lead to new ways of thinking … You have got to be a risk-taker and you have got to be an explorer. And people who are locked into whatever can't make that journey. That's where the incapacity is, because there is a new journey. We are going to new places, this is a new place in time, and whatever got us here, congratulations, it is very good, but it is not usable without crushing the next generation" (D55). This reflects a view of the past as static and the future as full of change that does not consider the past three decades of managerialism within the non-profit sector (Evans and Shields 2010; Milbourne 2013; Casey 2012) as well as cuts to health care programs. Another non-profit participant expresses a concern that "our world has become so obsessed with profit and profit-making that the question is: Where is the place for non-profit anymore? Where is the philanthropic desire to assist and support people? … This is critical in terms of supporting seniors and other vulnerable populations" (D8). Non-profits are proliferating but they are becoming more professionalized and economized, made to compete for predefined service programs despite their valuation as community-centric (Laforest 2013a). My research highlights that we have not forgotten the relationship between non-profits and philanthropy, but we have lost the concepts of solidarity and social services provided collectively as a right of citizenship. Aligning the AFC movement to the movement for a United Nations Convention on the Rights of Older Adults could be a platform to re-engage with this conversation.

There is increasing inequity in the non-profit sector between the smaller agencies and the larger, more corporate non-profits, as progress is equated with a larger size, professionalized sophistication, and economization (Smith 2013; Mitchell 2001). An academic policy expert explains: "I think that the larger agencies attract more money. They manage to do it because they have more resources to try to get it. Probably more experience and networks and so on that make it very difficult for those on the margins" (E20). This is consistent with Jenson and Phillips' (1996) observation that a shift to contractual service provision on the part of government funders has created a hierarchy of non-profits, with the large service-providers occupying the highest rung of power. Those non-profits best positioned for success have adopted a businesslike approach to demands for financial efficiency and accountability. Some larger agencies have seen their funding increase and believe that there is now a more equal partnership with funders, illustrating the need to understand the power dimensions and diversity within the sector. Thus, government is starting to listen to "community," but only to a particular segment of it. This is reflected in the following story:

> We were sitting in a room like this with all of the service providers for the catchment area and [the Local Health Integration Network staff] said … "Why don't we mutually design the decision criteria to evaluate your business case for funding to us" … we sat around and worked it up together. They had input from us, it was a collaborative process and at the end of the day, we know exactly what they are looking for. Either you provide what they are looking for or you don't get funding. We have some colleagues who are constantly saying, "Well, we didn't get funded." But we made the decision criteria, figure it out. We are not going to help you with that because we are actually going after the same dollars. (D12)

This is illustrative of changes in contracting where government is increasingly picking the winners with the type of expertise that they desire (McGoey 2015; Bar-Nir and Gal 2011). These are not small, mainly volunteer-led organizations, but highly professionalized and sophisticated entities with permanent staff.

I found that city staff members are particularly concerned about the nonprofits with whom they work, advising that many small agencies have little skill and capacity and very small budgets to develop these proficiencies. In particular, one city employee notes that some organizations "need a lot of capacity work, especially the smaller ethno-specific organizations, as they differ in the capacity to really run an organization and to provide all the services" (B7). A policy expert admits that "your size can also preclude how effective and big you can be in achieving economies of scale and how you run things" (E19). As these organizations compete for multiple funding streams from different institutions of the state as well as foundations, they need more sophisticated administrative infrastructures: "So all of a sudden, the infrastructure they would need, the back-office administration, is very important. You can't just run this out of a church basement which, frankly, a lot of them were doing for a long time. It is almost the level of sophistication that is needed to run these organizations and to understand how quickly the overall landscape is changing. It is hard for these organizations to be as stealthy and efficient and strategic as large big sophisticated organizations" (E19). As agencies try to become multi-service, some fail because they cannot cover their costs as they are getting grants from a fragmented variety of funders.

The question here is whether the goal should be for these agencies to provide "all the services." There are tensions here, as small agencies are also valued for their localized nature and community or "extended family" orientation, which results in popular programming and services that may be at risk in this funding climate.

NON-PROFIT CONSOLIDATION

I found a clear trend towards consolidation in the non-profit sector that relates to increasing pressure on agencies to deliver core services, as well as multiple services in competition with for-profit providers. A non-profit employee explains that "we do have an obligation to look at the population at large and where the needs are, and also to work together as a system of providers to make sure that we are not duplicating, triplicating, and fourplicating things. And create a more coherent systemic response to these issues" (D31B). In this regard, the non-profit sector is increasingly expected to address the service fragmentation created by the decades of public-sector restructuring discussed in chapter 2. A non-profit participant explains that "the non-profit sector is getting a lot more pressure to do it in a way that is a system response, which I think is excellent … I think that the non-profit sector has a responsibility … to come together and to work out the system glitches and to start to figure out, 'You are really good at that, and we are really good at this, why don't we stick to that, you stick to this, and let's get a system going'… I think that it is not just about getting your own little programs going and doing your thing in isolation but it's about how do we work together and what is working for people" (D7).

System fragmentation is understood as inefficient and wasteful, with several participants reflecting their responsibility to "cut fat" and "address bloat" in the provision of services for seniors. One agency employee notes that a "big push in non-profits is to do a really lean approach … the idea is to do a lot of value-stream mapping and quality-improvement exercises and that sort of thing to look at a process … So lean processes are taking a process and making sure that we are doing it in the most lean, efficient way because all of the rest of it is just wasted energy" (D7). Another agency employee critiques this allusion to bloat, explaining that it is based on a fundamental lack of understanding on the part of governments about how the sector operates:

> There seems to be an impression, I would say among the province and the LHINs [Local Health Integration Networks], not so much the city, but you can find efficiencies and cut the fat. Really!? I don't think that is really possible. The problem is that with our budget and the way we are organized as a business model, over 90 percent of our budget is labour and rent. So there is not a lot of discretion. Where am I going to find that $200,000? I mean by laying people off, I can't do the work. If I cut my marketing budget, people won't know about this new program. If I don't do the training, when it is mandatory training, then I am not in compliance with the legislation. There is not a lot of room to move. (D12)

Several agency employees link the notion of cutting fat to the push for greater consolidation in the sector through mergers: "If we merge there will be some efficiencies, but not many efficiencies because we really run a tight ship here. I have got some excellent staff and we are lean, so we are not very desirable as a merger partner. The good thing about a merger is that you see where there is fat and inefficiencies and you clean it up. I have no fat" (D35). Several agency employees advise that this push to merge is a stealthy manoeuvre on the part of the province: "[the province] won't say it out loud. So instead of saying 'amalgamate or die,' they are saying 'integrate services' because they know that is a political hot potato" (D35). This is a "hot potato" because the province claims to value local expertise and voice. This representative explains that "smaller agencies have a choice right now … we stay as we are, treading water, or we should seriously consider a merger" (D35). One agency employee explains that integration "gets cast as a reduction in funding … to a degree. Why do you fund fifteen organizations to buy office supplies? … If you centralize the purchasing, you will get a bigger bang for your buck" (D31B). This statement illustrates that mergers are about increasingly mass non-profit service delivery that offers "value for money." This is seen by some participants as a way to deal with new demands from government, such as the new accessibility (AODA) legislation and calls for them to engage in more service provision to seniors with acute health challenges, as well as a way to enhance their capacity to provide multiple services to clients. They see the need for universal service provision and a larger role for their sector in this regard and some agencies, particularly the larger ones, believe that mergers improve "client centeredness."

For some participants, the small community-centric role of the non-profit sector is a thing of the past: "The non-profit sector in Ontario and Canada is mature. Thirty years ago, it wasn't mature. The problem is that there are still people around who think that they are not mature, but it is. I think that the non-profit sector and certainly the larger non-profits can be trusted to do all sorts of things. They are bold, they are dynamic, and they are going to do great things" (E26). This policy expert predicts that "one of the big things that we are going to see with non-profits generally, and especially with the provision of seniors' housing, is non-profits that are currently operating one or two buildings will get bigger and bigger" (E26). Interestingly, some participants' critiques of government relate to scale and mass service provision, yet those same participants do not see a problem with non-profits becoming bigger and bigger, framing this as "maturation." Non-profits have grown to a size and a level of sophistication and professionalization that they can take on more and more of the work previously done by government, including the provision of social housing. This maturation is seen as a natural progression that improves client-centredness.

My findings suggest that there are different definitions of client-centeredness at play, reflecting different needs for universal and more a-spatial policy as well as personalized service supports. As government steps away, the non-profit sector is expected to provide both universal and niche services, though "one size fits all" provision appears to be prioritized despite the rhetoric of diversity and personal service delivery. As organizations get bigger and provide more "one size fits all" services, they risk getting further away from their distinct "extended family" nature (Smith 2013). This risk is elaborated by an agency staff member: "It is hard, because these organizations and ours as well have grown up from the ground. They were defined by the population needs at the time … every organization has their own history and they have grown up from communities and they have a sense of obligation to their community which continues to this day, so it is tricky" (D31B). It is this sense of obligation to the community that is being exploited by some government funders at the same time as they make it more difficult to maintain. Many non-profits and other policy experts see this as devastating for the local non-profit sector. One executive director complains that "the non-profit sector right now is being massacred. The funders aim to reduce their work and fund fewer agencies. The LHIN [Local Health Integration Network] basically doesn't want to fund as many community agencies as they do now. They are funding sixty-four different entities and they want only about ten" (D35). These agencies feel forced to merge to survive and feel they have no choice but to merge and thus would rather do it on their own terms than being forced by the government.

PRECARIOUS LABOUR

Non-profit staff feel the squeeze of these changes in the sector (Shields 2014; Baines et al. 2014; Hardill and Baines 2011; Chouinard and Crooks 2008). A number of interviewees suggest that non-profit staff go the extra mile to offer innovative and intimate service support, but this work is often unpaid (Hardill and Bains 2011). In this way, non-profit staff can get used by governments looking to offload responsibility because "they care" and "their hearts are in it." The sector is valued as a cheaper service delivery option to the state, and often this is on the backs of its labour: "People are doing multiple jobs and are taking work home to make sure it works or are trying to create free-ish type things, relying on volunteer-led initiatives, which is difficult to ask volunteers to give up so much energy and time. It is definitely a struggle, and this is an issue. I work at another non-profit, so I am here four days a week and I am in Hamilton one day a week and yes, we are constantly on the paper line. We have only got three paid employees and they do multiple different things" (D33). This can result in high staff turnover and burnout, which is particularly problematic for seniors because having the same person there to act as the "extended family" is familiar and reassuring.

In a context of non-profit economization, agencies are pressured to hire professionalized staff but cannot afford to pay people at a rate similar to public and private providers:

> Unfortunately, my workers, including myself, are getting a fraction of the salary. I tried to hire a social worker in a management position to manage the social services here. I interviewed someone that was working for a local hospital and she was fairly young, about three or four years' experience, and she would have

> loved to come here but she was getting paid more than I am. I can't do it. I am the executive director. I cannot hire someone to do what she would have been ideal for. And this is quite typical of the non-profit sector. We are being starved of resources. There is a gap between the public sector, the government sector, or the health services and the community agencies. (D35)

This participant advises that "if we cautiously were to privatize certain things, we could save a lot of money. If we cautiously slim down public services, we could save money" (D35). In other words, the solution is to reduce public services because public-sector salaries are so high, rather than bringing the salaries of the non-profit sector in line with public-sector workers. A senior citizen advocate disagrees, pointing out that we need "adequate salaries, full-time work, not exploiting your staff so that you can take benefits, health-benefits … And definitely pensions, access to a pension" (D54). A society that is "age-friendly for all" requires taking better care of those who care for seniors and who will one day become seniors themselves. This discussion also raises the question as to whether volunteering and non-profit delivery provides inherently better services or whether government must be less rigid and deliver care that is more humanized. Having well-paid public-sector staff do this work indicates that the nature of need is normal and worthy of a collective response.

Relations between Local Government and Non-profit Organizations

THE IMPORTANCE OF PARTNERSHIP BETWEEN LOCAL GOVERNMENT AND NON-PROFIT ORGANIZATIONS

Local governments are considered by many participants to be the most legitimate partners to support non-profits because they have similarities with respect to their place-based nature, service orientation, proximity to "ordinary citizens," and concern for vulnerable residents. "I don't think that they can work in isolation. I think that local government has its finger on the pulse of what they identify as local needs within the community and so does the non-profit sector" (D8). Many participants supported the idea that the local state and non-profit sectors can meet diverse needs. In addition, one non-profit employee explains that the city "take the really hard-to-serve groups. Maybe this is why we have a good relationship with them, because we get each other because we work with those marginalized seniors" (D7). A partnership with the non-profit sector is thought to enhance access by extending the city's outreach, especially to ethno-cultural groups. One city staff member notes that they "provide community funding through grants" and "rely on community agencies to do a lot of the work that we don't, that we can't do" (B3). However, I found that the limited rights of local government and of non-profit organizations has led to tensions in their relations.

A CONFUSED POLICY PARTNERSHIP

Although the city engaged in partnerships with non-profit actors to design the *Toronto Seniors Strategy* – specifically an expert panel consisting of both non-profit and academic leaders – there is confusion around the role of non-profits. While many of the panel's members claim that their presence provides accountability, this is not a formalized group that advocates for seniors on a regular basis, as is presented as a core component of a progressive city according to Clavel (2010). The expert panel only met in person three times, and many members that I interviewed appeared unaware that the *Toronto Seniors Strategy* lacked a formal budget and staff support. Furthermore, several panel members did not know who was driving and leading the *Toronto Seniors Strategy*, indicating that they had no contact or point person within the city bureaucracy. Despite a desire by many members to be involved in follow-up and to get back together, one member says, "I remember that there was a discussion about that, but I just can't recall whether we settled on anything definitive" (D8).

City staff leading *Toronto Seniors Strategy* implementation were also unclear on the role of the expert panel moving forward, pointing to vague language in the strategy report about maintaining an advisory body (City of Toronto 2013). One panel member relayed that when they contacted Councillor Josh Matlow about their involvement in the advisory committee, he had never heard of the concept. I learned from city representatives that some non-profits may be on smaller thematic tables.

A member of an advocacy organization involved on the expert panel voiced concerns about this: "I have now heard through the grapevine that there was a meeting with some sort of advisory group, some of whom had nothing to do with the original group … I have to get back to the person at the city … we should be on this advisory committee" (D49). This illustrates a discrepancy between large service agencies, considered natural partners in service implementation, and the development of an independent body that provides accountability to make sure the Toronto Seniors Strategy remains a "living document."

Several of the smaller non-profits I interviewed were involved only tangentially on *Toronto Seniors Strategy* development as they completed a survey with their seniors and attended larger open meetings as the strategy was being developed. The representative of one agency notes that "we get invited to some [city] meetings … but I am not sure how we fit into their planning. We do get consulted but there are so many people that go to those meetings, and there are so many players, and it is very complex" (D12). My interviews suggest that invitations to city-led open consultations occur haphazardly if an agency gets on the right mailing list, and that such processes are felt to be more about the city informing agencies than asking them for their input. Some agencies feel like their invitations to policy tables are merely window- dressing, and that local government does not actively reach out to non-profits: "It says it does by putting out documents and leaflets, but does it really? No. And to inform policy, even less … We're the junior, junior, junior partners. We are the sub-junior partner" (D49). A member of an advocacy organization expresses frustration with the advisory concept:

> There are many organizations, including many branches of the city, that want to reach out to seniors groups … But they want to do it in some kind of an advisory capacity. And one of the huge angsts of those of us who are members of [organization name] is that we don't want to just be advisors, we want to be actors. We want to be at the decision-making table around what form these take. You have been asking us for advice for years, it doesn't seem to go anywhere, and it is not that you don't put it forward but you need to have somebody who is at the table that is going to kick you in the ass in terms of actually doing it, because otherwise

> other priorities come up … An advocacy organization literally has to tell people that consultation and advising is not what we are about; we want to be where the decisions are being made and we were not invited to the decision-making table. So several times, we have just said, "Sorry, waste of time." (D29)

It is thus up to non-profits to insert themselves into these processes, and those that have taken the time to do this have had some success in ensuring that their voices are heard. In effect, this is what occurred with the expert panel, as the city had originally envisioned a panel of large service providers rather than advocacy organizations. Several smaller advocacy-based organizations pushed to have a seat at the table, including the Toronto Seniors Forum, who were not initially invited. This illustrates the way that expertise is defined as professional service-providers rather than citizens with everyday experience of policy and the smaller organizations that represent them. A representative of one small advocacy organization explains that if they did not insert themselves into the process, "it wouldn't have happened. No one was thinking about us. No one reached out to us and said, 'Would you like to be a part of this?'" (D49). The overarching finding is that agencies feel that they are always having to go to the city rather than the other way around. Several agencies noted how exhausting this can be, while others simply gave up.

Despite the critical importance of partnership between local government and non-profit organizations, the majority of non-profit participants expressed frustration that there is no coordinated and institutionalized relationship with the city in the policy field of aging. City staff members admit that while there are multiple arrangements with the non-profit sector that take place through separate local government organizations, they are not well understood or articulated in the *Toronto Seniors Strategy*. One city representative admits that the strategy is lacking in this area, and advises that "there could be a layer [to the *Toronto Seniors Strategy*] that we add on in the future about more clearly articulating how the city engages with non-profit organizations, because it is in and of itself very important" (B6). The same person suggests that a future project might include a more comprehensive mapping of the non-profit sector in Toronto. The implementation tables proposed by the city as part of a larger strategy for the non-profit sector may provide clarity and a strategic voice for how non-profits fit into city planning. Again, this appears to be happening more in the realm of service provision, though it could form a basis for a more institutionalized policy partnership.

Another advocacy strategy on the part of the non-profit sector is to bypass the bureaucracy and go to city councillors on an as-needed basis. A representative of an advocacy- oriented agency explains that in a context where there is no formal relationship between the city bureaucracy and the non-profit sector, "we've been lucky in some ways, because there have been some councillors on committees that are open to us. The fact that we ended up with an active seniors' group on the expert panel didn't have to happen; it wasn't in the mandate. So that had to be councillors who gave a damn and were willing to have seniors' groups be a part of this. That happens, but is it a policy? Not really" (D49). Several agency staff members spoke about efforts taking place between their executive directors and politicians rather than through the institutional channels of city administration. This local connection is important, but it depends on whether the agency is lucky enough to be located in a ward where the councillor is receptive. Again, this "local" strategy can result in spatialized fragmentation and inequity. Furthermore, this personal form of advocacy is not a substitute for institutional relationships where non-profits can inform policy, because politicians and bureaucrats can leave their posts and the relationships become lost.

Several non-profit participants warned that they had to limit advocacy because they received public funding. "If I am nasty to you, or I get sarcastic, I can wind up losing that particular line of funding … Or I won't be approached if some new opportunities come up, I won't be thought of favourably. So I watch my Ps and Qs" (D29). Those non-profit participants who have been in the field for a long time noted a change in the past few decades from an acceptance of advocacy to being seen by government as complainers, reflecting a general shift away from respecting the "voice" function of the non-profit sector (Evans and Shields 2010; Evans and Shields 2014). These power imbalances place the government's desire for partnership into question (Shields 2014; Zimmer 2011). The policy advocacy or voice function of non-profits is crucial but is often left out of rhetoric on civic engagement, which emphasizes individual volunteerism and community participation rather than political work (Martinson and Minkler 2006; Minkler and Martinson 2007). My findings suggest that there is a need to broaden rather than narrow the role of the non-profit sector so that it can act as a real partner through its voice and service functions. If AFCs are to be effective, innovative, and enhance access and equity, then the right of the non-profit sector to have a policy voice and institutionalized structures is imperative.

Conclusion

This chapter has explored the ways in which the AFC program is empowering both local government and non-profit organizations in Toronto to develop age-friendly environments. Participants understand the growing role of local government and non-profit organizations to meet the needs of seniors as a positive development. These sectors are valued for their capacity to meet everyday, ordinary, or personal care needs in a way that is respectful of difference. These characteristics are framed in opposition to the "thick," a-spatial, and seemingly dehumanized policy role of the federal and provincial levels of government. Yet, addressing "community needs" is undertaken equally by these governments, who support broader policy such as income support, infrastructure funding, and health care, and thus require an understanding of the impact of their policy work on diverse groups.

In a context where anti-statist sentiment is highly prevalent, local government retains a unique form of legitimacy given its proximity to "ordinary citizens," though it is still critiqued as lacking in innovation, failing to know citizens' needs, and being immobilized by political interests. These are understood as essential features of government and are used by participants to explain why we do not have effective approaches to address population aging while narrow projects of public-sector restructuring that work though the institutions of the state are often ignored. There is thus a major disconnect between the need for a public-sector response to population aging and the depth of anti-political and anti-statist sentiment among many interview participants. This understanding risks increasing anti-statism rather than engaging in a conversation as to how different types of institutional changes and investments by different governments are needed to realize AFCs.

While I have found a desire and some effort to establish the institutional norms, sanctions, and incentives (Lowndes 2009) to realize AFCs through the *Toronto Seniors Strategy*, my interviews illustrate that this change is not yet adequate. A strong bureaucratic infrastructure to sustain the strategy as well as partnerships to hold the local state accountable were underdeveloped. This challenges those progressive agents who really do care, seek to find meaning in their work, and want to embed the intent to consider the needs of diverse seniors into urban policymaking. Enhanced need for services and amenities when the city has been given responsibility for an increasing number of AFC policy domains without commensurate revenue tools challenges both an already thin policy level and the administrative capacity to implement and enforce strategies (Horak 2012).

Limitations on the rights of local government by the province, such as rescaled policy responsibility in the absence of enhanced resource and policy capacity, has resulted in resistance by some local government organizations to push for the rights to the city, or to recognize the needs of senior citizens and redistribute on this basis. Restructuring has thus, in some cases, resulted in inaction rather than fueling the city to act as a problem-solver, as the new localism literature suggests (Katz and Bradley 2013; Barber 2013). Amalgamation has also divided politics, with the anti-statism supported by right-wing councillors challenging the city's ability to obtain funding for services for seniors through new taxes or increased property taxes (Joy and Vogel 2015; Sancton 2008). At the same time, the leftists on council do not appear to be working together to offer their vision for a substantive AFC and few left-leaning councillors appear to be working with senior citizen advocates to push for a right to the city. I also found that the city is not working with non-profit organizations to advocate to other levels of government to provide the resources and tools necessary to achieve a meaningful AFC.

In Toronto, there is limited advocacy on the part of the non-profit sector to act in coalition to design an urban agenda for a progressive AFC. This relates to institutional changes because of which the sector is morphing into a small number of professionalized health care service-providers contracted to the provincial health care delivery system and working less and less with the city. Furthermore, my findings suggest that consolidation work is fundamentally reshaping the character and role of the non-profit sector. Service provision by local policy actors is both valourized and seen as a problem to be corrected because subsidiarity (Antonnen et al. 2012a) is resulting in a highly fragmented service landscape. Thus, while local small-scale provision and community are valourized, I found opposing trends towards the centralization and professionalization of the non-profit sector, which challenges accountability to community.

As non-profits increasingly take on the role of core service-providers, demands for accountability have changed to data-driven outcomes proving their worth to "the system," or their ability to show value for money. Servicing can narrow the relations between citizens and institutions (Clarke et al. 2014) as it becomes more about targeting vulnerable or so-called "risky" people who are considered costlier to society rather than advocating to support the social determinants of health and health care delivery. The precarity of the sector, in which both programs and labour are increasingly temporary (Shields 2014; Baines et al. 2014), is challenging the extent to which the *Toronto Seniors Strategy* acts as an opportunity to incorporate those who have significant expertise on the needs of senior citizens.

Rather than fighting for their rights, local government and non-profits are busy acting as residual providers of last resort, and this challenges the extent to which they can engage in the improvement of the social determinants of health. Public-sector restructuring has exacerbated bureaucratic fragmentation internally, intersectorally, and intergovernmentally. This has challenged partnership building between these sectors, as they remain overwhelmed in their own fields of work. As such, there is confusion as to who is responsible for coordinating aging strategies across fragmented urban spaces. There is a lot of finger-pointing, resistance to action, and non-profits and citizens who do not know where to direct their advocacy in this "landscape of antagonism."

Although the AFC model offers a holistic framework aimed at enhancing the quality of life for seniors, the program is decontextualized to urban governance challenges in a broader context of public-sector restructuring. If the WHO claims that the AFC program is about enhancing access in local environments, then it must incorporate tangible advice for how to action a substantive AFC through institutional change. Otherwise, AFCs risk being used as a program of "shallow decentralization" (Banting 2010) that offloads responsibility for meeting the needs of senior citizens onto those with the least capacity to act, as appears to be occurring in the Toronto case. As such, I find that the AFC program in Toronto is not only challenged in implementation by narrow projects of public-sector restructuring, as is suspected in the initial critical research (Scharlach 2012; Buffel et al.

2012; Modlich 2011), but may also extend these projects by encouraging the responsibilization of local policy actors as a substitute for higher level redistribution. The following conclusion begins to outline what is needed to establish an AFC based on the right to the city for senior citizens.

CONCLUSION

AFCs as a Right to the City in Toronto?

Introduction

My interest in age-friendly city policy and practice was motivated by personal circumstances: my observation of the everyday struggles and resilience of aging loved ones and neighbours with chronic, and then acute, health challenges. I became increasingly aware of the physical and cultural barriers limiting access to services and amenities for senior citizens in Toronto. I began to get angry as I developed an understanding of these barriers as a manifestation of our collective inability to recognize the needs of seniors, in all their intersecting identities. Seemingly private struggles to access the city became increasingly politicized in my mind and I began to search for a public response to aging in place. I soon learned that while such a response had been introduced with the *Toronto Seniors Strategy*, it had been criticized as mainly symbolic and inadequate (Goar 2013). I set out to learn more about this policy response and to understand its apparent insufficiencies.

The *Toronto Seniors Strategy* is based on the WHO's AFC program; I, like many others concerned about the wellbeing of senior citizens, was drawn to the concept. A holistic, place-based approach claiming to tackle ageism by improving social, physical, and institutional environments based on the needs of senior citizens and their non-profit representatives seemed an excellent antidote to the problems I was witnessing. By focusing on improving "the fit" between senior citizens and their environment, AFCs are positioned as a progressive policy alternative to ageist approaches that focus solely on the cost impact of a more dependent and supposedly unproductive population. AFCs are situated as an effective, inclusive, and even revolutionary program that promotes a positive aging identity, improves environments for everyone, and empowers local policy actors in the process (WHO 2007; Plouffe and Kalache 2010; Barusch 2013; Gonzoles and Morrow-Howell 2009; Halvorsen and Emerman 2013). However, while I remained enthusiastic about the concept of AFCs, some preliminary research on the program raised concerns about its achievements in practice (Scharlach 2012; Buffel et al. 2012; Ball and Lawler 2014; Biggs and Carr 2015; Buffel and Phillipson 2016; Winterton 2016). Like the critiques levelled against the *Toronto Seniors Strategy*, AFC programs elsewhere seemed to promote only minimal changes rather than substantive improvements to local environments. Why was the program struggling to fulfill its aims?

Initial research on AFCs speculated that the program was limited by narrow political projects of neoliberal austerity that reduce the role for the public sector in supporting social welfare and physical infrastructure projects (Scharlach 2012; Modlich 2011). The WHO's AFC approach, as well as mainstream literature, has tended to decontextualize the program from the changing political economy where cities are expected to compete for private investment, human capital, and tourism (Buffel et al. 2012; Buffel and Phillipson 2016). There is also an underlying assumption that local policy actors can accomplish age-friendly policy and service provision and very little insight is offered on the urban agents, policies, and institutions necessary (Modlich 2011; Canadian Urban Institute 2011). Under-analyzed in the AFC literature is that austerity urbanism also includes projects of devolution that transfer greater policy and service responsibility to local government and non-profit policy actors without commensurate resource capacity. The ensuing neoliberal policy package includes local tax cuts and social service disinvestment, especially for more vulnerable population groups (Harvey 1989). Common in this context are under-resourced urban policy strategies that target the local symptoms of social policy challenges (Peck 2012; Harvey 1989; Jessop 2009), such as the "priority neighbourhoods" approach to poverty discussed in chapter 2 (United Way Toronto 2005; Horak 2013). As a result, such strategies have been considered merely symbolic and may be dismissed by academic researchers and the public alike. In this book, I have cautioned against such a dismissal. I argue that in-depth analysis of place-based policy work can help to identify how neoliberal austerity actually works (Brenner and Theodore 2002) through ideas and administrative techniques, and how it generates conflicts and tensions that may create openings for alternative ideas and techniques rooted in social and spatial justice.

I speculated from the get-go that such alternative ideas and administrative practices were already present in the work of local government supporting seniors. This is because I believe that cities are not unitary actors that merely implement pre-defined policies but rather that they operate as "landscapes of antagonism" (Newman 2014) where multiple political actors, each with their own ideas, interests, and constraints, work to design and deliver public policy. In addition to translating and managing neoliberal approaches to aging, these ideas and practices might use AFCs to expand the role of the state to enhance equity and democracy for senior citizens. As such, I adopted a "seeing like a city" perspective that incorporates all of the different actors, institutions, and ideas operating in local spaces (Magnussen 2011). This form of critical analysis contributes to the literature on AFCs as it seeks to identify the ideas and practices that challenge the program, and in doing so offers insight into how the program might be made more substantive. Understanding how local policy actors make sense of their work is also crucial for political science analysis, as they are increasingly key agents in the delivery of public goods and the design of policy solutions to pressing social, political, economic, and environmental problems (Katz and Bradley 2013; Barber 2013). Given the prevalence of place-based policy or "task specific" rescaling (Bradford 2007; Horak 2013) in addressing major social policy issues today, a critical study of AFCs can tell us much about our capacity as a society to take care of each other.

I build on Buffel et al.'s (2012) call to study AFCs through a "right to the city" lens where senior citizens have full access to urban space and the amenities they need to survive and thrive. According to Isin (2008), a "right to the city" is a place where citizen similarities and differences are recognized through processes of democratic decision-making and material redistribution characterized by "universal inclusion," or universal programs complemented through niche programs of positive discrimination (Antonnen et al. 2012a). Isin (2008) argues that a right to the city requires complementary "rights of the city," or the resources and institutional mechanisms to actualize an expansive recognition and redistribution role. At the same time, cities are places affected by a multitude of political authorities that simultaneously affect the everyday experiences of citizens. As such, Isin (2008) argues that realizing the rights of the city will likely require new forms of inter-governmental or "translocal" policy action and institution-building. I argue that the rights of the city must also incorporate the rights of the non-profit sector representing citizens. Here I am informed by the work of Clavel (2010), who argues that a progressive city requires organized groups of non-profit organizations working with and pushing against local government administration. I adopt Isin's (2008) right to the city framework, including its three elements of redistribution, recognition, and the rights of the city to examine the three claims that AFCs improve local environments, promote a positive aging identity, and empower local policy actors.

Toronto presents an ideal case to study the anatomy of AFCs contextually, qualitatively, and critically (Merriam 1988; Flyvbjerg 2006). Toronto is a classic "landscape of antagonism" (Newman 2014): a big and diverse city with respect to its geography, social service landscape and infrastructure responsibility, and administrative structure. These features have been intensified through public-sector restructuring that has included a provincially mandated amalgamation and local service realignment (Joy and Vogel 2015). Toronto is also diverse in its demographics, which are being augmented through population growth, immigration, and aging. Finally, at the time of my research, Toronto had recently adopted the *Toronto Seniors Strategy* based on the WHO AFC framework and this strategy was being critiqued for being more symbolic than substantive (Goar 2013). I interviewed eighty-two policy actors, including city councillors, city staff, non-profit staff, senior citizens, representatives from the federal and Ontario government, and specialized policy experts. My research goal was to offer insights about aging-in-place policy through the lens of the actors undertaking this work on an everyday basis in Toronto. This concluding chapter brings together my findings to offer insights about the cultural and material changes needed to develop a right to the city for senior citizens both in Toronto and more broadly.

Improving Local Environments

Local environments are crucial for Toronto seniors because they dictate access to essential services and amenities. Place is thus an important lens through which to study gaps and inequities in access to public services for different population groups, and to identify the need for new forms of redistribution based on a model of universal inclusion. Here, participants identified a host of environmental problems in Toronto, such as a lack of accessible, appropriate, and affordable housing, transportation, and health care, as well as fragmentation and inequities in access to these services and amenities across neighbourhoods. There is ongoing controversy about city shelters operating at over capacity; housing prices skyrocketing; growing waitlists for public housing; public transit fares increasing; the subway system chronically malfunctioning; library workers facing job insecurity due to the increasing trend to "staff-less libraries"; and increases in pedestrian fatalities with seniors most at risk.

As I prepare this conclusion in the context of the COVID-19 pandemic, those over the age of seventy have been advised by Ontario's chief medical officer of health to self-isolate. Senior citizens are the most at risk of dying from the coronavirus and the pandemic has illuminated how our underinvestment in public services has created further risks for seniors and those who care for them. The situation in Ontario's long-term care facilities was so dire that the Canadian Armed Forces were called in to provide support. Military personnel documented both the lack of sufficient personal protective equipment for workers and understaffed facilities that left senior citizens without having their basic needs met (Carter 2020). As of 6 May 2020, senior citizens living in long-term care settings, as well as staff working in these facilities, have made up 82 percent of Canada's coronavirus deaths (MacCharles 2020). Such deaths have been considerably higher in for-profit homes (9 percent) as compared to those run by the non-profit sector (5.2 percent) and municipal government (3.62 percent) (Ontario Health Coalition 2020). In addition, death rates are increasing in both for-profit and non-profit homes at the rates of 28.52 percent and 14.15 percent respectively, yet are declining in municipal homes where the rate is -18.46 percent (Ontario Health Coalition 2020). This illustrates the importance of maintaining and investing in public services to support senior citizens. My research highlighted a mismatch between how most participants understand the scale of the problem of access and affordability to services and amenities for senior citizens and what is being done about it in Toronto. Large commitments and investments in the local environment, and particularly in the areas of supportive housing, accessible transportation, and home care, are unheeded in favour of pilot projects to activate seniors, community volunteers, the non-profit sector, and local government to fill gaps in social and physical infrastructures. While it is wonderful that the city has committed to budget $150,000 for a seniors' community transportation pilot project in Scarborough, this fully satisfies the *Toronto Seniors Strategy* action to fund community groups to increase non-medical transportation options for older adults (City of Toronto 2015b). But this is just one project, meagrely funded, on a pilot basis, and nowhere does the *Toronto Seniors Strategy* talk about expanding Wheel Trans services or the Community Bus Routes provided through the Toronto Transit Commission. A second version of the *Toronto Seniors Strategy*, passed by council in May 2018, continues to make no mention of these accessible forms of transportation, instead promising to develop a training program to teach seniors how to use public transit and an awareness program directed to transit riders to encourage a culture of civility towards and respect for senior citizens (City of Toronto 2018).

The AFC movement is occurring in a context where local policy actors have already been transferred greater responsibility for public services and amenities through previous rounds of public-sector restructuring. This has led to a crisis in social service provision and physical infrastructure in Toronto, particularly in the areas of social housing, long-term care, and public transportation. Local government struggles to maintain its aging infrastructure, let alone make investments to improve accessibility and affordability. The city cannot even afford to support non-profit agencies to transport seniors to a library or shovel the snow in front of a seniors' home, let alone invest publicly in Wheel Trans and snow removal. Several city staff members remarked on the tension between what they understand as efficiency and equity in a context where they are measured foremost on short-term cost effectiveness. They also complain that they are continuously required to freeze or reduce their budgets to meet municipal budget shortfalls because council refuses to increase the property tax rate above the rate of inflation or use other taxing powers at its disposal. By voting for these cuts, city council is ignoring its own policy direction to support Toronto seniors. This is also a matter of political decision-making regarding where to direct revenue. In the wake of widespread protests in Canada and the United States against police brutality against Black and Indigenous peoples and people of colour, councillors Josh Matlow and Kristyn Wong-Tam have tabled a motion to defund Toronto's police force by 10 percent. It is estimated that this would result in savings of up to $122 million that could be spent on other community initiatives (Casey 2020), such as elder abuse prevention programs.

Where competition for money is fierce and the social investment approach to social policy is dominant (Saint-Martin 2007; Chen 2008), some staff members admit that city programming for youth and newcomers provides more "value for money" than programming for seniors. However, more and more seniors are placing demands on emergency services, so the city is increasingly concerned about targeting those with the most acute needs: those who end up in shelters and use paramedic services, for instance. Similarly, the non-profit sector is contracted by the province to assist seniors with acute health challenges to prevent them from entering hospitals and long-term care homes and, increasingly, to care for them when they are released back into the community. Where need is growing and public investment is waning, non-profit organizations are taking on more social and physical infrastructure in the big-ticket AFC domains of housing, transit, and health care. However, small-scale pilot programs cannot replace the need for universal redistribution in these policy areas at other levels of government. Both local government and non-profit staff admit that they are struggling to invest in prevention-oriented programming and these programs are increasingly subject to user fees and means testing. In some policy domains such as elder abuse, the city's role working with non-profits to reach out to seniors has been discontinued.

Substantive redistributive policy investments by all governments in the areas of health care, housing, and transportation are essential foundations for the social determinants of health and without them, the local government and non-profit sectors are scrambling to meet increasingly complex, acute, and emergency needs. In this context of restructuring, improvements in local environments cannot be made by residual policy efforts alone and my research suggests the need for a much more coordinated effort to engage in universal service provision through the AFC program. Ball and Lawler (2014) agree, arguing that the "exclusive focus on pilots, forums, and toolkit resources is potentially a new form of disengagement, trading the denial of the 20th century for procrastination in the 21st" (20). The authors critique both the literature and practice of AFCs for its fleeting and faddish nature and unambitious incrementalism and argue that large-scale paradigmatic change or "creative destruction" is needed to truly achieve age-friendly places. Ball and Lawler (2014) advise that this scale of change requires a response that can only be undertaken via leadership on the part of the state. My research strongly suggests that this is true in Toronto and that all levels of the state need to be involved in realizing AFCs.

Promoting a Positive Aging Identity

I found the claims that the movement towards AFCs necessarily supports a move away from a negative aging identity incorrect in the Toronto case, as many participants continued to see aging as a problem of cost amid a growing "non-contributing" population. There is a general concern among participants that population aging will result in a crisis to our welfare systems, particularly in the realm of health care. Governments are at once worried about a fiscal crisis associated with population aging because of reduced labour and greater dependency, as well as what they see as a moral crisis where individuals are inadequately caring for themselves and families, neighbours, and communities are not filling the role.

The dominant cost-effective solution to the "aging crisis" is to prevent or slow it down by encouraging active aging for individual seniors. In this way, AFCs can represent a project of social investment where its dominant value is to save money in present and future public programs (Saint-Martin 2007; Chen 2008). This obsession with saving money operates in fundamental tension with the need for public investment to build and service environments that are socially just. Participants talked about the importance of information campaigns and service programs targeting the behaviour of seniors to more actively engage in self care and develop resilience in their local environments. Active seniors are encouraged to keep contributing through employment as well as providing care for spouses, children, grandchildren, and their communities. In fact, the original intent of the AFC approach was to activate grassroots community groups of seniors to improve their local environments, illustrating a co-production agenda (Minkler and Martinson 2007; Newman and

Clarke 2009) from conceptualization. We see such an agenda at play with the *Toronto Seniors Strategy* as the city is using its policy advisory group of seniors, the Toronto Seniors Forum, to advertise its own work and, in so doing, limit the advocacy role of this group. But the co-production agenda is flexible and could involve such groups replacing the role of the state or working in partnership with a more mobilized state.

In addition to language of "prevention through activation," I found a great anxiety among participants about those seniors with the most acute needs who use or are at risk of using emergency services, particularly in the realm of health care. The *Toronto Seniors Strategy* and the work of many non-profits in the city is predominantly focused on this group. I found that seniors are targeted according to the degree of risk that they present to society, and those whose needs are the costliest are prioritized (Newman and Clarke 2009). This residual approach to social policy, whereby local governments and non-profit organizations become last-resort service providers, can encourage seniors to feel ashamed for having needs while others are seen as healthy, able-bodied contributors. This targeting envisions little collective response to the desires and needs of seniors, nor does it understand how public policies that fail to heed these needs create greater vulnerability. We see this to some degree with the *Toronto Seniors Strategy*, in both its first and second versions, which narrowly delineate the city's jurisdictional role in its support for seniors and limit the discussion topics in its public consultations to only those problems the city can "solve." That said, this residual approach is challenged by several city and non-profit sector employees who argue that more systems-oriented work that tackles the roots of inequality in cities is needed.

The "aging as a crisis" metaphor illustrates how the AFC program does not necessarily promote a positive aging identity, as it may still embody the assumptions that aging is bad and that seniors must prevent themselves from becoming a burden on their families and society. This is a framing where vulnerability, need, and ultimately care are considered a drain on society rather than rights of citizenship. There is an unproblematized assumption here that dependence and vulnerability are negative, even unnatural human states, whereas independence, self-care, and economic contribution are positive and normal. Public programs such as long-term care and supportive housing are believed by some to segregate seniors and encourage their dependency and passivity while limiting their voice and empowerment. The risk is that these public programs of care, that are desperately needed, will get dismissed as "ageist" because they assume that seniors are vulnerable and needy (Dannefer et al. 2008). As such, large programs of care for seniors are subject to underinvestment in favour of programs that activate seniors and thus offer value for money by limiting future health care costs. Rather than focusing on the social rights of senior citizens in place, the "active aging" approach on which AFCs are based can also be used to support the claim that seniors are no different than everyone else and thus do not need special treatment (Biggs and Carr 2015). My interviews illustrate considerable emphasis on aging as an opportunity to make environmental improvements for all population groups and not just seniors; however, this understanding also risks ignoring the distinct needs of senior citizens aging in place. These needs have been made more visible in the context of the COVID-19 pandemic. In the wake of the pandemic, there will likely be more calls to invest in aging in place as the population at large now fears long-term care facilities. The risk here is that this could lead to further underinvestment in long-term care. Yet, we will continue to need these 24-hour care facilities just as we will need home care and other social and recreational services. My research suggests that it is important to incorporate long-term care homes into the AFC model so that they are available in neighbourhoods and are redesigned as community places. Toronto has made strides here to incorporate long-term care into its AFC strategy and has used AFC principles to align these facilities with community needs. Yet both the first and second versions of the *Toronto Seniors Strategy* make clear that further improvements to these facilities require money from central governments. The pandemic has illustrated systemic ageism in the most horrific way. These facilities are in dire need of public investment to protect the rights of senior citizens.

I argue that the problem with ageism is not equating aging with vulnerability and dependency but the underlying consensus that vulnerability and dependency are fundamentally abnormal and negative human states (Joy 2018). The reality is that as we age, we are faced with new vulnerabilities such as health challenges and the deaths of loved ones, and this is absolutely normal. Abrahamson (2015) explains that how we manage these vulnerabilities depends very much on our identities and how they are linked to systems of inequity such as class, race, and gender and, of course, whether we live in societies that provide care to meet our needs.

Vulnerability because of old age is a complex intermingling of biological and social characteristics that must be more fully recognized in order to design adequate policy responses. My research illustrates that aging as a form of difference is being ignored by narrow political projects that seek to limit more substantive redistribution, and that the AFC program does not fundamentally challenge this willful blindness. For this reason, the program can be limited in improving the lives of seniors. My research illustrates Buffel et al.'s (2014) warning that "the idea of age-friendliness itself carries limitations unless linked to wider debates about rights and citizenship with the urban environment" (68) and this means fundamentally challenging our ideas about ageism and what a positive aging identity really means.

Empowering Local Policy Actors

Participants agree that the local government and non-profit sector are on the frontlines when it comes to serving seniors and see this as a good thing. Particularly prevalent are notions of local actors operating in closer proximity to "ordinary citizens" (Newman and Clarke 2009) than other levels of government and thus being better able to serve them. While local government and the non-profit sector may have their own insights into the needs of seniors, they currently have the least capacity to redistribute services and engage in substantive policy programs (Joy et al. 2018). Nonetheless, because this vantage point addresses bureaucratic professionalism by humanizing service provision and addressing diverse needs, it is also understood as an ideal site for pilot programs to responsibilize seniors or target the most vulnerable. In this case, the local can be understood to reduce the role of the state and enhance the role of individuals, families, communities and the non-profit sector to care for seniors as a residual strategy.

Participants envisioned a role for local policy actors as important advocates based on their day to day recognition of access and equity challenges for senior citizens. Non-profits and local government can advocate for improvements to universal policy at other levels of government and develop niche programs to address difference. While this illustrates an important role for local government and non-profit organizations in a model of universal inclusion (Antonnen et al. 2012a), the policy and administrative structures needed to facilitate this were not well understood by participants. This policy advocacy role is challenged by the degree of anti-statism and anti-politics prevalent in the current conjuncture. Several participants blamed inadequacies in actioning AFCs on seemingly insincere, self-interested, and conservative politicians and bureaucrats.

The *Toronto Seniors Strategy* does represent an effort to understand the role of local government in fostering age-friendly environments and supporting senior citizens across the vast bureaucracy. Thus, there is an effort to devise a persuasive institutional discourse (Lowndes 2009) to recognize and redistribute to senior citizens. However, this form of "positive discrimination" is challenged by an ideology of procedural universalism (Antonnen et al. 2012b) according to which special treatment for senior citizens is seen as unfair to other population groups, thus leading to a focus on improvements that are "age-friendly for all." Staff are also reluctant to admit that they serve seniors because they are provided with no institutional incentives (Lowndes 2009) to action their recommendations as the *Toronto Seniors Strategy* is unfunded. Furthermore, the *Toronto Seniors Strategy* has no power of institutional sanction (Lowndes 2009) as there are no paid staff dedicated solely to coordinate implementation, and the one staff member charged to support implementation has no power to enforce the strategy. These governance challenges are exacerbated in a big-city context of public-sector restructuring where service responsibility and demand has increased (Horak 2012). There is concern among some staff that admitting that they serve seniors will see their already unsustainable service demands increase, despite the fact that they are operating without adequate policy and funding support from central governments. There is a fear that AFCs may represent more devolution in the realm of health care. In this case, senior citizens are understood as "health problems" that are foremost under provincial jurisdiction. Here, narrow practices of restructuring solidify the discourse that seniors are a burden (Joy 2018).

In the Toronto case, there are challenges to developing the political leadership necessary to move the strategy forward with respect to funding, policy, and administrative tools. This has been made much more difficult where the political wards are massive post-amalgamation and different policy issues and their advocates compete for attention from local councillors, and will likely become even more challenging because

Ontario premier Doug Ford unilaterally increased the size of Toronto wards and cut the size of council in half. The fact that Toronto is prevented by the province from operating local political parties may also make it more difficult for councillors to build coalitions. Obtaining greater insight on these issues merits further case based and comparative urban politics research.

There are also significant institutional changes in the non-profit sector serving seniors that challenge their capacity to advocate for AFC policy and to deliver AFC services. There is pressure on the sector to become bigger, more marketized, and more professionalized as it is contracted by the province to take on more of a support role for increasingly acute "patients" (O'Connor 2004; DeSantis 2013). As such, non-profits relate in their policy focus more to the provincial health care sector and less to the social service and community development work of local government, despite the discourse of health promotion. Several agencies spoke to me about pressure to merge to address increasing needs of seniors and the fragmentation of services for them, particularly in the domains of health care, housing, and transportation. Several agencies, and particularly small non-profits, are concerned about their ability to provide personalized services and to inform AFC policy as they are bombarded with demands from seniors with increasingly acute health challenges. This has led to staff burnout and turnover (Shields 2014; Baines et al. 2014; Hardill and Baines 2011; Chouinard and Crooks 2008), a precariousness that is particularly problematic for seniors who benefit from familiarity and agencies that operate like an "extended family."

My findings illustrate that the diversity of the non-profit sector is not being respected and, paradoxically given the localized nature of AFCs, it is the smaller agencies that are most at risk. This economization of the non-profit sector challenges the ability of agencies to develop innovative niche programs and to inform wider, more universal policy domains such as health, housing, and transportation. Local actors become emergency providers of last resort while, at the same time, they are expected to fill gaps in universal provision to the extent that they are becoming core public service providers. Large unelected agencies are becoming the new public service providers, making decisions about who is worthy of recognition and redistribution. This raises a larger question about democracy in the current era and, as the sector is asked to prove positive health outcomes, whether value for money should be the sole guide for accountability. State retreat in the realm of redistribution is legitimized via localization, but in doing so, the state is becoming increasingly controlling and coercive, which limits the ability of local actors to provide personalized service that addresses difference, enhances access, improves self-worth, and promotes democracy (Evans and Shields, 2010; Shields 2014; Wells 2008).

At the time of the original *Toronto Senior Strategy* development, the City of Toronto lacked a formal governance structure to incorporate advice from the non-profit sector in the field of aging. While there was a desire to engage in coalition-building within the non-profit sector, ad hoc advisory committees of experts appeared too busy to actively push for *Toronto Seniors Strategy* implementation. The city's formal advisory committee of senior citizens was also struggling to check in on strategy implementation in a confusing bureaucratic landscape, while much of their organizing time was being used to legitimate the city's own AFC work. The Toronto Seniors Forum's struggles have led to some effort to establish coherent advocacy within the bureaucratic structure and to engage in coalition-building with other senior citizen advocates. Small agencies wanted to be active in AFC development but did not know how to advocate in such a fragmented system. Overall, I found that non-profits are valued more as service agencies than as critical policy voices by city staff. However, some advocates have been able to insert themselves into participatory processes and reorient policy discussions. This work on the part of senior citizen advocates to democratize the local state through the AFC program should be the subject of further research. The *Toronto Seniors Strategy* progress report indicated that an accountability table that includes both city staff and some of the non-profits as well as policy experts from the expert panel was being struck to support the implementation of the strategy (City of Toronto 2015b). The second version of the *Toronto Seniors Strategy* clarifies that this is now a formal Accountability Table. There are members of the Toronto Seniors Forum on the table, and apparently more support is being given to the forum to enhance their role. Further research to update this case should assess whether this Accountability Table equates to a real voice in decision-making for non-profits and senior citizens and the impact of this voice on implementation of the *Toronto Seniors Strategy.*

My findings suggest that AFCs do not actualize the rights of the city in the Toronto case. I find that other levels of government laud local government and non-profits as key actors actioning AFCs without designating and solidifying the rights of the city, illustrating either a troubling naiveté or a lack of sincerity. There are very few resources to support the development and implementation of AFC strategies locally other than small-scale grants and information guides for local actors voluntarily adopting the AFC framework. Cities and non-profits are expected to engage in both service delivery and policy work, while other levels of government steward this process and blame local actors when their capacity is limited. Although there is rhetoric about health prevention, the real motivation appears to be to save money on hospitals and long-term care facilities rather than focusing on wellbeing that requires significant public investment in supportive housing, home care, and public transportation. Ball and Lawler (2014) argue that "without a strategic framework that provides broader context for local initiatives and helps to clear the way at the federal and state levels, pilot programs will rely too heavily on the ingenuity, energy, and bureaucratic acrobatics of highly motivated individuals and organizations willing to swim upstream against policies that do not provide the options people need throughout their lifetimes" (25). The Toronto case illustrates this empirically. For other levels of government, AFCs are more about "do it yourself urbanism" (Iveson 2013) than real policy openings, illustrating a form of "shallow decentralization" (Banting 2010) at the root of place-based policy.

My findings suggest a paradox: AFCs claim to broaden the role of local policy actors but actually narrow them by burdening them with more and more unrealistic demands. Local government focuses only on those items within its jurisdiction despite growing need, and the non-profit sector is increasingly refusing to meet unrealistic demands to squeeze more out of less. While these are understandable responses, they are obviously not in the best interests of senior citizens. Rather than this crisis creating an opportunity for actors to innovate, as is posited in the "new localism" literature (Katz and Bradley 2013; Barber 2013), they are becoming more rigid in their behaviours because further innovation requires the rights of the city. This is a serious problem because need for social services and amenities based on a model of universal inclusion will only grow with population aging.

In the context of the pandemic, just as urban services and amenities that keep people safe both in the community and in long-term care settings are needed the most, cities such as Toronto face unprecedented budget shortfalls. Toronto's city manager has estimated that the pandemic could cost municipal government between $1.5 to $2.8 billion in 2020 alone, a sum that will result in drastic service cuts and rising user fees (City of Toronto 2020). Toronto and other cities in Canada are calling for crisis funding from central governments (Federation of Canadian Municipalities 2020). A movement is also building among Canadian cities for more systemic change that includes consistent funding transfers and new revenue tools (City of Toronto 2020). Similarly, Imagine Canada – the national advocate for the charitable non-profit sector – is calling on the federal government to initiate a grant program to address an estimated $9.5 to $15.7 billion in financial loses and to support the sector in recovery efforts (Imagine Canada 2020). These are all rallying cries for the rights of the city, but they require local non-profits, charitable and otherwise, to work with municipal governments in a formalized recovery effort. In the realm of seniors' care, these voices could be aligned through the AFC approach.

Moving Forward

Identifying tensions and contradictions in the everyday practice of AFCs is the first step in searching for openings for more expansive discourses and actions based on a model of universal inclusion. In this way, the Toronto case offers broader insights for how the AFC program could more substantially improve local environments, promote a positive aging identity, and empower local policy actors.

Perhaps the most central and troublesome finding from my research is the normalization of a fundamentally dehumanizing and ageist neoliberal discourse that equates human worth with economic contribution and considers dependency and care as a burden. Those scholars and activists fighting for rights-based AFCs must understand, critique, and challenge the instrumentalization of human life. Rather than seeking to change or activate seniors to fit this economization of citizenship, I argue that a positive aging identity recognizes seniors as citizens fundamentally worthy of social and physical infrastructure supports in local environments (Buffel et al. 2014). Rights-based AFCs would be founded on a recognition of the complex vulnerabilities that come with age. This recognition understands these vulnerabilities as worthy of public care that is universal and tailored to unique needs as well as socialized. At the same time, Biggs and Carr (2015) remind us that while AFCs should create new channels to make more substantive claims on urban space based on citizenship rights, there is a need to better understand and theorize citizenship beyond economic contribution that involves emotion, play, leisure, solidarity, and creativity. In other words, seniors should have the right to play and to relax. Rights-based AFCs must ensure that all seniors have access to the social services and physical amenities that they need to survive and thrive. We can understand the latter as access to parks, libraries, and community centre programming that support these quality of life endeavours. If we seek to enhance human life, these pursuits must be valued intrinsically, not just because they produce more active seniors who are less burdensome to the health care system.

Local government and non-profits may be best situated to recognize senior citizens, given their role in the design and delivery of human services and physical amenities. An expansive process of recognition is much more extensive than one-off consultations, bounded to specific jurisdictional policy domains. This process must be thorough and ongoing because it requires understanding the experiences, desires, and needs of seniors in all their diverse identities living in every corner of the city. This could consist of more localized processes of recognition in neighbourhoods through the development of social planning structures that better understand issues of geographic fragmentation in access to services and amenities. This is a process of recognition that necessitates both quantitative data collection on the use of different services disaggregated to different identities based on age, income, gender, and ethnicity for instance, as well as more qualitative research on the experiences of services to identify where there might be gaps, overlaps, and great programming that should be expanded. Within these neighbourhoods, specific groups of seniors, such as LGBTQ+ elders, should be identified for deliberative initiatives to involve them in program decision-making.

A more localized process of recognition could inform city-wide AFC policy programs and form the basis for an intersectional seniors' policy lens applied to all local government organizations. All existing and new policy could be required to go through this lens, which would examine how seniors in their differing identities might be affected and how any potential problems would be addressed. An "age-friendly for all" city could design various lenses specific to different age groups – children, youth, young adults, the middle-aged, senior citizens – based on an understanding of intersecting and niche needs. Age lenses could also be intersected with other diversity dimensions in each age cohort such as ability, income, ethnicity, sexuality, and gender. This would require forms of research where local actors differentiate each age group to assess their needs, examine how this intersects with other diversity characteristics, and then examine how these needs are both similar and different from other age cohorts and how they conflict and cooperate in shared space. This could then form the basis for a wider age-friendly city strategy that focuses on meeting the needs of citizens through the life cycle; one that seeks to foster intergenerational solidarity. This would mean going beyond the AFC framework to address, for instance, intergenerational issues of caregiving where seniors provide care to grandchildren as well as where children provide care to parents.

The second version of the *Toronto Seniors Strategy* advises that a much more concerted effort to seek out diverse senior voices was sought. There is a greater focus on senior citizen employment, via the promise to work with community partners to develop a workplace anti-ageism campaign and to expand employment supports, targeted to those who already receive social assistance. There is also a promise on the part of the city to work with community partners to develop a public awareness and education campaign to address homophobia and transphobia affecting seniors (City of Toronto 2018). The second version of the strategy also commits to working with the province and community partners to develop a Toronto Caregiving Strategy aimed at informal caregivers of senior citizens. While this direction is important, there is a lack of clarity as to the role of the city in resourcing these "community partnerships," what looks to be a focus on developing awareness campaigns and resource guides over and above funding support for city staff and agencies, and a continued targeting of programs. Further research should explore the ways in which these initiatives meet the needs of Toronto seniors and their caregivers.

This work requires a "seeing like a city" lens on the part of local policy actors. These actors must remain open and curious about the ways in which areas under the domain of different levels and departments of the state intersect in local places and in the lives of seniors citizens, rather than remaining confined only to what is within the jurisdictional mandate of local government. Furthermore, this work must strive to inform central governments who claim to support AFCs about the lived reality of their own policies, such as fragmented geographic access to public health programs or the lack of health care support for newcomer seniors. This work requires time, effort, and dedicated resources to provide outreach to seniors and their organizations and to develop trust and lasting partnerships. Local policy actors are well positioned to bring all these factors together through research and collaborative approaches, which is what is potentially progressive about the place-based policy agenda. Such an approach is not possible without significant institutional development and resources.

One example of such an institutional development would be a municipal aging office that is funded and staffed to engage in ongoing research and the policy design and implementation of AFC strategies and action plans. This office could coordinate city departments and special-purpose bodies, age-related training protocols, and enforce policy lenses and age-friendly actions to address problems. This office would be bolstered by an advisory committee consisting of senior citizens, policy advocacy organizations, and service providers who could be organized by neighbourhood and linked to local social planning offices. We are seeing some institutional work being done in the second version of the *Toronto Seniors Strategy*, which now has one full-time staff member dedicated to the file and commits to developing a new seniors' housing and services entity. It is not clear whether this entity would be part of a new "aging" office that also convenes policy work. Politicians and municipal political parties, should they exist, need to think much more extensively about the types of institutional innovations needed in local government to design and action substantive AFCs. This is also an important avenue for further research on AFCs.

A municipal aging office could create a clear space for non-profits to direct their advocacy, working both in partnership with and to push the city, as in Clavel's (2010) progressive city model. It is especially important for progressive non-profit movements to problematize homogeneous and undifferentiated understandings of the state and politics in order to seek out, work with, and push its more expansive agents and institutional elements (Graefe 2002). A broader coalition of advocacy and service non-profit agencies rallying behind the AFC concept as an effort to enhance everyday access to services and amenities for senior citizens in cities is crucial. These agencies must challenge the assumption of vulnerability as a burden, reframing it as both a normal and socially produced feature of life deserving of a collective response. This is a response whereby these agencies play a fundamental role through personalized care, innovative community development activities, engaging volunteers, community-based research, as well as policy advocacy based on local expertise. This also requires that the non-profit sector advocate for public investment in the social determinants of health such as supportive housing, hospital and long-term care, and accessible public transit, rather than attempting to take over these service domains.

AFCs must promote the rights of the non-profit sector that respect its ability to represent and service diverse seniors and advocate for policy. This means that AFC research and practice must understand the work and needs of non-profit agencies representing and supporting seniors in different policy areas. This work should be undertaken with non-profit agencies to inform a clear role for the sector in designing and implementing AFC strategies in partnership with government. Supporting the rights of the sector means that all "levels" and departments of the state that fund non-profits must provide the financial and legislated support to enhance the wages and benefits of workers, offer grants that cover core and project costs, design evergreen contracts to enhance the stability of agencies and programs, and design institutional structures where the sector can inform policy decision-making (Shields 2014; Janes 2008; Phillips and Smith 2010; Graefe 2002).

AFCs based on a right to the city, and especially in the Canadian context of federalism, must be by nature intergovernmental. This requires a much more coordinated effort at place-based policymaking and institution-building than currently exists. An intergovernmental AFC body situated at the federal level of government could outline the policy responsibilities of all levels of government in each domain of the AFC framework and create an associated map for non-profit organizations working locally in these areas; coordinate and resource the design of AFC strategies and action plans at all levels of government; coordinate the development and implementation of an intersectional seniors lens to policy at the federal level and create toolkits for how to undertake this work at the provincial and local government levels; and pool funding to support big ticket infrastructure improvements as well as smaller niche projects to address diverse needs in place. The latter point is crucial, as AFCs based on a right to the city require the federal and provincial governments to invest much more substantially in health care, affordable housing, public transit, and infrastructure such that these policy domains are appropriate, affordable, and accessible to seniors. The extensive recognition process required by local governments and non-profit organizations in AFC development would inform these wider policy domains based on local experience and hence should be funded through an intergovernmental AFC body.

Given the federal and provincial dependence on the work of local governments and non-profit organizations to deliver supports to senior citizens, more formal coalition-building between these local actors to advocate for central government policy support for AFCs coordinated through an intergovernmental AFC body is needed. Such pressure on central governments could also be exerted at the international scale by the cities participating in the WHO's Global Network for Age-Friendly Cities and Communities to push for the development of a United Nations Convention on the Rights of Older People. This activism is only more relevant in the wake of the pandemic and the horrific rights abuses experienced by senior citizens. Local governments and non-profits could call other levels of government to account in their claims to support AFCs by working with researchers to estimate the costs of a substantive AFC program plan that includes accessible and affordable transportation, appropriate and affordable housing, home care, and infrastructure improvements that can then be contrasted with inadequate seed funding on the part of other levels of government. Ball and Lawler (2014) recommend designing AFC indicators that measure how local projects have informed and shifted specific higher-level policy that causes problems on the ground. This requires ways to measure intra- and inter-governmental cooperation, such as the breaking down of silos within departments, across departments, and between levels of government (Ball and Lawler 2014). This institutional work should be the focus of further research on AFCs and on place-based policy more broadly. A group of mainly health researchers has begun to advocate for a National Seniors Strategy in Canada and this can be more clearly linked, with the help of political science and policy studies researchers, to the policy and administrative challenges of local governments and non-profits doing this work in local places.

APPENDIX

Interview Guide

The interview guide below is comprehensive, and in practice differed slightly in length and depth depending on the participant in question to reflect their level of involvement in AFCs in Toronto specifically and as experts more broadly and to reflect their level of involvement in the embedded case of the *Toronto Senior Strategy* development and implementation.

Interview Guide

A. POLICY ISSUE

1. How have you been involved in the area of population aging?
2. How important is it to understand population aging from a local policy perspective?
   a. Is there anything unique about population aging in big cities, generally and in Toronto?
3. How is population aging a challenge and an opportunity for cities?

B. POLICY RESPONSE

4. Have you noticed a general trend towards more local responses to population aging, such as Age-Friendly Cities?
   a. Based on your experiences working with seniors, are there any challenges and opportunities associated with this trend?
5. How does local policy action in response to population aging fit within the broader field of aging policy at other levels of government?
6. How was your (Division, Organization) involved in the development of the *Toronto Seniors Strategy?*
   a. Has your work changed with the development of the *Toronto Seniors Strategy*?
7. What do you think motivated the development of the *Toronto Seniors Strategy* (or local aging strategies more broadly)?
8. What would you say is the core purpose of the *Toronto Seniors Strategy* (or local aging strategies more broadly)?
9. Do you think that the policy actions contained in the *Toronto Senior Strategy* can address the opportunities and challenges of local population aging?
10. How will the policy actions contained in the *Toronto Seniors Strategy* be implemented?
11. How will the *Toronto Seniors Strategy* be sustained in future political contexts?

C. POLICY ACTORS

12. What is the role of local government to respond to population aging?
    a. Did you find that there was a real opening for city staff to be creative in their role in developing the *Toronto Seniors Strategy?*
    b. How do different city departments work together to address population aging through the *Toronto Seniors Strategy*?
13. What is the role of the non-profit sector to respond to population aging?
14. What is the relationship between local government and the non-profit sector in responding to population aging?

a. Is there anything unique about the relationship between local government and the non-profit sector?
   i. Does the city actively outreach to and support non-profits to engage in service delivery and to inform policy in the field of aging?
b. How was the non-profit sector involved in the development of the *Toronto Seniors Strategy*?
c. Does the *Toronto Seniors Strategy* support and strengthen the role of the non-profit sector in the field of population aging?

15. What is the role of local residents in developing policy responses to population aging?
    a. How were local residents involved in the development of the *Toronto Seniors Strategy*?
    b. How does the city ensure that a diversity of resident voices are heard?
16. What is the role of other levels of government to support the development of local aging strategies?

D. POLICY CAPACITY

17. Does local government have the adequate resources and capacity to address the opportunities and challenges of local population aging?
18. Has the city encountered any political challenges developing and implementing the *Toronto Seniors Strategy*?
19. Has the city encountered any administrative challenges developing and implementing the *Toronto Seniors Strategy*?
20. Do non-profit organizations have the adequate resources and capacity to meet the needs of local seniors?
21. Are the resources and capacities of local government and non-profit organizations taken into account by other levels of government that promote aging in place and age-friendly communities?
    a. Are there efforts at other levels of government to support cities and non-profit agencies struggling to serve aging populations?
    b. Are local government and non-profit policy actors able to inform and influence aging policy at other levels of government?

REFERENCES

Abrahamson, C.M. 2015. *The End Game: How Inequality Shapes Our Final Years*. Cambridge, MA: Harvard University Press.

Anttonnen, A., L. Haikio, K. Stefansson, and J. Sipila. 2012a. "Universalism and the Challenge of Diversity." In *Welfare State, Universalism and Diversity*, edited by A. Anttonen, L. Haikio, and K. Stefansson, 1–15. Cheltenham: Edward Elgar.

Anttonnen, A., L. Haikio, and K. Stefansson. 2012b. "The Future of the Welfare State: Rethinking Universalism." In *Welfare State, Universalism and Diversity*, edited by A. Anttonen, L. Haikio, and K. Stefansson, 187–96. Cheltenham: Edward Elgar.

Association of Municipalities of Ontario. 2011. *Coming of Age: The Municipal Role in Caring for Ontario's Seniors*. Toronto: Author.

Bacchi, C. 2009. *Analysing Policy: What's the Problem Represented to Be?* Australia: Pearson.

Baines, D., J. Campey, I. Cunningham, and J. Shields. 2014. "Not Profiting from Precarity: The Work of Nonprofit Service Delivery and the Creation of Precariousness." *Just Labour: A Canadian Journal of Work and Society* 22: 74–93.

Ball, S., and K. Lawler. 2014. "Changing Practice and Policy to Move to Scale: A Framework for Age-Friendly Communities across the United States." *Journal of Aging and Social Policy* 26: 19–32.

Banting, K. 2010. "Decentralization, Welfare, and Social Citizenship in Contemporary Democracies." *Environment and Planning C: Government and Policy* 28: 381–8.

Banting, K., and J. Myles. 2013. "Introduction: Inequality and the Fading of Redistributive Politics." In *Inequality and the Fading of Redistributive Politics*, edited by K. Banting and J. Myles, 1–39. Vancouver: UBC Press.

Bar-Nir, D., and J. Gal. 2011. "Who Has the Power? The Role of NPOs in Local Authorities." *Voluntas* 22: 1–25.

Barber, B.R. 2013. *If Mayors Ruled the World: Dysfunctional Nations, Rising Cities*. New Haven, CT: Yale University Press.

Barusch, A. 2013. "Age-Friendly Cities: A Social Work Perspective." *Journal of Gerontological Social Work* 56(6): 465–72.

Berg, B.L. 2009. "Introduction." In *Qualitative Research Methods for the Social Sciences*, 7th ed., by B.L. Berg, 1–20. Boston: Allyn and Bacon.

Biggs, S. 2001. "Toward Critical Narrativity: Stories of Aging in Contemporary Social Policy." *Journal of Aging Studies* 15: 303–16.

– 2008. "Aging in a Critical World: The Search for Generational Intelligence." *Journal of Aging Studies* 22: 115–19.

Biggs, S., and A. Carr, 2015. "Age- and Child-Friendly Cities and the Promise of Intergenerational Space." *Journal of Social Work Practice* 29(1): 99–112.

Boudreau, J.A., R. Keil, and D. Young. 2009. *Changing Toronto: Governing Urban Neoliberalism*. Toronto: University of Toronto Press.

Brenner, N. and N. Theodore. 2002. "Cities and Geographies of 'Actually Existing Neoliberalism.'" *Antipode* 34(3): 349–79.

Brenner, N. 2009. "A Thousand Leaves: Notes on the Geographies of Uneven Spatial Development." In *Leviathan Undone: Towards a Political Economy of Scale*, edited by R. Keil and R. Mahon, 27–50. Vancouver: UBC Press.

Brown, M. 1968. "Home Care Program for Metropolitan Toronto." *Canadian Family Physician* 14 (2): 49–52.

Bradford, N. 2002. *Why Cities Matter: Policy Research Perspectives for Canada*. Ottawa: Canadian Policy Research Networks.

– 2005. *Place-Based Public Policy: Towards a New Urban and Community Agenda for Canada*. Ottawa: Canadian Policy Research Networks.

– 2007. "Placing Social Policy? Reflections on Canada's New Deal for Cities and Communities." *Canadian Journal of Urban Research* 16(2): 1–26.

Buffel, T., C. Phillipson, and T. Scharf. 2012. "Ageing in Urban Environments: Developing 'Age-Friendly' Cities." *Critical Social Policy* 32(4): 597–617.

Buffel, T., P. McGarry, C. Phillipson, L. De Donder, S. Dury, N. De Witte,

A. Smetcoren, and D. Verte. 2014. "Developing Age-Friendly Cities: Case Studies from Brussels and Manchester and Implications for Policy and Practice." *Journal of Aging and Social Policy* 26: 52–72.

Buffel, T., and C. Phillipson. 2016. "Can Global Cities Be 'Age-Friendly Cities'? Urban Development and Ageing Populations." *Cities* 55: 94–100.

Buffel, T., S. Handler, and C. Phillipson, eds. 2019. *Age-Friendly Cities and Communities: A Global Perspective.* Bristol: Policy Press.

Calasanti, T. 2008. "A Feminist Confronts Ageism." *Journal of Aging Studies* 22: 152–7.

Canadian Urban Institute. 2011. *Re-positioning Age-Friendly Communities: Opportunities to Take AFC Mainstream.* Toronto: Author.

Casey, J. 2012. "Impact of the Economic Crisis on the Nonprofit Sector in the United States." In *Taking Stock of Government-Nonprofit Relationships in Times of Recession,* edited by R. Laforest, 41–60. Montreal and Kingston: McGill-Queen's University Press.

Casey, L. 2020. "Toronto Councillors Put Forward Motion to Defund Police Budget by 10 Per Cent." *The Canadian Press.* 8 June. https://www.cp24.com/news/toronto-councillors-put-forward-motion-to-defund-police-budget-by-10-per-cent-1.4974590.

Carter, A. 2020. "Military Report Reveals What Sector Has Long Known: Ontario's Nursing Homes Are in Trouble." CBC News. 27 May. https://www.cbc.ca/news/canada/toronto/military-long-term-care-home-report-covid-ontario-1.5585844.

Charmaz, K. 2006. *Constructing Grounded Theory: A Practical Guide.* London: Sage.

Chen, X. 2008. "The Child-Citizen." In *Recasting the Social in Citizenship,* edited by F.E. Isin, 162–86. Toronto: University of Toronto Press.

Chouinard, V., and V.A. Crooks. 2008. "Negotiating Neoliberal Environments in British Columbia and Ontario, Canada: Restructuring of State-Voluntary Sector Relations and Disability Organizations' Struggle to Survive." *Environment and Planning C: Government and Policy* 26: 173–90.

City of Toronto. 1999. *Toronto – Building a City for All Ages.* Toronto: Toronto Seniors' Taskforce.

– 2002. "A Reconstituted Toronto Seniors Assembly." *Community Services Committee,* 18–19 June. Toronto: Author.

– 2006. *City of Toronto Roundtable on Seniors: Housing Toronto Seniors.* Toronto: Author.

– 2013. *The Toronto Seniors Strategy: Towards an Age-Friendly City.* Toronto: Author.

– 2014. "Staff Report: Improving the Equity Impact Statement." *Executive Committee,* 12 May. Toronto: Author.

– 2015a. "Staff Report: Provincial Funding for Enhanced Long Term Care Renewal Strategy." *Community Development and Recreation Committee,* 24 March. Toronto: Author.

– 2015b. "Progress Report on the Toronto Seniors Strategy." *Community Development and Recreation Committee,* 10 November. Toronto: Author.

– 2016a. "Long-Term Care: Community Programs." http://www1.toronto.ca/wps/portal/contentonly?vgnextoid=8e4b3293dc3ef310VgnVCM10000071d60f89RCRD.

– 2016b. "Mental Health: Vulnerable Adults and Seniors." http://www1.toronto.ca/wps/portal/contentonly?vgnextoid=9a313f66be832410VgnVCM10000071d60f89RCRD.

– 2016c. "Falls Prevention: Prevent Falls in Older Adults." http://www1.toronto.ca/wps/portal/contentonly?vgnextoid=6463214f65a32410VgnVCM10000071d60f89RCRD.

– 2016d. "SPIDER Program – Specialized Interdivisional Enhanced Response." http://www.toronto.ca/311/knowledgebase/01/101002792801.html.

– 2018. *Toronto's Seniors Strategy 2.0.* Toronto: Author.

– 2020. "City of Toronto Response and the Ongoing Management of Emergency City Business during the COVID-19 Pandemic." *City Council.* 27 April. Toronto: Author.

Clarke, J. 2004. "Putting People in Their Place: The Contested Social in Social Policy." In *Changing Welfare, Changing States: New Directions in Social Policy,* by J. Clarke, 52–71. London: Sage Publications.

Clarke, J., J. Newman, N. Smith, E. Vidler, and L. Westmarland. 2007. *Creating Citizen-Consumers: Changing Publics and Changing Public Services.* London: Sage.

Clarke, J., and J. Newman. 2012. "Brave New World? Anglo-American Challenges to Universalism." In *Welfare State, Universalism and Diversity,* edited by A. Anttonen, L. Haikio, and K. Stefansson, 90–105. Cheltenham: Edward Elgar.

Clarke, J., K. Coll, E. Dagnino, and C. Neveu. 2014. *Disputing Citizenship.* Bristol: Policy Press.

Clavel, P. 2010. *Activists in City Hall: The Progressive Response to the Reagan Era in Boston and Chicago.* Cornell University Press.

Cruickshank, M. 2008. "Aging and Identity Politics." *Journal of Aging Studies* 22: 147–51.

Dannefer, D., P. Stein, R. Siders, and S.R. Patterson. 2008. "Is That All There Is? The Concept of Care and the Dialectic of Critique." *Journal of Aging Studies* 22: 101–8.

Darab, S., and Y. Hartman. 2013. "Understanding Single Older Women's Invisibility in Housing Issues in Australia." *Housing, Theory and Society* 30(4): 348–67.

DeSantis, G. 2013. "Voluntary Social Service Organizations Working on the Social Determinants of Health: Cause for Concern?" *The Philanthropist* 25(1): 57–71.

DiGiacomo, G., K. Rabheru, L. Garcia, L. Plouffe, M. Gillis, and M. Lagacé. 2017. "Protecting the Rights of Older Persons: Canada Should Lead the Push for an International Convention on Older Persons' Rights." *Policy Options*, 1 March. https://policyoptions.irpp.org/magazines/march-2017/protecting-the-rights-of-older-persons/.

Dowling, E. and D. Harvie. 2014. "Harnessing the Social: State, Crisis and (Big) Society." *Sociology* 48(5): 869–86.

Du, P., and L. Xie. 2015. "The Use of Law to Protect and Promote Age-Friendly Environments." *Journal of Social Work Practice* 29(1): 13–21.

Eidelman, G., and Z. Taylor. 2010. "Canadian Urban Politics: Another 'Black Hole'?" *Journal of Urban Affairs* 32(3): 305–20.

Elson, P. 2011. *High Ideals and Noble Intentions: Voluntary Sector-Government Relations in Canada*. Toronto: University of Toronto Press.

Evans, B., and J. Shields. 2010. "The Third Sector and the Provision of the Public Good: Partnerships, Contracting and the Neo-Liberal State." In *The Handbook of Canadian Public Administration: Second Edition*, edited by C. Dunn, 305–18. Toronto: Oxford University Press.

Fanelli, C. 2016. *Megacity Malaise: Neoliberalism, Public Services and Labour in Toronto*. Halifax: Fernwood.

Federal/Provincial/Territorial Ministers Responsible for Seniors. 2007. *Age-Friendly Rural and Remote Communities: A Guide*. Ottawa: Author.

Federation of Canadian Municipalities. 2020. "Protecting Vital Municipal Services: Urgent Federal Recommendations to Address the Financial Crisis in Our Cities and Communities due to COVID-19." Ottawa: Author.

Flyvbjerg, B. 2006. "Five Misunderstandings about Case Study Research." *Qualitative Inquiry* 12(2): 219–45.

Frisken, F. 2007. *The Public Metropolis: The Political Dynamics of Urban Expansion in the Toronto Region, 1924–2003*. Toronto: Canadian Scholars Press.

Goar, C. 2013. "Toronto Leaves Its Seniors Behind." *Toronto Star*, 12 November. http://www.thestar.com/opinion/editorials/2013/11/12/toronto_leaves_its_seniors_behindgoar.html.

Golant, S. 2014. "Age-Friendly Communities: Are We Expecting Too Much?" *Institute for Research on Public Policy* 5: 1–20.

Golden, A., and E. Slack. 2006. "Urban Governance Reform in Toronto: A Preliminary Assessment of Changes Made in the Late 1990s." In *Metropolitan Governing: Canadian Cases, Comparative Lessons,* edited by E. Razin and P.J. Smith, 29–74. Jerusalem: The Hebrew University Magnes Press.

Gonzales, E., and N. Morrow-Howell. 2009. "Productive Engagement in Age-Friendly Communities: A Natural Intersection." *Journal of the American Society on Aging* 33(2): 51–8.

Graefe, P. 2002. "The Social Economy and the State: Linking Ambitions with Institutions in Quebec, Canada." *Policy and Politics* 30(2): 247–62.

Green, G. 2012. "Age-Friendly Cities of Europe." *Journal of Urban Health: Bulletin of the New York Academy of Medicine* 90: 116–28.

Hackworth, J. 2006. *The Neoliberal City: Governance, Ideology, and Development in American Urbanism.* Ithaca: Cornell University Press.

Halvorsen, C.J., and J. Emerman. 2013. "The Encore Movement: Baby Boomers and Older Adults Can Be a Powerful Force to Build Community." *Journal of the American Society on Aging* 37(4): 33–9.

Hardill, I., and S. Baines. 2011. *Enterprising Care? Unpaid Voluntary Action in the 21st Century.* Bristol: The Polity Press.

Harvey, D. 1989. "From Managerialism to Entrepreneurialism: The Transformation in Urban Governance in Late Capitalism." *Geografiska Annaler* 71(B): 3–17.

HelpAge International. 2019. *FAIR Guidelines: Four Steps Towards a UN Convention on the Rights of Older People.* London: Author.

Horak, M. 2012. "Multilevel Governance in Toronto: Success and Failure in Canada's Largest City. In *Sites of Governance: Multilevel Governance and Policy Making in Canada's Big Cities,* edited by M. Horak and R. Young, 228–62. Montreal and Kingston: McGill-Queen's University Press.

– 2013. "State Rescaling in Practice: Urban Governance Reform in Toronto." *Urban Research & Practice* 6(3): 311–28.

Imagine Canada. 2020. *Imagine Canada Open Letter to PM – June 2020.* https://live-imagine-canada.pantheonsite.io/sites/default/files/Imagine%20Canada%20open%20letter%20to%20PM%20-%20June%202020.pdf.

Ingram, H., A.L. Schneider, and P. deLeon. 2007. "Social Construction and Policy Design." In *Theories of the Policy Process, Second Edition*, edited by P.A. Sabatier, 93–126. Boulder: Westview Press.

Isett, K., I.A. Mergel, K. Leroux, P.A. Mischen, and R.K. Rethemeyer. 2011. "Networks in Public Administration Scholarship: Understanding Where We Are and Where We Need to Go." *Journal of Public Administration Research and Theory* 21(i): 157–73.

Isin, E., J. Brodie, D. Juteau, and D. Stasiulis. 2008. "Recasting the Social in Citizenship." In *Recasting the Social in Citizenship*, edited by E. Isin, 3–19. Toronto: University of Toronto Press.

Isin, E. 2008. "The City as the Site of the Social." In *Recasting the Social in Citizenship*, edited by E. Isin, 261–80. Toronto: University of Toronto Press.

Iveson, K. 2013. "Cities within the City: Do-It-Yourself Urbanism and the Right to the City." *International Journal of Urban and Regional Research* 37(3): 941–56.

Janes, J. 2008. "Mapping Aging in Place in a Changing Neighbourhood." *Institute for Life Course and Aging.* Toronto: University of Toronto.

Jenson, J., and S. Phillips. 1996. "Regime Shift: New Citizenship Practices in Canada." *International Journal of Canadian Studies* 14 (Fall): 110–35.

Jessop, B. 2009. "Avoiding Traps, Rescaling Cities, Governing Europe". In *Leviathan Undone: Towards a Political Economy of Scale*, edited by R. Keil and R. Mahon, 87–104. Vancouver: UBC Press.

Joy, M., 2018. "Problematizing the Age Friendly Cities and Communities Program in Toronto." *Journal of Aging Studies* 47: 49–56.

Joy, M., P. Marier, and A-M. Séguin. 2018. "La démarche villes-amies des aînés. Un remède universel pour vieillir chez soi?" In *Les vieillissement sous la loupe: Entre mythes et réalités*, edited by V. Billette, P. Marier, and M.-M. Séguin, 75–84. Laval: Presses de l'Université Laval.

Joy, M., and J. Shields. 2013. "Social Impact Bonds: The Next Phase of Third Sector Marketization?" *Canadian Journal of Nonprofit and Social Economy Research* 4(2): 39–55.

– 2018. "Austerity in the Making: Reconfiguring Social Policy through Social Impact Bonds." *Policy & Politics* 46 (4): 681–95.

Joy, M., and R. Vogel. 2015. "Toronto's Governance Crisis: A Global City under Pressure." *Cities* 49: 35–52.

Kalache, S. 2016. "Active Ageing and Age-Friendly Cities – A Personal Account." In *Age-Friendly Cities and Communities in International*

Comparison: Political Lessons, Scientific Avenues, and Democratic Issues, edited by T. Moulaert and S. Garon, 65–77. New York: Springer.

Katz, B., and J. Bradley. 2013. *The Metropolitan Revolution: How Cities and Metros Are Fixing Our Broken Politics and Fragile Economy.* Washington: Brookings Institution Press.

Keil, R., and S. Kipfer. 2003. "The Urban Experience and Globalization." In *Changing Canada: Political Economy as Transformation,* edited by W. Clement and L.F. Vosko, 335–62. Montreal and Kingston: McGill-Queen's University Press.

Kemshall, H. 2002. *Risk, Social Policy and Welfare.* Buckingham: Open University Press.

Kendall, J. 2008. "Voluntary Welfare." In *The Student's Companion to Social Policy,* edited by P. Alcock, M. May, and K. Lingston, 212–18. Oxford: Blackwell.

Kendig, H., A. Elias, P. Majwijiw, and K. Anstey. 2014. "Developing age-friendly Cities and Communities in Australia". *Journal of Aging and Health* 26(8): 1390–414.

Laforest, R. 2013a. "Introduction." In *Government-Nonprofit Relations in Times of Recession,* edited by R. Laforest, 1–7. Montreal and Kingston: McGill-Queen's University Press.

– 2013b. "Muddling through Government-Nonprofit Relations in Canada." In *Government-Nonprofit Relations in Times of Recession,* edited by R. Laforest, 9–17. Montreal and Kingston: McGill-Queen's University Press.

Lefebvre, H. 2003. *The Urban Revolution.* Translated by R. Bononno. Minneapolis: University of Minnesota Press.

Lehning, A.J. 2014. "Local and Regional Governments and Age-Friendly Communities: A Case Study of the San Francisco Bay Area." *Journal of Aging & Social Policy* 26: 102–16.

Lexler, M. 2015. "42–2: John Tory, Toronto City Council and the Austerity Consensus." *Rabble.ca,* 16 March. http://rabble.ca/blogs/bloggers/michael-laxer/2015/03/42-2-john-tory-toronto-city-council-and-austerity-consensus.

Lightbody, J. 1999. "Finding the Trolls under Your Bridge: The New Case for Party Politics in Canadian Cities." *Journal of Canadian Studies* 34(1): 172–83.

Lowndes, V. 2002. "The Institutional Approach." In *Theory and Methods in Political Science, Third Edition,* edited by D. Marsh and G. Stoker, 60–79. New York: Palgrave Macmillan.

– 2009. "New Institutionalism and Urban Politics." In *Theories of Urban Politics, Second Edition*, edited by J.S. Davies and D.L. Imbroscio, 91–105. London: Sage Publications.

Lum, J., J. Shields, and B. Evans. 2016. "Co-constructing Performance Indicators in Home and Community Care: Assessing the Role of NGOs in Three Canadian Provinces." *Canadian Journal of Nonprofit and Social Economy Research/Revue canadienne de recherche sur les OBSL et l'économie sociale* 7(1): 46–73.

MacCharles, T. 2020. "82% of Canada's COVID-19 Deaths Have Been in Long-Term Care, New Data Reveals." *Toronto Star*. 7 May. https://www.thestar.com/politics/federal/2020/05/07/82-of-canadas-covid-19-deaths-have-been-in-long-term-care.html.

Magnussen, W. 2011. *Politics of Urbanism: Seeing Like a City*. London, New York: Routledge.

Mahon, R., C. Andrew, and R. Johnston. 2007. "Policy Analysis in an Era of "Globalization": Capturing Spatial Dimensions and Scalar Strategies." In *Critical Policy Studies*, edited by M. Orsini and M. Smith, 41–64. Vancouver: UBC Press.

Mahon, R., and R. Keil. 2009. "Introduction." In *Leviathan Undone: Towards a Political Economy of Scale*, edited by R. Keil and R. Mahon, 3–26. Vancouver: UBC Press.

Mahon, R., and L. Macdonald. 2010. "Anti-poverty Politics in Toronto and Mexico City." *Geoforum* 41(2): 209–17.

Martinson, M., and M. Minkler. 2006. "Civic Engagement and Older Adults: A Critical Perspective." *The Gerontologist* 46(3): 318–24.

Marutto, P. 2004. "Charity and Public Welfare in History: A Look at Ontario, 1830–1950." *The Philanthropist* 19(3): 159–67.

Maxwell, J.A. 2005. *Qualitative Research Design: An Interactive Approach, Second Edition*. Thousand Oaks: Sage Publications.

– 2012. *A Realist Approach to Qualitative Research*. Los Angeles: Sage Publications.

McBride, S. 1996. "The Political Economy Tradition and Canadian Policy Studies." In *Policy Analysis in Canada: The State of the Art*, edited by L. Dobuzinskis, D.H. Laycock, and M. Howlett, 49–66. Toronto: University of Toronto Press.

McBride, S., and H. Whiteside. 2011. *Private Affluence and Public Austerity: Economic Crisis and Democratic Malaise in Canada*. Halifax and Winnipeg: Fernwood Publishing.

McGoey, L. 2015. *No Such Thing as a Free Gift: The Gates Foundation and the Price of Philanthropy.* London, New York: Verso.

McKeen, W., and A. Porter. 2003. "Politics and Transformation: Welfare State Restructuring in Canada." In *Changing Canada: Political Economy as Transformation,* edited by W. Clement and L.F. Vosko, 109–34. Montreal and Kingston: McGill-Queen's University Press.

Merriam, S.B. 1988. *Case Study Research in Education: A Qualitative Approach.* San Francisco: Jossey-Bass Publishers.

Mette Kjaer, A. 2009. "Governance and the Urban Bureaucracy." In *Theories of Urban Politics, Second Edition,* edited by J.S. Davies and D.L. Imbroscio, 137–52. London: Sage publications.

Milbourne, L. 2013. *Voluntary Sector in Transition: Hard Times or New Opportunities?* Bristol: The Polity Press.

Minkler, M., and M. Martinson. 2007. "Charity Work Isn't the Solution for All Older Americans." *The Chronicle of Philanthropy* May: 33.

Minkler, M., and M.B. Holstein. 2008. "From Civil Rights to … Civic Engagement? Concerns of Two Older Critical Gerontologists about a 'New Social Movement' and What It Portends." *Journal of Aging Studies* 22: 196–204.

Mitchell, K. 2001. "Transnationalism, Neo-Liberalism and the Rise of the Shadow State." *Economy and Society* 30(2): 165–89.

Modlich, R. 2011. "Age-Friendly Communities – A Women's Issue." *Women and Environments* Fall/Winter: 28–31.

Moody, H.R. 2008. "The Maturing of Critical Gerontology." *Journal of Aging Studies* 22: 205–9.

Moulaert, T., and S. Garon, editors. 2016. *Age-Friendly Cities and Communities in International Comparison: Political Lessons, Scientific Avenues, and Democratic Issues.* New York: Springer.

Neal, M.B., A.K. DeLaTorre, and P.C. Carder. 2014. "Age-Friendly Portland: A University-City-Community Partnership." *Journal of Aging & Social Policy* 26: 88–101.

Newman, J. 2014. "Landscapes of Antagonism: Local Governance, Neoliberalism and Austerity." *Urban Studies* 51(15): 3290–305.

Newman, J., and J. Clarke. 2009. *Publics, Politics and Power: Remaking the Public in Public Services.* London: Sage Publications.

O'Connor, D. 2004. "The Dark Side of Contracting with Government: The Case of VHA Hamilton and the Province of Ontario." *The Philanthropist* 19(3): 201–10.

Office of the Ombudsman. 2010. *A Duty to Care: An Investigation into Municipal Licensing and Standards' Treatment of a Resident with Dementia*. Toronto: Author.

– 2013. *Housing at Risk: An Investigation into Toronto Community Housing Corporation's Eviction of Seniors on the Basis of Rent Arrears*. Toronto: Author.

Ontario Government. 2007. *Long Term Care Homes Act*. https://www.ontario.ca/laws/statute/07l08.

– 2012. *Ontario's Action Plan for Health Care: Better Patient Care through Better Value from Our Health Care Dollars*. Toronto: Author.

– 2013a. *Finding the Right Fit: Age-Friendly Community Planning*. Toronto: Author.

– 2013b. *Independence, Activity and Good Health: Ontario's Action Plan for Seniors*. Toronto: Author.

– 2015. *Seniors Community Grant Program*. http://www.seniors.gov.on.ca/en/srsorgs/scgp.php.

– 2019. "Keeping Seniors Healthy, Safe and Active: More Community Support for Seniors across the Province." Ontario News Release, 23 September. https://news.ontario.ca/oss/en/2019/09/keeping-seniors-healthy-safe-and-active.html.

Ontario Health Coalition. 2011. *Still Waiting: An Assessment of Ontario's Home Care System after Two Decades of Restructuring*. Toronto: Author.

– 2020. "Release & Analysis: COVID-19 Death Rates in Ontario Long-Term Care Homes Significantly Higher and Increasing in For-Profit Homes vs. Non-Profit and Publicly-Owned Homes: New Data Analysis." 6 May. https://www.ontariohealthcoalition.ca/index.php/death-rates-in-long-term-care-by-ownership-release/.

Ontario Seniors' Secretariat. 2013. *Finding the Right Fit: Age-Friendly Community Planning*. Toronto: Author.

Orsini, M. 2007. "Discourses in Distress: From 'Health Promotion' to 'Population Health' to 'You Are Responsible for Your Own Health.'" In *Critical Policy Studies*, edited by M. Orsini and M. Smith, 347–63. Vancouver: UBC Press.

Orsini, M., and M. Smith. 2007. "Critical Policy Studies." In *Critical Policy Studies*, edited by M. Orsini and M. Smith, 1–18. Vancouver: UBC Press.

Osborne, S. 2010. "The (New) Public Governance: A Suitable Case for Treatment." In *The New Public Governance? Emerging Perspectives on* the *Theory and Practice of Public Governance,* edited by S. Osborne, 1–16. London, New York: Routledge.

Peck, J. 2009. "The Cult of Urban Creativity." In *Leviathan Undone: Towards a Political Economy of Scale,* edited by R. Keil and R. Mahon, 159–76. Vancouver: UBC Press.

– 2012. "Austerity Urbanism: American Cities Under Extreme Economy." *City,* 16:6, 626–55.

Phillips, S.D., and R.D. Smith. 2010. "Between Governance and Regulation: Evolving Government-Third Sector Relationships." In *Governance and Regulation in the Third Sector: International Perspectives, edited by S.D. Phillips and S.R. Smith, 1–36.* London, New York: Routledge.

Plouffe, L., and A. Kalache. 2010. "Towards Age-Friendly Cities: Determining Urban Features that Promote Active Aging." *Journal of Urban Health: Bulletin of the New York Academy of Medicine* 87(5): 733–9.

Plouffe, L., A. Kalache, and I. Voelcker. 2016. "A Critical Review of the WHO Age-Friendly Cities Methodology and Its Implementation." In *Age-Friendly Cities and Communities in International Comparison: Political Lessons, Scientific Avenues, and Democratic Issues*, edited by T. Moulaert and S. Garon, 19–36. New York: Springer.

Provencher, C., N. Keating, J. Warburton, and V. Roos. 2014. "Ageing and Community: Introduction to the Special Issue." *Journal of Community and Applied Social Psychology* 24: 1–11.

Public Health Agency of Canada. 2012. *Age-Friendly Communities in Canada: Community Implementation Guide – Toolbox*. Ottawa: Author.

– 2016. "Age-Friendly Communities." http://www.phac-aspc.gc.ca/seniors-aines/afc-caa-eng.php.

Purcell, M. 2003. "Citizenship and the Right to the Global City: Reimaging the Capitalist World Order." *International Journal of Urban and Regional Research* 27(3): 564–90.

Rebick, J. 2014. "Toronto Election: The Left Has Some Work to Do." *Rabble.ca*, 5 November. http://rabble.ca/news/2014/11/toronto-election-left-has-some-work-to-do.

Rémillard-Boilard, S. 2019. "The Development of Age-Friendly Cities and Communities." In *Age-Friendly Cities and Communities: A Global Perspective*, edited by T. Buffel, S. Handler, and C. Phillipson, 13–32. Bristol: Policy Press.

Rice, J.J., and M.J. Prince. 2000. *Changing Politics of Canadian Social Policy.* Toronto: University of Toronto Press.

Richmond, T., and J. Shields. 2004. "NGO Restructuring: Constraints and Consequences." *Canadian Review of Social Policy* 53: 53–67.
Rochester, C., A.E. Paine, and S. Howlett. 2010. *Volunteering and Society in the 21st Century.* London: Palgrave Macmillan.
Saint-Martin, D. 2007. "From the Welfare State to the Social Investment State: A New Paradigm for Canadian Social Policy." In *Critical Policy Studies,* edited by M. Orsini and M. Smith, 279–98. Vancouver: UBC Press.
Sancton, A. 2008. *The Limits of Boundaries: Why City-Regions Cannot Be Self-Governing.* Montreal, Kingston: McGill-Queen's University Press.
– 2015. *Canadian Local Government: An Urban Perspective, Second Edition.* Don Mills: Oxford University Press.
Sassen, S. 2005. "Global City: Introducing a Concept." *Brown Journal of World Affairs* 11(2): 27–43.
Scharlach, A. 2012. "Creating Aging-Friendly Communities in the United States." *Ageing Int* 37: 25–38.
– 2014. "Does the Village Model Help to Foster Age-Friendly Communities?" *Journal of Aging and Social Policy* 26: 181–96.
Scott, A.J. 2011. "Emerging Cities of the Third Wave." *City* 15(3–4): 289–321.
Senate of Canada. 2009. *Canada's Aging Population: Seizing the Opportunity.* Ottawa: Author.
Shields, J., and B.M. Evans. 1998. *Shrinking the State: Globalization and Public Administration Reform.* Halifax: Fernwood.
Shields, J. 2014. "Constructing and 'Liberating' Temporariness in the Canadian Nonprofit Sector: Neoliberalism and Nonprofit Service Providers." In *Liberating Temporariness? Migration, Work and Citizenship in and Age of Insecurity,* edited by R. Latham, V. Preston, and L. Vosko, 255–81. Montreal, Kingston: McGill-Queen's University Press.
Sinha, S.K. 2012. *Living Longer, Living Well: Recommendations to Inform a Seniors Strategy for Ontario.* Toronto: Author.
Smith, S.R. 2013. "The New Reality of the Government-Nonprofit Relationship in the United States." In *Government-Nonprofit Relations in Times of Recession,* edited by R. Laforest, 19–40. Montreal, Kingston: McGill-Queen's Press.
Soja, E. W. 2010. *Seeking Spatial Justice.* Minneapolis: University of Minnesota Press.
Stake, R. 1995. *The Art of Case Study Research.* Thousand Oaks: Sage Publications.
Stone, C. 2009. "Who Is Governed? Local Citizens and the Political Order of

Cities." In *Theories of Urban Politics, Second Edition,* edited by J.S. Davies and D.L. Imbroscio, 257–73. London: Sage Publications.

Szreter, S., and A. Ishkanian. 2012. "Introduction: What Is Big Society? Contemporary Social Policy in a Historical and Comparative Perspective." In *The Big Society Debate: A New Agenda for Social Welfare?* edited by A. Ishkanian and S. Szreter, 1–24. Cheltenham: Edward Elgar Publishing.

Taylor, M. 2013. "England's Big Society: Can the Voluntary Sector Manage without the State?" In *Government-Nonprofit Relations in Times of Recession,* edited by R. Laforest, 79–95. Montreal, Kingston: McGill-Queen's University Press.

Thomlinson, N. 2000. "When Right Is Wrong: Municipal Government and Downloading in Toronto." In *Restructuring and Resistance: Canadian Public Policy in an Age of Global Capitalism,* edited by M. Burke, C. Mooers, and J. Shields, 226–60. Halifax: Fernwood Publishing.

Thompson, G., S. Hudson, N. Wilson, and R. Edwards. 2010. "A Qualitative Case Study of Policy Makers Views about the Protection of Children from Smoking in Cars." *Nicotine and Tobacco Research* 12(9): 970–7.

Toronto Community Housing. 2016. "About Us." http://www.torontohousing.ca/about.

United Way of Greater Toronto. 2001. *A Commitment to Care: Community Support Services for Seniors.* Toronto: Author.

United Way Toronto. 2005. *Strong Neighbourhoods: A Call to Action.* Report for the Strong Neighbourhoods Task Force. Toronto: Author.

Vromen, A. 2010. "Debating Methods: Rediscovering Qualitative Approaches." In *Theory and Methods in Political Science, Third Edition,* edited by D. Marsh and G. Stoker, 249–67. New York: Palgrave Macmillan.

Walks, R.A. 2001. "The Social Ecology of the Post-Fordist/Global City? Economic Restructuring and Socio-spatial Polarization in the Toronto Urban Region." *Urban Studies* 38(3): 407–47.

Wells, P. 2008. "The Third Sector and Community Cohesion in Deprived Neighbourhoods." In *Community Cohesion in Crisis? New Dimensions of Diversity and Difference,* edited by J. Flint, J. and D. Robinson, 139–57. Bristol: The Polity Press.

Winterton, R. 2016. "Organizational Responsibility for Age-Friendly Social Participation: Views of Australian Rural Community Stakeholders." *Journal of Aging & Social Policy* 28(4), 261–76.

World Health Organization. 2007. *Global Age-Friendly Cities: A Guide.* Geneva: WHO Press.
Zimmer, A. 2011. "Third Sector-Government Partnerships." In *Third Sector Research*, edited by R. Taylor, 201–17. New York: Springer.

INDEX